Austin Music Is a Scene Not a Sound

Other Books By Michael Corcoran

Ghost Notes: Pioneering Spirits of Texas Music

All Over the Map: True Heroes of Texas Music

Washington Phillips and His Manzarene Dreams

He Is My Story: The Sanctified Soul of Arizona Dranes

Austin Music Is a Scene Not a Sound
An Illustrated History of the First 100 Years

MICHAEL CORCORAN

TEXAS MUSIC SERIES

Fort Worth, Texas

Library of Congress Cataloging-in-Publication Data

Names: Corcoran, Michael, 1955- author.
Title: Austin music is a scene, not a sound / Michael Corcoran.
Description: Fort Worth, Texas : TCU Press, [2024] | Summary: "Michael Corcoran culminates forty years of writing about Austin music with a history of the scene, going back to the German singing societies of the late 1800s and ending with the ascent of South by Southwest, whose registration line would become the Ellis Island of new Austin. Over fifty legendary Austin live music venues, starting with the Skyline and Victory Grill in the wake of WWII, are profiled in a rolling "Clubland Paradise" subsection. Told are the stories of Willie Nelson and the Armadillo, nascent Black radio DJs Lavada Durst and Tony Von, the making of Stevie Ray Vaughan, the significance of Sixth and Red River Streets, and how Aquafest went from Austin's biggest annual event to belly-up in five years. As a daily newspaper journalist for over twenty years, Corcoran is first about the facts in this dig for interesting stories and context from the Live Music Capital of the World"– Provided by publisher.
Identifiers: LCCN 2023040295 | ISBN 9780875658667 (hardcover)
Subjects: LCSH: Popular music–Texas–Austin–History and criticism. | Nightclubs–Texas–Austin–History. | Music-halls–Texas–Austin–History. | Musicians–Texas–Austin.
Classification: LCC ML3477.8.A97 C67 2024 | DDC 781.6409764/31–dc23/eng/20230829
LC record available at https://lccn.loc.gov/2023040295

OPPOSITE PHOTO: A 21-year-old Stevie Ray Vaughan and mentor Denny Freeman of the Cobras 1975. Photo Diana Ray.

PAGE VIII:: David Yow and Scratch Acid play a Sunday barbecue at the OAF House, 1983. Seattle bands have acknowledged Scratch Acid, along with other Austin bands Poison 13 and Butthole Surfers as influences on the grunge sound. Photograph by David Sprague.

TCU Box 298300
Fort Worth, Texas 76129
www.tcupress.edu

Design by Bill Brammer

"One of the good things about Austin is the way musicians fall in love with each other and give so much support. And the most loyal and curious audience in the world."

—**BONNIE RAITT**

IN MEMORIAM

Michael Corcoran (1955–2024)

Michael Corcoran, 68, was found dead at his home in Austin, Texas, on Monday, July 1, 2024.

Described as the "greatest chronicler of the Austin music scene," Michael Corcoran lived his life and conducted his writing on his own terms, much to the amusement and sometimes to the chagrin of those around him. He could frequently infuriate people, but then turn around and charm them with his quirky sense of humor, which was often at his own expense.

Michael Corcoran left an indelible impression as a music journalist who wrote copiously about unsung, obscure, and often unknown Texas music and musicians. His writing will forever be preserved as an essential part of Texas, particularly Austin, music history.

* * *

My father's death on July 1, 2024, sent a shockwave through Austin's music community. Of the literally thousands of comments about his writing and career, I think Senator Sarah Eckhardt said it best in the Texas Senate Proclamation:

"[His] biting humor and descriptive eloquence [was] unmatched by his industry peers. . . . He quietly stood as an exemplar of fearless and brilliant journalism to countless colleagues and fellow writers; his influential canon of work reflects the true spirit of Texas music and Austin's vibrant music community. His remarkable legacy will continue to inform, entertain and inspire Texans for generations to come."

Austin is a vibe, an idea that only exists when you believe in it, and Michael Corcoran was the Truest Believer. His voice, his humor, and his curation of Austin's immense musical past in this book distills its essence perfectly.

My father took painstaking efforts to canonize Austin music's saints in this book. His untimely death adds another saint to the wall.

—JACK HENRY CORCORAN

THE FOLLOWING QUOTES ARE TAKEN FROM A TRIBUTE PUT TOGETHER FOR THE *Austin American-Statesman*:

Beyond his prodigious journalism, Michael Corcoran's first books, *Ghost Notes: Pioneering Spirits of Texas Music* and *All Over the Map: True Heroes of Texas Music*, represent truly remarkable and deep cultural history. They will be read for decades to come. You should read them now. And we should make a pact that they never fall out of print.

MICHAEL BARNES, columnist, *Austin American-Statesman*

Michael Corcoran, arguably the greatest chronicler of the Austin music scene, has died. Corky was a gleeful provocateur. The original troll. He made a name for himself shooting down Austin's stars, and throughout his career, he never shied away from a hot take. But his opinions were malleable. Once dubious of the band Blue October, late in his career at the *Statesman*, he became the greatest champion of San Marcos's favorite sons.

DEBORAH SENGUPTA STITH, *Austin360* editor, *Austin American-Statesman*

End of an era. He was his own man. He was singular talent, equal parts frustrating and brilliant. He was the GOAT of Austin music journalism. Those are all clichés, but with the added advantage of being true.

ANDY LANGER, journalist and radio host

One thing I always admired about Michael, and why I loved working with him, was that he saw stories everywhere. And when it came to music, which was his beat for so long, he was never satisfied by the easy reach. He wanted to dig deep into everything, and was especially passionate about making sure overlooked musicians, especially those of color, got their due.

KATHY BLACKWELL, executive editor, *Texas Monthly*

Contents

ne Fabulous Thunderbirds were the ultimate Austin band. They were blues traditionalists ith a Gulf Coast bent that set them apart. This photograph was taken at the Continental Club r a Miller Lite commercial , circa 1982. *Left to right:* Conni Hancock, bassist Keith Ferguson, onnie Vaughan, Jimmie Vaughan, painter Julie Speed, singer Kim Wilson. Photograph by om Wright. Courtesy of Dolph Briscoe Center for American History.

PREFACE

Welcome to Clubland Paradise

Just as a scene is not only the music, clubs are much more than stages and walls. They are the folks who work there and go there and play there. I knew these were my people the night I arrived at age twenty-eight. After I found Austin, I had to chuckle inside when someone called Hawaii paradise.

The natural beauty of my home state was nothing compared to the former dry cleaners, pizza parlors, and used furniture stores where I saw Lou Ann Barton, Little Joe y la Familia, the Offenders, Albert Collins, the Commandos, Dino Lee, and Herman the German in my first couple weeks in town.

Forget the white sand and ocean blue, my favorite Beach was on the north shore of the University of Texas, where Daniel Johnston played between acts for five dollars a song—good money for a McDonald's janitor.

I loved how the scenes intersected, how you'd see some of the same people at Voltaire's punk basement as you would at a LeRoi Brothers show. Everyone seemed to know (and secretly envy) everyone else, which made Austin perfect for the kind of music/gossip column I was made for. That I was the ultimate outsider ("He's from fucking Hawaii!"–Charlie Sexton in *Creem*, 1986), writing as an insider, was a joke many didn't get.

My acerbic "Don't You Start Me Talking" column in the *Austin Chronicle* from 1985–88 made me some enemies—I was voted "The Worst Thing to Happen to Austin Music" in 1986 by the readers of the *Chron*—but everybody read it. I was clickbait before the click.

The way I saw it, Austin was a city full of itself (was?), and it was my job to bring it down a few pegs. "Every overinflated balloon needs a prick" is how Brian Beattie of Glass Eye described my role. But Austin wasn't wrong about itself. This is the only place I had to move away from, in 1988, because the good times were getting out of hand.

This is a city people have flocked to since the '60s for the "quality of stimulation," which is the quality of life. The Austin icebreaker: "What boring town are you from?" The Austin cliché: "You got here too late." Nah, I'd counter, you peaked too soon. I couldn't imagine any time and place being more alive than this Clubland Paradise in the '80s.

The present was so good I had little interest in the past, aggressively ignoring every three-name act that rated a chapter in Jan Reid's *The Improbable Rise of Redneck Rock* (1974).

When I was a young writer, I didn't really know anything, so I relied on a fearless attitude to get folks to read me. But with experience and research comes knowledge that can entertain in a more satisfying way. In the past few years, I've become consumed with history I never thought much about before.

When old timers taunt new arrivals with tales of the city's glorious past, they lay a cattle guard to that history. But the lucky ones are actually those who just got here. ("Huh? You must also love those assholes that try to squeeze into a full elevator.") There's no sad sense of UBT—Useta Be There—for those who've always had to dial 512 for local calls. There's not a CVS in town that can make them cry.

The Black Cat was a hub of activity on Sixth Street in the 1980s.
Photograph by Bill Leissner.

Yes, it used to be better here. So what? Living in this city is like sex in that what happened in the past has only sentimental value, which when it comes to sex is no value. Who would you rather be, the old guy hunched over his cereal who made out with Farrah Fawcett one night at the Jade Room, or the insufferable hipster in the trucker hat who goes home to that hot barista, the one with only two tattoos?

There's nothing like the first stroll in your new town, which for me and Austin was Sunday, April 1, 1984. I was walking down South Congress (which wasn't nearly as seedy as developers will have you believe) when I happened upon the grand opening of the costume store Lucy in Disguise with Diamonds. The party spilled out onto the sidewalk, while zydeco music pumped out of the speakers. What a cool town!

Next stop was the Continental Club, where the sign said, "Butthole Surfers $3." I was the first one in the door at 9 p.m., and it was just me and owner Mark Pratz for a while. Cheryl Newlin, a bartender on her day off, was the second person in. My first friend in Austin!

They didn't have opening acts in Hawaii clubs, so when Happy Death came onstage at about 10:00 p.m. I thought they were the Butthole Surfers. I was surprised to see another band set up afterwards. And wonderfully unprepared for the strangeness that would follow.

Not many people have seen the Butthole Surfers without knowing a thing about them. This was before all the visual insanity—the penis reattachment films and the flaming cymbals and the stripper who covered her teeth in aluminum foil. It was just the music, and it was both abrasive and hypnotic. As Gibby yelped and howled his brilliant gibberish, my brain was locked in on the primal stand-up rhythms of Teresa and King, and I've been chasing that beat ever since.

"This guy just moved here from Hawaii," Cheryl introduced me around after the show.

"Why the hell would you leave Hawaii to come here, man?" growled Xalapeno Charlie Duggan, who owned a legendarily spicy Mexican restaurant on Barton Springs Road.

"I'm into bands, not beaches," I answered.

"Well, then, welcome to Austin," he said with a handshake.

As an irreverent rock critic, I was in love with the notion that opinions can't be proven incorrect. But history has a very definite right or wrong. Making sure your information is accurate requires a work ethic akin to, as Kurt Vonnegut described, inflating a blimp with a bicycle pump. Anybody can do it, but most give up when the effort seems futile. Sometimes obsession is the talent.

This history starts with yodeling tavern owner Kenneth Threadgill, the granddaddy of them all, whose performance and encouragement of Austin music dates to the 1933 repeal of Prohibition. Then we step back even further to the German singing societies, which preceded the Volstead Act by several decades. Beer has always played a big part in the history of Austin music.

We end with the launch of South by Southwest (SXSW), whose registration line would become Ellis Island of the New Austin. SXSW was born in March 1987, the month Kenneth Threadgill died at age seventy-seven of a pulmonary embolism.

You'd think the end of one era in Austin and the beginning of another couldn't be more succinctly defined, but six years earlier— April 1, 1981—Austin's first punk club, Raul's, closed for good on the night hip-hop made its live concert debut here. As Sugarhill Gang, Grandmaster Flash, and other acts drew three thousand to Municipal Auditorium on a Wednesday, rap perched to replace punk as the sound of rebellion in Austin and around the world.

Austin music is not defined by genres, however. Sammy Allred of the Geezinslaw Brothers, the second Austin act (after folk singer Carolyn Hester) to sign with a major label in 1963, used to say, "Austin music is not a sound. It's a scene."

Yellow lights on South Lamar . . . capital punishment . . . "Don't Move Here" t-shirts. What are, things that don't deter?

Austin's a mulligan town, a fresh start–ville, a land of opportunity for those with low expectations. Some moved here for jobs. They're called Round Rock residents. But most of us came because we loved the party,

Roky Erickson found new fans at Raul's. Photograph for the *Daily Texan*. Courtesy of Dolph Briscoe Center for American History.

Joe Ely and Butch Hancock at Dobie Mall, once home for the Other Place folk club. Photograph by Nancy E. Goldfarb LeNoir. Courtesy of AusPop archives.

This is how the Butthole Surfers looked on my first night out in Austin. Drummer Teresa Taylor is hidden by guitarist Paul Leary. Photograph by Pat Blashill.

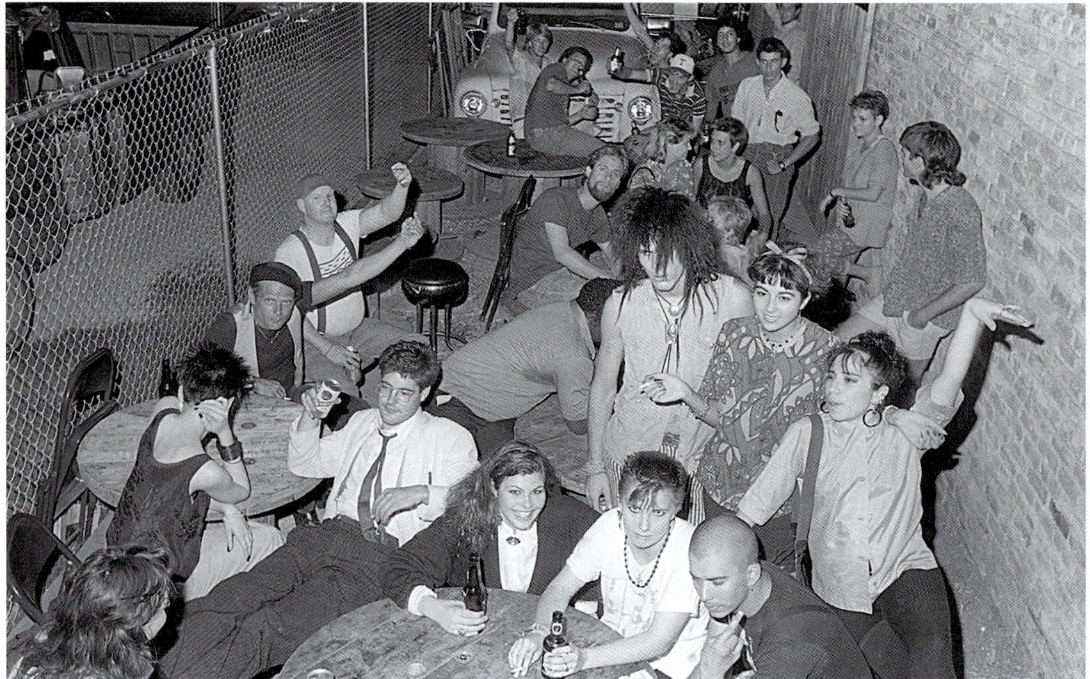

Scenes intersect on the patio of the Black Cat, circa 1987. That's Clara Portillo Reed, the future go-go dancing bartender at the Continental, in the right corner. Photograph by Bill Leissner.

you know, the vibe. It started as a room full of conversations on Goodwill couches and someone pulled out a guitar and everyone sang "Blister in the Sun." We needed only songs and Tamale House #3 to survive.

In the 1970s, Austin had the cheapest cost of living of the one hundred largest cities in the United States. Today, it's one of the most expensive. The average one bedroom in Austin costs more to rent than did the Armadillo World Headquarters!

The only Austin we get is the one we got, so let's make the best of it. Let's ditch the once-accurate "Live Music Capital of the World" like an itchy scarf. A better city slogan: "Austin: It's the People!"

Clubs come and go, but what's always made this community special are the folks who understand how lucky they are to be in the middle of all that music. They were schooled in the essentials by the deejays—Lavada Durst, Joe Gracey, Larry Monroe, Dan Del Santo, Paul Ray, Jody Denberg, and more—and graduated to the clubs, where they worked hard and partied harder to keep this thing of ours going. This book is dedicated to the musicians, the club owners, the bartenders, the fans, the sound techs, the journalists, the scenesters, the faces we used to see out in the clubs who passed away too soon. It could've been us, but they took the hit. Death is especially cruel when you've got somewhere to go.

As a late-blooming Austin nostalgist (Austalgist?), who didn't move here until the '80s, I was greatly aided in this research by a newspaper archive database provided for free by the Austin Public Library. Faded memories had backup. Lockdown became livable. Insomnia made a friend.

Special thanks to the Dolph Briscoe Center for American History, a vital research center on the University of Texas campus which provided many of the facts and photos in this book. The Austin Museum of Popular Culture (AusPop) was also a great help with the vintage images. The Austin History Center was another invaluable source for photos and history. I had a lot of help from dedicated archivists.

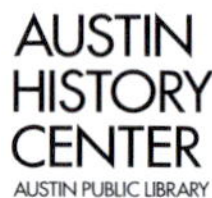

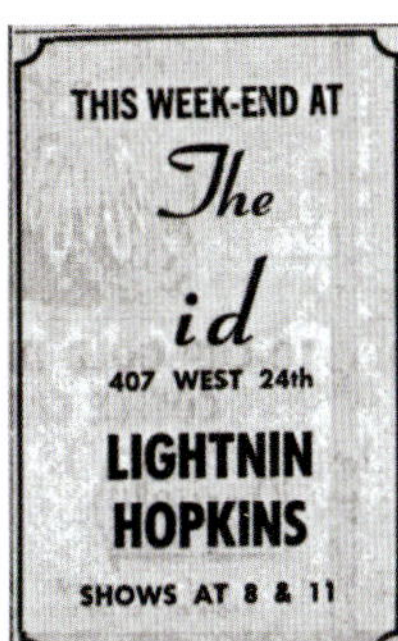
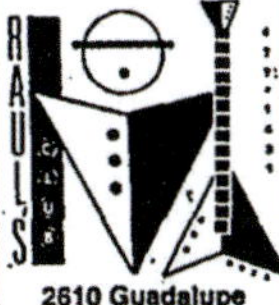

Three decades of club ads. Collage by Dave Prewitt.

Threadgill and the Hootenanny Hoots, including Julie Paul on the far left with Chuck Joyce and Bert McGuire on the right, at the recently enclosed Split Rail patio, February 1967. Courtesy of *Austin American-Statesman* Photographic Morgue at the Austin History Center.

I.

Kenneth Threadgill: Father of the Austin Music Scene

Willie Nelson famously brought the rednecks and the hippies together in musical affinity when he debuted at the Armadillo World Headquarters in August 1972. But Kenneth Threadgill laid the groundwork for the comingling of the species the previous seven years when he played every weekend at the Split Rail Inn, a country beer joint on South Lamar, across the street from the Pitch & Putt.

Mr. Threadgill was a hardcore country singer, but he often had longhairs in his band. "Where the heads meet the necks" was the Rail's unofficial slogan. "Live and let live" was Threadgill's.

This yodeler with the bushy white sideburns and prominent beer belly had counterculture bona fides for giving Queen Janis her spiritual breakthrough at his namesake beer joint on North Lamar in 1962. The tavern owner's enthusiasm for how she put a song across at his Wednesday night hootenannies was the validation Ms. Joplin so desperately needed—and she never forgot. What set Threadgill apart from the UT students who applauded Janis at the "folk sings" in reserved rooms at the Texas Union, was that he had seen it all. He knew his hero Jimmie Rodgers personally, had been hosting music since the '30s, and sang with local country bands in the '40s and '50s. Threadgill was the impromptu opener for Hank Williams at Dessau Hall in 1948, plucked from the audience by co-owner Hallie Price when the headliner looked to be a no-show. Backed by the house band, Threadgill was singing "Lovesick Blues" when Hank walked in with a big smile.

Janis, Chuck, and Julie

Threadgill always celebrated his September 12, 1909, birth at the Split Rail, so the "KT Jubilee" in July 1970 was a "thanks for everything" tribute not tied to the calendar. A crowd of about five hundred was expected at the BRW Party Barn in Oak Hill, with an advertised lineup of Mance Lipscomb, Shiva's Head Band, Bill Neely, folklorist Stan Alexander, and Threadgill's Hootenanny Hoots. But a crowd of about five thousand, "a mind-boggling assortment of bearded youths, overalled farmers and laborers, and fraternity boys trying to look casual" (*Statesman*), showed up after the first female rock star checked into the Holiday Inn on Town Lake the night before. Janis Joplin didn't do incognito. She blew in from the Islands with a present for "Daddy" that she put around his neck. "Here's something from Hawaii I knew you'd like," she said, "a good lei." As the crowd roared, Threadgill said, barely audible, "Now that's something I wouldn't know what to do with."

She sang two songs at the Jubilee by her new friend Kris Kristofferson, "who's gonna be famous, I give him a year," she said introducing "Me and Bobby McGee." Janis also sang "Sunday Morning Coming Down," backed on both songs by Julie Paul and Chuck Joyce, the married couple who played in Threadgill's band. Janis recorded "Bobby McGee" just a few days before she died of a heroin overdose in October 1970. It became her first and only #1 single in 1971.

Julie Paul was especially devastated by Joplin's demise just three months after the Jubilee, as the one-time lovers had remained close. It was a flash affair in '62, with Janis seeming to prefer men, but Julie had a red Triumph TR3 convertible prone to sudden road trips to New Orleans, and "took care of Janis and treated her like a boy would treat her," according to biographer Alice Echols (*Scars of Sweet Paradise*).

Julie Paul became Mrs. Chuck Joyce in '67, months after Chuck's wife Angela died in a car accident at age twenty-five, leaving him with two young children.

The Joyces left Threadgill's band in August '70 to form Cross Country with another couple, Roy and Linda Robinson from Whistler. They went on tour opening for Delaney and Bonnie and Friends, but this rootsy version of the Mamas and the Papas didn't take and split up in less than a year, with the Robinsons reforming Whistler. Chuck and Julie went back to Threadgill and their day jobs—he as a pressman for the *Statesman* and she cutting hair.

Blues/country singer Bill Neely plays the KT Jubilee 1970. Photograph by Van Brooks. Courtesy of AusPop Archives.

After Janis passed, Kristofferson followed up on her promise to get Ken Threadgill a record deal. Kris heard him yodel at Darrell Royal's afterparty for 1972's Dripping Springs Reunion, then flew Threadgill and the Joyces to Nashville the next month for four sessions at Jack Clement's recording studio. Using royalties from "Bobby McGee," "Help Me Make It through the Night," "For the Good Times," and "Sunday Morning Comin' Down," all from his 1970 debut, Kristofferson paid for everything, but he had to go on tour, so he left Clements and half-hearted coproducer Waylon Jennings in charge. Clements was focused on developing a new singer from Corpus Christi named Don Williams, and nobody wanted Jimmie Rodgers covers in '72, so the tapes gathered dust for years. Threadgill's Nashville album was never released, but one number, "Going Back to Texas," was included on the million-selling soundtrack to the film *Honeysuckle Rose*, so cowriters Threadgill and the Joyces did get to experience the thrill of mailbox money.

Threadgill's only album, 1981's *Silver-Haired Daddy* on Armadillo Records, was credited to Velvet Cowpasture, which played regularly at Bevo's Westside Tap Room at 24th and Rio Grande (later Abel Moses's Bar & Grill).

Threadgill the throwback was one of those singers you had to see if you were visiting Austin, Texas, yeehaw! One night at Bevo's, the writer Richard Brautigan (*Trout Fishing in America*) showed up, overserved in a sombrero, and picked the wrong guy's girlfriend to hit on. As Brautigan kept trying to whisper in the annoyed woman's ear, Cowpasture bassist Bill Campbell came offstage and confronted the scribe, who bolted. Campbell chased him outside, where Brautigan found an unlocked car and frantically locked himself inside.

Bill Neely's Country Blues

Of all the musicians who've backed Threadgill, who didn't play an instrument, he had a special kinship with Bill Neely, whose life also changed after an encounter with Jimmie Rodgers as a teenager. Neely was a thirteen-year-old farm kid from North Texas who saw Rodgers play in a tent in 1929, then shadowed him afterward. "Why you following me, kid?" asked Rodgers, to which Neely replied, "I want to learn how to play guitar." Rodgers showed the earnest bumpkin how to strum a C-chord—and gave him his thumbpick. "You're the only one to ever play this guitar besides me," said "the father of country music." You can't not be a country blues picker after that.

Neely was a dust bowl refugee during the Depression, riding the rails until he was of army age. Then came marriage in Arizona, kids in Oregon, and city road work in Dallas. He settled down in Austin in '62, driving a truck for the State Hospital, and never missing a Wednesday night open mic at Threadgill's. That's where he met Mance Lipscomb, a deep bluesman from East Texas who'd finally found an audience with folk revivalists and blues-loving hippies.

ABOVE: Janis Joplin was a "surprise" guest of the Threadgill's Jubilee, backed by Julie Paul and Chuck Joyce on guitars. Photograph by Van Brooks. Courtesy of AusPop archives.

RIGHT: Kenneth Threadgill and his '70s band Velvet Cowpasture, featuring Janie Hart, at the Split Rail. Photograph by John Christian. Courtesy of Dolph Briscoe Center for American History.

Ken Threadgill and unidentified man take in the Jubilee scene at night. Photograph by Van Brooks. Courtesy of AusPop Archives.

Like Lipscomb (1895–1976) and Lightnin' Hopkins (1912–82), who both played Austin clubs regularly, Neely brought grit to a '60s music scene of copy bands aimed at college students. He played the Split Rail even before Threadgill and then, with his State Hospital coworker Larry Kirbo on guitar, did all the folk clubs. Neely was authentic enough for the roots police at Arhoolie Records to put out his *Blackland Farm Boy* in '74. A career highlight was representing Central Texas at the Smithsonian Folklife Festival in DC in 1976.

When hotshot LA band Rank and File relocated to Austin in 1981, they were looking for real Texas music and found it in Neely, who opened for them at the Shorthorn Bar on North Lamar.

"He was like a bit of history I could go and talk to," said Alejandro Escovedo, whose first Austin band was Rank. Both had wives named Bobbi, and Alejandro's wife worked at Threadgill's where Neely played often. "He was always trying to sell me stuff—guitars, Western shirts, cars," said Alejandro. "My daughter Maya's first bike was bought from Bill Neely." He remained a child of the Depression, in both music and survival instinct.

Neely passed away March 22, 1990, at age seventy-three, just three weeks after he'd been diagnosed with leukemia. His pallbearers were musicians he'd inspired including Sean Mencher of High Noon, who called Neely's sound "the perfect marriage of country and blues, the two prominent styles of music in Austin." Bassist J. C. George slipped a pick on the thumb of Neely's right hand before they closed the casket.

Bill Neely's life in music began when "the Singing Brakeman" gave him a thumbpick and "learnt me my first chord," as Neely put it. He deserved to go out the same way.

The son of a Pentecostal preacher, Ken Threadgill is remembered less for his music than for the community he nurtured with his example of love, kindness, and, especially, acceptance.

ABOVE: Mance Lipscomb with Bill Neely and Taj Mahal looking on, backstage at the Armadillo. Photograph by Burton Wilson.

RIGHT: Janis Joplin as she looked when she sang at Threadgill's every Wednesday. Photograph by the *Daily Texan* from the July 27, 1962, feature "She Dares to Be Different," by Pat Sharpe.

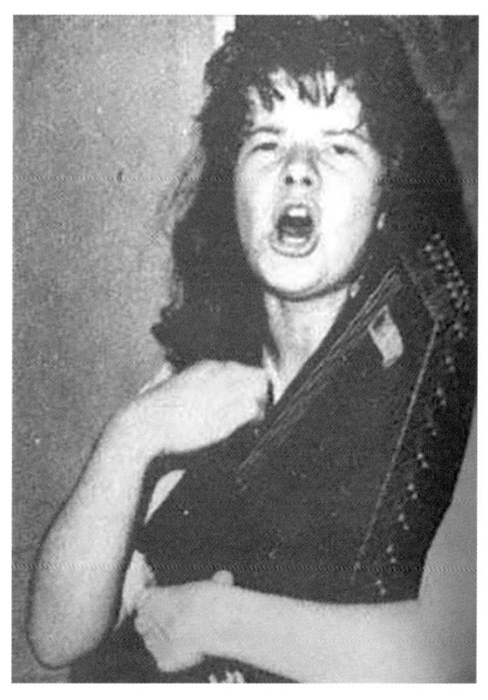

That was the spirit Rod Kennedy was looking for when he launched the Kerrville Folk Festival in 1972. In acknowledgement of Jimmie Rodgers living in Kerrville before his 1933 passing, Kennedy christened the event with Threadgill singing "Blue Yodel # 1 (T For Texas)" the first night. His cover of the old Shelton Brothers hillbilly number "Just Because" got former President Lyndon Johnson bopping in the aisle, so soon after a massive heart attack. (The fatal one would come the next year.) Today, the covered Threadgill Memorial Theater is the second stage at Kerrville.

John Kenneth Threadgill wasn't a traditionalist, he was the tradition. Born in Hunt County just outside of Greenville, the ninth of eleven kids, Ken's family came to Austin in 1923 when he was fourteen. After graduating from Austin High in 1928, Threadgill moved back to Beaumont, where his father had led a Church of the Nazarene for four years before Austin. Beaumont was where a nineteen-year-old Kenneth first heard Rodgers, who replaced Al Jolson as his singing obsession.

Back in Austin, he worked at a Gulf Station on the Dallas Highway (North Lamar) and made a little extra selling copies of the *Austin American* morning paper, wrapped around bootleg liquor. Eventually, he bought the gas station and when Prohibition ended in 1933, Threadgill waited in line overnight to get the first license to sell beer in Travis County. The fillin' station became Threadgill's Tavern.

Threadgill's closed during WWII, when Kenneth got a job as a welder for the US Army Corps of Engineers, repairing bridges and other structures on area bases.

After the war, Threadgill's reopened and stayed open, twenty-four hours a day. He took out the gas pumps in 1947 and concentrated on the tavern. "I didn't have a key for nine years," Threadgill told the *American-Statesman* in a 1970 profile that provides much of the information here.

After the clubs closed, the party would end up at Threadgill's. "Pop Wheeler would come by with his bass, Mildred Womack would sit at the piano, and Joe Ramon would be on fiddle," Threadgill said of the afterhours jams that would sometimes serenade dawn. Threadgill had his own string band at the time with Shorty Zeiger, Ole Peterson, and Herman Thompson, the one-legged fiddler.

Kenneth and wife Mildred started keeping business hours in the mid-'50s, when the Saturday night jam sessions were getting so crowded that they moved to midweek. At 9 o'clock every Wednesday night, Threadgill would come from behind the bar, still wearing his apron, and yodel a short set that would end with a crowd-pleasing jig. Threadgill otherwise forbade dancing, lest he be hit with a dancehall tax.

There was always a big groan at last call, but Threadgill would say, "We don't make the laws, we just try to get along with them." On one particularly chaotic Wednesday night, Threadgill was told he had a lot of patience. "Thanks," he said, "but I prefer to call them customers."

Split Rail Inn

The fire marshal wasn't thrilled to see well over two hundred people crammed into Threadgill's, so the Wednesday night songfests were discontinued in 1965. Kenneth and his Hootenanny Hoots sought a club residency, and Bob Bass of the Split Rail gave them Saturday nights, then Sundays, too, when they brought in a nice crowd.

The Rail had been more of a hangout with cheap pitchers and touted fried chicken than a music venue, though such honky-tonk singers as Roger Beck and Barney Tall also played there. Cedar choppers, softball players, and stoners all drank beer together, an inclusionary mindset found in "Split Rail Inn," written by the Joyces. "Are you straight, are you hippie, are you Klan?" went the chorus.

With his smattering of pot-smoking, war-protesting fans growing into a throng, Threadgill was the link between Barney Tall and Marcia Ball. What he started at the Split Rail, Freda (Marcia) and the Firedogs turned into a local sensation, packing the Rail every Sunday night from 1972–74. One of their regular guests was Doug Sahm, in the process of being dropped by Atlantic. "I'd go into the Split Rail and sing 'Is Anybody Goin' to San Antone' and everybody would flip out," Sahm told Ed Ward of the *Statesman*. "There was all this love that I needed."

While Willie Nelson gave Austin's music scene a name and a face for the world, it had already been established that Texas hippies loved country music. That's why Willie moved here in the summer of '72.

Leon Russell and Willie Nelson open the first Willie Picnic. Photograph by Watt Casey.

Waylon Jennings plays the first Willie Picnic July, 4, 1973, Hurlbut Ranch.
Photograph by Van Brooks. Courtesy of AusPop Archives.

II.

Dripping with Significance

Nobody protested when developers built million-dollar homes at Hurlbut Ranch, thirty-five miles west of Austin. But that's sacred land, where "progressive country," Willie's Picnic, and "grunge" were born.

"The Country Woodstock"

The three-day Dripping Springs Reunion in March 1972 anticipated crowds of sixty thousand a day for a mix of country legends—Buck Owens, Loretta Lynn, Merle Haggard, Roy Acuff, etc.—with hip, offbeat favorites Willie Nelson, Waylon Jennings, Kris Kristofferson, Roger Miller, and Tom T. Hall. Tickets were ten dollars, or twenty-five dollars for all three days, but a total of only twenty thousand came through the gates. The crowd for Friday's bluegrass lineup, including Bill Monroe and Earl Scruggs, was a paltry two thousand. The biggest day was Sunday, with Willie, Kris, Rita Coolidge, and Waylon playing to twelve thousand. The fest was "a successful failure," according to Mike McFarland, one of the four promoters from Dallas.

"They lost a fortune," Willie said in a 1973 interview with the *Statesman*, blaming too much money spent on advertising in New York and Nashville and not enough in Texas. Indeed, much of the hometown crowd was unaware of the festival until Townsend Miller raved in the *Statesman* about the quality of the music, and good-time festival air, calling the event, "the greatest family picnic ever."

Willie Nelson picked up on that vibe when he brought his first Fourth of July Picnic to Hurlbut Ranch the next year because the infrastructure was in place. Those poor Dallas guys had to clear roadways, bring in electricity, and drill wells.

The rock festival format apparently didn't appeal to hardcore country fans, who preferred seating and shade and plumbing. But Texas music history was made, nonetheless, at Hurlbut in '72, not only because the cordial coexistence of pot smokers and beer drinkers convinced Willie that Austin was where he needed to be but for the live music debut of an unbilled Billy Joe Shaver. Though the size of the crowd was disappointing to promoters, it was overwhelming to a hayseed poet from Waco, pushed onstage by Kristofferson during a set change. Singer Bobby Bare, whose publishing company had hired Shaver, warned him not to, under any circumstances, sing "that interracial song or the rednecks'll kill you." So, of course, a defiant Billy Joe opened with "Black Rose," and when he got to "Well the devil made me do it the first time / the second time I done it on my own," the crowd roared and gave Shaver a standing ovation at the end of the song. He tried to walk offstage, but emcee Tex Ritter (UT class of '29) turned him around. "I'm not any good," said Shaver. But the crowd ate him up.

A guitar pull in a backstage trailer was even bigger for Shaver's confidence. After Billy Joe sang "Willie the Wanderin' Gypsy and Me," Waylon Jennings poked his head in and asked if he had any more of them ol' cowboy songs. "I have a whole sack full of 'em," Shaver told his favorite singer, which led to Waylon's *Honky Tonk Heroes* LP, featuring nine Billy Joe compositions. *Heroes* came out the month before the first Willie Picnic, as did *Shotgun Willie*, which introduced Nelson's version of Johnny Bush's "Whiskey River." Though now regarded as classics, neither LP sold very well, except in Austin.

Charlie Rich performs at the first Fourth of July Picnic with Willie and Leon looking on. Photograph by Watt Casey.

Willie's "Picnic"

Willie would be a Red Headed Stranger-to-the-charts for another two years, until "Blue Eyes Crying in the Rain" ended a thirteen-year drought on the country singles Top Ten. So how did he and his scruffy friends draw forty thousand fans to Hurlbut Ranch in July heat just a year after the biggest bust in country music concert history? They treated the Picnic as a counterculture festival of country music, hiring the crew from the Armadillo to run things, and buying ads on KLBJ-FM and other rock stations in Texas and neighboring states.

The secret weapon was Leon Russell, whose gospel-infused piano turned concerts into spiritual revivals, making him one of the biggest touring rock acts. Promoting 1973's triple-LP *Leon Live*, which reclaimed "Delta Lady" from Joe Cocker, Leon had his own headlining dates in Texas so he couldn't be advertised. But word-of-mouth confirmed him coming to help his new best friend Willie celebrate the births of not only the USA but the new country music individual—a figure so foreign to the way Nashville ran things they were called outlaws.

The Cult of Willie went national when *Rolling Stone* and the *New York Times*, among others, covered the Picnic as if it was the Super Bowl of the hippie cowboy lifestyle. Willie's July 4 soiree was an endurance event, a test of loyalty and sunscreen, as much as a concert. The press release for the second Picnic, at the Texas World Speedway in College Station, was honest about year one's problems: "Traffic backed up 10 miles . . . water and restrooms were inadequate . . . the sound system blew out. The temperature reached 100 degrees and there was no shade. Texans love their music, however, and at 2 a.m. on July 5, 1973, happily exhausted fans headed home, unanimously looking forward to Willie's Second Annual Fourth of July Picnic in 1974."

Folks always look so happy at Willie's Picnics no matter how miserable they should be.

The Dharma Bums at Woodshock with Joe McDermott,
Garrett Williams and Steve Spinks, 1985. Photograph by Deb Pastor.

ABOVE (TOP): Townsend Miller and Willie Nelson at the 1972 Dripping Springs Reunion, a precursor of the Fourth of July Picnic. Photograph by John Jefferson. Courtesy of Dolph Briscoe Center for American History.

Devil's Hole on the Hurlbut Ranch offered a refreshing respite from the punk onslaught at Woodshock, 1985. Photograph by Pat Blashill.

The Offenders play Woodshock 1986, their final show until the inevitable reunion twenty years later. Photograph by Jerry Milton.

Woodshock, 1985

The only thing the Woodshock punk festivals had in common with the Reunion and the Picnic was Hurlbut Ranch, which required a long drive up a rocky road, so your car would get fucked up, too. Anarchy was tamed by nature in "Tripping Springs," when punks turned into hippies if only for the longest day. Woodshock was at Hurlbut from 1983–85.

In that third year, my mind's camera clicked on the moment of the day just before the sun rises, when the darkness positively glows. Next to the stage was a wild party revolving around members of Seattle's U-Men, San Francisco's Tales of Terror and the Austin bands Poison 13 and Scratch Acid. They were toasting the performances they'd given earlier in the evening, which demonstrated an uncanny musical kinship. They were all considered punk bands, but there was something different going on, from the U-Men's melding of Captain Beefheart and Gang of Four, Tales of Terror's manic metallica, Poison 13's assertion that Howlin' Wolf was the original punk rocker, and Scratch Acid's big bottom sound, which was closer to Led Zeppelin than to the Sex Pistols. It was the morning of June 30, 1985, the last day that ecstasy was legal, and pop music had changed right before the dilated pupils of the six hundred or so still in attendance. This blessed fest had kicked off eighteen hours earlier with Daniel Johnston singing "The Marching Guitars."

This new style of music—slowed metal/art rock played with punk attitude—wouldn't have a name until six years later, when Kurt Cobain, a big fan of the aforementioned bands, led Nirvana to the top of the charts, and the U-Men's manager Susan Silver guided Alice in Chains and Soundgarden to the platinum promised land. They called it "grunge," and it sold almost as many albums as flannel shirts and combat boots.

Every young man and woman should have an experience like Woodshock, where you lose yourself in the music and the camaraderie, shaking up your mind to get rid of the excess brain cells that are holding you down. Even the skinheads were mellow.

The 1981 debut, organized by Chris Wing of Sharon Tate's Baby, was a free BYOB event on the deck near the west entrance of Waterloo Park downtown. Only a hundred or so were on hand, but it was an amazing day by all accounts.

An unlikely trio of bouncer/actor Charles "Doug the Slug" Gunning III and musicians Mike Alvarez (Max and the Make-ups) and Jeff Smith (the Hickoids), got with Blaine Hurlbut, the cool ranch heir, to make Woodshock an annual campout/passout in '83. After three years at the Hurlbut Ranch, protests from neighbors moved the fest to Camp Ben McCulloch, just across from Salt Lick barbecue in Driftwood. That '86 Woodshock is remembered for two things: 1) a stupefying set by the Butthole Surfers, whose singer Gibby Haynes used a bullhorn after the PA went out, and 2) someone giving psychedelics to Daniel Johnston.

Daniel that night was charming, funny, ecstatic to be part of such a cool event. But weeks later, he'd be up to his knees in Waller Creek, yelling incoherently until the cops took him away. He was never the same.

Neither was Woodshock. Though there'd been a few half-assed productions in subsequent years using the Woodshock name, the last real one was '86 at Camp Ben. You can't call an all-day punk festival Woodshock without a swimming hole and psychedelics.

Bobbie Nelson joined brother Willie's band on piano in 1973, just before the first Picnic. Photograph by Nancy E. Goldfarb LeNoir.

1889
WILLKOMMEN ZUM SAENGERFEST.
CAPITOL CLOTHING HOUSE
MEYER MINCHEN MERCHANT TAILOR
TRUNKS
VALISES

III.

The Singin' and Swingin' Germans: 1860s to the Jazz Age

Liberty Lunch . . . bulldozed. Armadillo . . . gone. One Knite . . . Stubb's. Charlie's Playhouse and the Skyline and Soap Creek and the original Antone's were all wiped off the face of Austin to make way for office buildings, parking lots, condos, and other boring shit. Workers at One Texas Center park their stupid cars where Jimmy Cliff once sang "The Harder They Come" for an audience which had never heard live reggae before.

Almost all the lionized Austin clubs are long gone, but one of the city's first live music venues—beating Millett Opera House (the Austin Club today) by six years—is still standing.

Turner Hall

Turner Hall was built in 1872 by the Turn Verein social and athletic club. Turn comes from *turnen*, which means "to practice gymnastics." *Verein* is German for "club." Physical fitness was a big part of Turner Hall (a common Americanization), which had a gymnasium and a bowling alley.

It was one of many halls erected in Texas by German and Czech immigrants in the years between the Civil War and World War I to help keep their cultural identity alive. Most of the plays and operas staged at Turner were in German.

Since 1914, that limestone edifice on Lavaca St. at 18th has been home to the Scottish Rite Theater.

Designed by San Antonio mayor C. A. Thielepape, Turner Hall had a capacity of four hundred inside and a couple thousand more in the back biergarten, in the shadow of the state capitol, which burned down in 1881. You could have a beer at Turner and watch the dome being rebuilt.

Turner Hall became more easily accessible in 1874 when Austin's mule-drawn trolley system extended lines down Lavaca to the venue. Turner's Saloon opened in the basement in 1885.

Scholz Garden was built earlier, 1866, and occasionally hosted musical events, but it was primarily a restaurant/bar, not a dedicated venue. The Austin Saengerrude vocal group met at Turner every Thursday because their own hall, next to Scholz's, wasn't built until 1879. Turner was also home to Austin's Maennerchor Society, a men's choir that would also relocate to Saengerrunde Hall.

The first documented music venue in Austin was Buaas Garden on the E. 400 block of Pecan (Sixth) Street. It opened six years before Scholz's but was cleared in 1874 to make way for buildings that are still there. The middle one was home of rock club Steamboat 1874 from 1978–1999.

Besserer and Ludwig: The Music Men

John L. Buaas was the stepfather of Carl William Besserer, who would go on to be Austin's John Phillip Sousa. Buaas sent him to Germany as a teenager to be trained by future New York Philharmonic leader Leopold Damrosch.

Besides owning a musical instrument store with Buaas, Besserer was active at Turner Hall since the beginning. According to *Limestone to Legacy*, Gordon W. Kelso's essential history of the building, one of the first big productions at Turner was "Laila," a three-act operetta featuring forty students from Austin Female College under the direction of Besserer. In 1873, he married the daughter of August Scholz (who called his place "Garden," not "Garten"). After Scholz died in 1891, the Besserers inherited Scholz's but sold it after a few years so Carl could dedicate himself to music. The Austin Saengerrunde has owned Scholz's since 1908. It's the longest-operating business in the state and the oldest beer garden in the country.

If you needed something done, musically, Besserer was your man. From 1895 until the boat's destruction in the 1900 flood, Besseser led the orchestra of the Ben Hur paddle wheel riverboat on its excursions on Lake Austin when it was called Lake McDonald. In 1906, he put together, on short notice, a string quartet to back French actress Sarah Bernhardt at Hancock Opera House (120 W. Sixth St.), on a performance of *Camille* the *Statesman* called "decidedly the greatest ever seen in Austin." Playing cello was Carl T. Widen, the son of Swedish immigrants, who would cofound the Austin Symphony in 1911.

Though Besserer is "the Father of Austin Music," many considered pianist Edmund Ludwig, whose Conservatory of Music trained many at 301 E. 14th St., its finest musician.

Ludwig went against the town's classical music establishment in 1897, when he canceled a concert at the Millett Opera House because segregation was practiced—with Blacks in the balcony. The scheduled dual piano recital was with African American Maud Cuney, the head of the music department for the Texas Institute of Deaf, Dumb, Blind Colored Youth on Bull Creek Road. When Cuney made Ludwig aware of the seating inequality, they held the concert at the blind school instead. In attendance was an eight-year-old student named Arizona Dranes, who would go on to pioneer "the gospel beat," with piano-driven recordings on Okeh Records in 1926. Born in 1889, Dranes attended the Austin Institute for Deaf, Dumb, and Blind Colored Youths from age seven to twenty-one.

Austin's first two great musicians, Carl William Besserer (1851–1931) and Edmund Ludwig (1858–1909), are both buried at Oakwood Cemetery.

Turner Hall was prominent in the 1889 Saengerfest, a German singing celebration which rotated each year between New Braunfels, San Antonio, Galveston, and Austin. *The Austin Daily Statesman* covered the hometown's turn like it would later obsess over SXSW and ACL Fest.

"This will be one of the grandest displays Austin has ever had," the *Statesman* correctly predicted on April 13, 1889. Saengerfest's motto was German for "When men sing there are no bad men, for bad men have no song."

The fest opened with a torchlight procession up Sixth St. and down Congress towards the state capitol. The parade, which featured two marching bands and Governor Sul Ross, followed the streetcar tracks to Turner Hall, where a smaller arch on Lavaca marked the end of the procession.

The *Statesman* writer was in top form: "The blare of music, the tramp of marching men and the shifting line of torches formed one panoramic phantasmagoria, beautiful to contemplate, grand to behold and pleasant to remember." The banquet at Turner Hall found "long tables" which "fairly groaned beneath the burden of delicacies." The Saengerfest concluded April 24 with a picnic concert under the live oaks at Pressler's Garden (1327 W. Sixth) during the day and, at night, a grand ball at Turner Hall, featuring a forty-piece orchestra of German musicians from around the state, organized and led by Besserer.

Schools closed early that day so families could go to Pressler's, a former brewery with a bandstand in the middle of beautifully landscaped grounds that extended south to the river.

Here's the *Statesman* again: "He who could not find pleasure in such surroundings has no place on Earth—Heaven's his home."

Turner Hall fell into disrepair at the turn of the twentieth century, with Saengerrude Hall and the Hancock Opera House (est. 1898) hosting most of the German musical and indoor athletic events. The building was sold in 1912 to Ben Hur Temple, who passed it on just two years later to the Scottish Rite folks. A massive renovation changed the façade while keeping the core.

So, this town's oldest venue is still there, you just can't see it anymore.

When UT Dances Were Called "The Germans"

The 1920's Austin music scene revolved around the University of Texas—as it would for decades—so if you wanted to make a living as a musician you played frat dances, which back then were called "Germans" because the first ones were organized by the German Club. This handpicked interfraternity supergroup of popular kids hosted Saturday night dances at the Knights of Co-

This German singing society met at Turner Hall for seven years before Saengerrude Hall was built next to Scholz's Garden. Courtesy of Texas Music Museum.

lumbus Hall at Eighth and Colorado Streets. Claiming that the six hundred-capacity venue could barely handle their members, pledges, and dates, the Germans denied admission to "barbs"—for barbarians—students socially independent of fraternities and sororities.

Such snobbery didn't sit well with the board of regents, which voted to dissolve the German Club in 1929, along with other exclusive "ribbon clubs" on campus like the Skull and Bones. Even after student dances were officially labeled all-university, they were called Germans until the ascent of Adolph Hitler in the late 1930s.

One of the first popular jazz orchestras to play at the Germans was the Howell and Gardner Band-its of 1919, led by Jay and Hilton Howell of Cameron, and Steve Gardner, who also played sax for the Longhorn Band.

Steve Gardner put together his own orchestra in 1923, with brothers Fred on sax, John on tuba, and Derry on banjo. That same year, banjo-playing sister Bernice Gardner joined the Texette Sextette, an all-female pop/jazz band from the Scottish Rite dorm.

For a city of less than fifty thousand, Austin had a vibrant music scene in the '20s, but the stock market crash of 1929 led to the Great Depression, for the country as well as the music scene. Multi-instrumentalist Gardner cut his twelve-piece orchestra to a combo—Steve Gardner and His Hokum Kings—who kept active until 1941. A 1965 *Statesman* interview of oldest brother J. Harris Gardner, Travis County's first juvenile judge and namesake of Gardner House detention facility (now Gardner-Betts), told the history of the musical Gardners, who moved to Austin from West Texas circa 1914. After a 1917 performance at University Baptist Church, attended by Col. Haston Smith of Camp Mabry, Steve Gardner was recruited to lead the 131st Artillery Band during World War I.

While Steve Gardner's bands (one called "Steve's Stevedores") battled Gertrude Shoch's Varsity Peacocks and Jimmie's Joys, led by Jimmie Maloney (whose gimmick was playing two clarinets simultaneously), for lucrative German gigs, the Texettes played "gym-jams" for barbs most Friday nights. With a repertoire of popular songs like "Carolina in the Morning" and Sophie Tucker's "You Gotta See Mama Every Night," the Sextette played live on the Statesmen's radio station WNAS to promote those shows at UT's women's gymnasium. The group also played between movies at the Queen Theater, at the 1923 opening of the pavilion at Barton Springs and at fundraisers for the Memorial Stadium construction. Nobody'd ever seen an all-female jazz group before, so the Texettes usually got wild ovations, "forced to encore every selection they played," according to one review.

Led by Miss Clyde Watkins on violin and featuring drummer Etelka "Tech" Schmidt, Bernice Gardner on banjo, Jane Worthington on piano, and the sax duo of Bernice Milburn and Maizine Grady in the original lineup, the Texettes formed the same year as California's Helen Lewis and Her All-Girl Jazz Syncopators, who are often credited as the first all-female band.

The Texettes were active only two years, with no known recordings, but they own a piece of history.

Steve Gardner went on to head UT's band and orchestra department, while keeping a steady schedule of night gigs. But one job he'd probably liked to have turned down was playing the debut concert at the Ku Klux Klan hall at E. Fifth and San Jacinto Streets in 1924. Still in the bask of 1915's Klan-glorifying blockbuster *Birth of a Nation*, the white-robed bigots did not have the despicable reputation in '24 they would have just a few years later. The Klan posed as a Christian organization out to make America great again, and in February '24, they put on a circus attended by thousands. Their giant burning cross at the entrance, just south of the Congress Avenue Bridge, could be seen from miles away.

In the late 1920s to mid-1930s, one of the most popular dance bands in town was George Corley and His Royal Aces, a nine-piece "colored orchestra" from Sam Huston College in East Austin, which included brothers Reginald, John, and Wilford Corley. The Aces played swanky gigs for fraternity parties, at the Avalon Dinner Club on far North Lamar, and at the Driskill and other hotels. After the Avalon closed in late '38 amid noise complaints from neighbors, Corley's group moved to the Rocky River Tavern on Burnet Highway. The Aces' homebase on the Eastside was the Paradise Inn at 813 E. 11th St.

The Corley name was well-known around Austin from "the Ol' Lamplighter," George M. Corley Sr. (born 1878), who serviced as many as nine hundred gas lamps—trimming wicks and relighting pilots—for decades before widespread electricity. In a 1961 *Statesman* profile, before he died that year at age eighty-three, Corley Sr. touched on dreams of being a musician before he found his trade. He made sure music was important to the family he started. All five kids played in bands, with George Jr. and Reginald eventually becoming music teachers at Black high schools in Oakland and DC, respectively.

ABOVE (TOP): The Ben Hur pleasure boat was destroyed during the 1900 flood. Courtesy of Austin History Center.

ABOVE: An all-female pop/jazz band from the Scottish Rite dorm, the Texette Sextet formed in 1923. Courtesy of Dolph Briscoe Center for American History.

EAST 6 TH-ST. BAR
Coca-Cola
Dr Pepper
NEW LOOK Beauty Salon
REGAL BEAUTY SALON
7up
Calvert
EAST
STREET

IV.

Sixth and Red River

Eleven Blocks That Make Up "The Devil's Dogleg"

Austin's most famous street has earned the nickname "Dirty Sixth" over the past few years, with an unruly Bourbon Street-like atmosphere and a YouTube driven reputation for violence. It's where teens beef with bullets on weekends, and sometimes the scent of danger makes you forget the history of the street whose buildings, even those housing tattoo parlors and frat bars, were erected mostly in the late 1800s. East Sixth, from Brazos to the interstate has, what's believed to be the greatest concentration of limestone Victorian commercial buildings west of the Mississippi.

The close proximity of nightclubs on Sixth, many of which change to live music venues for a week to catch a whiff of the windfall, was key to the success of South by Southwest in the early years. Modeled after Manhattan's New Music Seminar, SXSW had a big logistical advantage in that music industry attendees could see bands in clubs a few steps from each other all the way down Sixth and up Red River Streets. It was possible to sample several acts an hour. Equal exposure in Manhassle would require major cab fare, and four hours of your time.

The '80s and '90s were the heyday for live music on Sixth, with the Black Cat and Steamboat rockin' a block apart, and the Cannibal Club across the street. The cursed 222 E. Sixth location, where even the Hard Rock Café failed, had a good run in the '80s from Sixth Street Live (James Brown!) to Mirage, where Nine Inch Nails doused sweaty ringsiders with gallons of water, then ripped open bags of flour to send the crowd into the night air like white-caked zombies.

The Ritz Theater went through several incarnations, including a hardcore punk phase in the early '80s, then you had funk and hip-hop at Homer Hill's Catfish Station, reggae at Flamingo Cantina, punk at Emo's, blues at Joe's Generic, country at Headliners East, Irish music at B. D. Riley's and Maggie Mae's, and everything in-between at Babe's and Lucy's Retired Surfers Bar. And that's not counting piano bars and cover band joints.

But Sixth was still tame enough that the Coen brothers could make their first film *Blood Simple* undisturbed there in 1984. Multiple-Oscar-winner Frances McDormand also made her screen debut, with her character moving into an apartment above the Old Pecan Street Cafe (314 E. Sixth) that was the scene of the bloody finale.

By the '90s, "Dirty Sixth" had gotten so popular that the street was closed to cars on weekends and during SXSW, which created a hangout for teenagers too young or adults too broke to get into the bars. It's called "parking lot pimpin'," and the mob that mills between the barricades triples during South by Southwest, calling for cops in riot formation. The few miserable-looking, badge-wearing registrants move through the roving street gangs and drunken frats like they're navigating chest-high swamp water. This was not in the brochure!

Some Sixth Street merchants and club owners made news in 2013 when they closed and boarded up the Saturday night of the Texas Relays track meet, the Super Bowl for Black Austin. Their venues didn't cater to that demographic—predominately teenagers—and none of their usual customers could get through the throng, they argued, but the moves smacked of racism.

The Ritz has gone through many hands since Jim Franklin brought live music there in '74, including a late '80s phase managed by Paul Sessums of the Black Cat. Note the cheap beer prices from the sidewalk bar. Photograph by Bill Leissner.

History reminds us that Sixth Street, which was platted as Pecan Street in 1839, was built on true diversity. While most of the rest of Austin abided by rules of Jim Crow segregation, East Sixth was always open to every race. Black businesses were next to Lebanese, Chinese, Jewish, and Hispanic storefronts. Jonas Silberstein's store at 305 East 6th St. was one of the few in Austin where Black customers could try on clothing before they bought it. White businesses, like Hyman Samuelson's Crown Tailors at 408 E. Sixth, advertised on Black radio shows, such as Lavada Durst's "Dr. Hepcat" on KVET. "Now if you want to be draped in shape, hop on down and get your frantic fronts at Crown," Durst would say.

Street of Dreams

Sixth (Pecan) Street became Austin's east-west Main Street because it was the most level path from the east. And it was the closest street to the Colorado River that didn't flood in the years before a huge granite dam was constructed in 1893 (and collapsed in 1900), where Tom Miller Dam is today. It was safe to build on well-traveled Sixth Street, so settlers and immigrants opened dry goods stores, saloons, sporting houses, and hotels. When the Houston and Texas Central Railroad came to Austin in 1871, the town's population doubled to ten thousand in a year. Pecan Street was dubbed "The Street of Dreams."

Congress Avenue was segregated, so Blacks couldn't go to the Paramount Theatre. They were welcome at the Ritz, which opened in 1929, though they had to sit in the balcony. There were no such restrictions at the Lyric Theater (419 E. Sixth St.), which was opened in the '20's by prominent African American dentist Everett Givens, "the Bronze Mayor of Austin." By the time Bessie Smith played there in 1931, the Lyric was called the Dunbar Theater.

Musician Jimmie Jones, who worked at the Tip Top barbershop, three doors down from the Nicholas Brothers shoe shop, recalled the 400 block of Sixth as where a Black clientele would converge on weekends. "People would come there from all over—Bastrop, Giddings, Lockhart, Round Rock, Manor, all those," he told the *Austin Chronicle*.

The 700 block of E. Sixth became mostly Hispanic at the turn of the twentieth century, with Garza's Meat Market and Austin's first Tex-Mex restaurant, El Original. There were also Chinese laundries on Sixth, and Joe Lung's Cafe, which opened in 1916 at the 301 E. Sixth St. location of Shawn Cirkiel's Parkside eatery.

Much of this information comes from *Sixth Street*, a good history book by Dr. Allen Childs, whose family owned Kirby's shoe store on the street for decades.

Waterloo Becomes Austin

Austin and Sixth Street were both born in 1839. Mirabeau B. Lamar, who succeeded Sam Houston as president of the Republic of Texas, discovered Waterloo, as Austin was originally called, while camping near the mouth of Shoal Creek on a buffalo hunt. The town was home to two or three families at the time. Lamar suggested the location to the commission created to select a permanent site for the capital of Texas and they agreed, renaming Waterloo after "the Father of Texas," Stephen F. Austin. Lamar's agent, Judge Edwin Waller laid out the town in a fifteen-block square, naming the north-south streets after Texas rivers and the east-west streets after indigenous trees.

Sixth Street was Pecan Street until 1884, when the city had overgrown available tree names and decided to go numerical. Two years later, Sixth Street had its crown jewel when cattle baron Col. Jesse Driskill built Austin's first grand hotel at the corner of Sixth and Brazos. A late spring freeze killed three thousand of Driskill's cattle in 1888 and wiped him out financially, forcing him to sell the hotel. Or he lost it in a card game, the version favored by those who believe the colonel haunts his namesake hotel to this day.

Sixth and Red River Streets changed drastically after the repeal of Prohibition in 1933. The majority of liquor stores and bars were owned by Lebanese Americans, many descendants of Cater Joseph, who led the Lebanese immigration to Austin in the 1880s. His father put him on a ship at age fourteen, with younger brothers to follow, to avoid mandatory enlistment to the Turkish Army at the tail end of the Ottoman Empire.

Twin brothers Theodore and Arthur Jabour opened a package store on East Sixth that served as the foundation for the Twin Liquors empire of over a hundred stores in Central Texas today. Their main competition was from the Attal brothers Wolfred and Gus, whose A&A Drugs across the street engaged in alcohol price wars with the Jabours. But that was only business. The sets of brothers were part of a bigger family—Catholic and patriotic—that would send a few men to sleep at Zilker Park the night before Easter and the Fourth of July, to reserve enough tables for the whole Lebanese clan. Wolffred Attal is the grandfather of concert promoter Charles Attal, whose Austin City Limits Music Festival takes over Zilker's Great Lawn every October.

The Sabb family owned the Diamond Bar, next door to the Ritz, where Gene Snowden, "Austin's Original Hillbilly Poet," began performing in the late '40s. Backed by the great guitarist Curly Top Clayton, Snowden was perhaps the first local musician on Sixth Street that folks came out see, specifically. "I'm the son of a railroad bum, with a one-track mind," Snowden sang to appreciative crowds at the Diamond, whose six-foot-tall stage was designed to let the musicians keep playing during brawls. Like many Sixth Street sensations that would follow, Snowden could not break out of Austin's clubs for a national career. His hard-drinkin' ways didn't help.

For the first half of the twentieth century, Sixth Street was bustling, but it started getting seedy after World War II, when Austin's first shopping centers drew away customers. You could buy a reefer on any streetcorner on Sixth, claimed a 1953 *Statesman* article that detailed the downtown decline. When I-35 was built in 1959, erasing the prosperous East Avenue melting pot, it created a barrier from East Austin.

The almighty Driskill closed in 1969 and was saved from demolition only through a campaign that raised $900,000. The next year the Ritz became a porno movie house, as did other theaters on the strip, including the former Yank Theater, which changed its name for obvious reasons. Cross-dressing streetwalkers strolled in front of the dirty peep shows, as "The Street of Dreams" had become Sleaze Central.

But various Austinites wouldn't give up on what was once a vibrant thoroughfare. Architect David Graeber paid $13,000 for the former Rob the Robin Cafe building at 410 E. Sixth St. in 1968 and turned it into an *Architectural Digest*-worthy townhouse, with an indoor swimming pool.

Four years later, the Old Pecan Street Café, with its "continental cuisine," turned the block into a destination for whatever they called foodies back then. Sixth was still sketchy, but worth exploring.

After the legal drinking age dropped to eighteen in 1973, new Sixth Street bars like Gordo's and Toad

The Twin Liquors empire began on Sixth Street in the 1930s.
Courtesy of Texas Historical Commission.

The original Antone's at 141 E. Sixth St. brought
blues greats to Austin. Photograph by Diana Ray.

Hall started drawing UT students. With the October '74 reopening of the Ritz Theater as a concert hall, with Weather Report, Dr. John, J.J. Cale, and Pretty Things in the first few weeks, "skid row" was becoming the new entertainment district.

But funding was funky for the Jim Franklin Ritz, which lasted only a few months before the requisite Willie Nelson benefit/stay of execution. In April '75, filmmakers Eagle Pennell and Maureen Gosling organized Austin's first film festival—"Change the Reel"—at the Ritz, debuting the *Austin City Limits* pilot. In September '75, after extensive renovations, the Ritz became the new home of the Center Stage theater company for about a year. "Esther's Follies" moved in, temporarily in the '80s, before Shannon Sedwick and Michael Shelton bought the former JJJ Bar at the corner of Sixth and Red River.

Valmon Records

The south side of the 300 block of E. Sixth had long been vital as a hub for Spanish-language music, with La Plaza, and the Green Spot next door, pumping out accordion-driven conjunto. Austin's first Mexican American record label Valmon opened at 313 in the late '50s when watchmaker Ben Moncivais leased space upstairs from the Martin Valdez furniture store and opened Valmon Jewelry (Val for Valdez and Mon for Moncivais). A big fan of Chicano soul and Mexican polka music, Moncivais began recording local acts for the label he operated on the side with wife Lupe. Little Joe and the Latinaires put Valmon on the map in 1963 with "Por Un Amor," and the label with the diamond logo also had some success with 45s (recorded live to tape at the Pan-American Center on E. 3rd St.) by Roy Montelongo, Los Sonics, Alfonso Ramos Jr., Shorty and the Corvettes, and more.

The 300 block of E. Sixth St., with Lamplite Saloon and Green Spot in 1974. Photograph by Mack Royal. Courtesy of AusPop archives.

The jewelry/record store relocated to South First in 1978, replaced at 313 E. Sixth by Midnight Cowboy Oriental Modeling, a massage parlor. Valmon continued putting out records until 1980, with about two hundred releases in the catalog. Today, that upstairs space is still called Midnight Cowboy, but it's a craft cocktail bar where a happy ending is getting the check and it's less than fifty dollars.

Clubland Paradise: Sixth Street

ANTONE'S #1, 1975–79

There'd already been blues on Sixth, with Brooks' Home Cooking (418 E. Sixth) much more than a restaurant, and the Lamplite Saloon (currently Blind Pig Pub), where the Fabulous Thunderbirds played their first gigs in 1974 with original singer Lou Ann Barton. Hell, John Lee Hooker played the Ritz in March '75. But no club elevated the local blues scene like Antone's, which opened at 141 E. Sixth on July 15, 1975. The former Levine's department store became "Home of the Blues" almost overnight.

Port Arthur native Clifford Antone was a blues fanatic who wanted to meet all the living Chicago legends, so he opened a club that would treat them like royalty. Antone's hosted the likes of Muddy Waters, Albert King, Albert Collins, Eddie Taylor, and Jimmy Reed for five nights in a row, giving them a break from the road. The audiences would be filled with blues-crazed young musicians, who got to hang out with their idols after the show. That's how Stevie Ray Vaughan met Albert King, and the mutual appreciation began.

But the city council voted to bulldoze the musical classroom in 1979, along with the rest of the one hundred-year-old Bremond Building, which included the great Cajun restaurant Moma's Money, O.K. Records, Ed's Shine Parlor, and Don Politico's Tavern. In its place came a parking garage for the Littlefield Building.

Antone's moved far north, the first of five relocations through the years. Though the club's longest tenure was at 2915 Guadalupe St. (1982–97), some say the original, which also served those Famous Antone's Po' Boys from Uncle Jalal's Houston shops, has never been topped.

ABOVE: Junior Wells, Muddy Waters, and Kim Wilson clowning around at the original Antone's, circa 1978. Photograph by Watt Casey.

LEFT: Clifton Chenier band at Antone's, 1978. They'd played opening night three years earlier. Photograph by Nuri Valbona for the *Daily Texan*. Courtesy of Dolph Briscoe Center for American History.

BLACK CAT LOUNGE, 1985–2002

Austin has had some remarkable club owners, and still does, but there's never been one like Paul Sessums, a biker who grew up in Austin, married an artist and raised their children in a raging nightclub in the heart of Sixth Street. When Sessums would stand on the sidewalk and rail about this and that, leaning on a parking meter as his pulpit, all was right in his world as long as the guitars were ringing through the doors of the Black Cat.

Wife Roberta den-mothered the lost, as little Sasha picked up empty beer bottles. Paul Jr. ("Martian"), a former punk rocker in Criminal Crew, designed the t-shirts that everyone wore, including Timbuk3 on *The Tonight Show*. Sasha ran the club in the late '90s, after her parents semiretired to Palacios, on the Gulf Coast.

The night Sasha was arrested for refusal to turn down the band after repeated noise complaints, Paul Sr. was both proud and livid. The next night there was a big handmade sign that said "Shhh! People are trying to sleep." Another one declared Austin "the Dead Music Capital of the World."

What's sometimes overlooked about all the mythical Austin music clubs is that their calendars had a lot of filler. Even the Armadillo had its cricket nights, but the all-ages Black Cat was almost never dead, seven nights a week, even if the music that night was not your thing. It was a whole scene, lorded over by a biker in a beret with a devilish smile, who gave bands weird sound advice: "Turn up the guitar 23% and turn down the bass 8%."

Groups that played the Black Cat had to do three-to-four-hour sets, no breaks, and for that they were paid handsomely. Paul gave them all the door, which for top acts like Soulhat (with Frosty the drummer), Joe Rockhead, Chris Duarte, Little Sister, Johnny Law, and Ian Moore, could be as much as $3,000 a night if they turned the house. Which isn't hard to do when you're playing for four hours. The only rule was no whining.

Evan Johns and the H-Bombs were the first act to draw music fans to that biker bar at 313 1/2 E. Sixth, the original BC location. The tip jar was on a pulley overhead, and if you'd been there awhile and hadn't tipped, Sessums would make the jar dance over your head until you were shamed to throw in some coin. The Black Cat moved to the bigger 309 E. Sixth in '88, and that's where it really took off. When Sessums was told he needed a permit to sell hotdogs in his club, he gave them away, for years, until the health department shut the free weiners down. They took away dinner to many.

The first real sensation was Two Hoots and a Holler, who packed the place every Monday night from '89 to about '91. They had the songs and the attitude and major frontman talent in Ricky Broussard. One night Broussard decided to take a break after landing wrong on one of his trademark leaps, and Sessums was in his face. "What's the matter, is your pussy sore?" The pair had to be separated. And that was it. The lucrative "Two Hoots and a Hotdog" residency, for both club and band, was over. But that was Paul. He didn't seem to care about money. The Black Cat was never a SXSW venue. It never had a phone and didn't advertise.

Rick Broussard of Two Hoots and a Holler at the Black Cat. Photo by Robin Sullivan. Courtesy of Rick Broussard.

Paul Sessums was not a joiner, and when the East Sixth Street Merchants Association would host a street fair, he'd undercut their four-dollar beer cups by selling ice cold tallboys from a table in front of his club for $1.50 each. It was never considered breaking even when Sessums got a chance to stick it to the man.

ABOVE: Soulhat was one of the most popular Black Cat bands of the 1990s. Photograph by Lisa Davis. Courtesy of Austin History Center.

PAGES 30-31: Joe King Carrasco at Steamboat circa 1986. He and the Crowns always put on a high-energy show. Photograph by Bill Leissner.

ABOVE: The Black Cat had a unique tip jar. Photograph by Bill Leissner.

BELOW: Paul Sessums and artist wife Roberta St. Paul. Photograph by Bill Leissner.

The original Black Cat at 313½ E. Sixth had an "Oriental" massage parlor upstairs. Here are the two owners. Photograph by David C. Fox.

He had more respect for the Korean woman who ran the massage parlor upstairs from the original Black Cat location because she was a true outlaw. Sessums also welcomed Leslie Cochran, the homeless eccentric who paraded up and down Congress Avenue with his butt cheeks on display, causing oglers to shiver when they saw the beard.

You want weird? In the beginning, the Black Cat had the band start the minute the doors opened at 10 p.m. Paul could've sold more beer by letting the milling crowd in an hour earlier, but he didn't like people waiting around in his joint. Plus, it made the bands start on time. This rule changed in the '90s glory years, when cover charges started and it took longer to get the crowd inside.

The Black Cat nurtured many different scenes in its seventeen-year run. It was the home of country, rockabilly, funk, jamband, blues, soul, and whatever you'd call Flametrick Subs with Satan's Cheerleaders (Sasha's favorite band). The club was also the first on Sixth to regularly book hip-hop—every Thursday night in 1990—when a short-term transplant from DC named Citizen Cope made his stage debut.

When Paul Sessums died in a single car accident near Bastrop in 1998, the Black Cat opened for business as usual the next night. There were signs in front—one proclaiming that the Black Cat didn't sell martinis or cigars (this was during the swing fad)—but no memorial of the founder's passing. But that's how Paul Sr. would've liked it. He never could stand crybabies.

The Black Cat Lounge burned down in 2002 and has never been rebuilt or relocated. Or recreated.

STEAMBOAT, 1978–99

The first real rock club on Sixth Street, Steamboat was originally a restaurant/bar with bands at night, like the original Steamboat Springs on Burnet Road. But Sixth Street was rockin' and it didn't take long for music to win out.

Owner Sonny Neath opened Steamboat II in 1978 at the former location of Billy Shakespeare's disco, which had backgammon in the basement. Though it was never really the cool club, Steamboat on Sixth was a consistent positive on the scene for twenty-one years until it was priced off the block in 1999.

Stevie Ray Vaughan recorded *In the Beginning* there April 1, 1980 (it aired live on KLBJ-FM), and regulars included Eric Johnson, Van Wilks, Extreme Heat, and the Bizness. Steamboat was also a cover band paradise where a pre-Grammy Christopher Cross sang "Horse with No Name" just six months before America was opening for him on a national tour.

In the mid-1980s, Steamboat owner Craig Hillis and manager Hank Vick started regularly booking national acts like Los Lobos, Red Hot Chili Peppers, and Jason and the Scorchers. But many consider the club's glory years in the '90s when bar manager Danny Crooks took over booking and built a clubhouse scene on local bands like Joe Rockhead/Ugly Americans (with Bob Schneider), Vallejo, Little Sister, Pushmonkey, Ian Moore, Breedlove, Sunflower, and many more. It was an old-fashioned rock box, where you went to hear loud music and tried to find someone to sleep with. And you got drunk.

Crooks eventually bought the club in the mid 1990s but had only a few years before his landlady gave him sixty days to vacate. She leased the building to a nightclub group from San Antonio at a rent 2 1/2 times higher than the $3100 a month Crooks was paying.

On Steamboat's last night, September 26, 1999, reunited headliners Joe Rockhead led amped-up club regulars in trashing the place—spray-painting the walls, smashing mirrors and bathroom fixtures, and demolishing the stage and sound booth. "I don't think Danny's going to get his deposit back," KLBJ FM's Bob Fonseca said the next morning.

"The new owners said they were going to gut the place," said Crooks, who was already home when the carnage erupted. "We just helped 'em get started."

Antone's was the first renowned club on Sixth in 1975, and Steamboat had the longest run, but the Black Cat left the greatest mark, from 1985 through the 1990s. The Sessums family made Sixth Street weird and wild and outlaw. But the Black Cat was also a place where

The future home of Emo's was Raven's Garage for several decades, then a C&W club named that. Courtesy of Texas Historical Commission.

you could leave your seventeen-year-old daughter and her friends to see Soulhat (as you parked across the street to make sure they were safely inside).

Clifford Antone and Paul Sessums were two maverick Austin clubowners who both died in their mid-fifties—Antone of a heart attack in 2006—whose impact was immeasurable. We didn't move to New York or LA or Nashville because we had Antone's and the Black Cat, and they didn't.

Let's ignore how things are now on Sixth Street, until they get better. And they will on that resilient strip. So much of our foundation as a city, as a people, is built on six blocks from Congress Avenue east to Waller Creek. Six blocks "with just enough danger to make it interesting," as the *Austin Sun* reported in '78.

Six blocks that have represented all of Austin since 1839.

Red River: Street On the Edge

The same could be said for the five blocks of Red River Street, from Sixth to 11th, which also ignored the rules of segregation like a "no jaywalking" sign.

Red River was at the eastern edge of Austin when the street plan was laid out and became a main north-south thoroughfare because it was the first street east of Congress Ave. that wasn't uphill. Red River was home to automobile businesses like Raven's Garage (later Emo's) and Crenshaw Garage (later Beerland), which opened in the 1920s and 1930s.

The neighborhood was originally nicknamed Germantown after the colony of immigrants who settled around 10th and Red River in the mid-1800s, with the German Free School anchoring the community. Aloes Wulz Grocery opened in 1877 at 1101 Red River, the future home of the 11th Door folk club and the Austin Symphony offices.

Ida Pecht, who grew up on Red River between Hickory (8th St.) and Ash (9th St.), married Andrew Zilker in 1888 and gave birth to four children. The family had planned to build a mansion on Barton Springs, but after Ida died in 1916, a distraught Zilker donated the land and the springs to the city as a park.

For most of the '50s, '60s, and '70s, the Red River corridor was dominated by used furniture stores and junk shops with names like Williams Do-Rite Swap Shop, Fairyland Antiques, Dutch Meyer's Trading Post, Red River Rats, and Hurt's Hunting Grounds. Doug Sahm's Austin anthem "Groover's Paradise" was a play on Snooper's Paradise, a thrift store at 705 Red River. Many of the old junk stores became clubs.

The Red River walk has always had a bit of a desperado gait, starting with the 13th Floor Elevators at the New Orleans Club in '66, and the '67 opening of the One Knite biker/hippie bar at the future Stubb's. Cave Club brought industrial in '86, then in the early '90s, the BYOB Cavity Club installed a half-pipe for skateboarders and hosted G. G. Allin. Miss Laura of the Blue Flamingo turned her drag bar into a punk club, with the action spilling out onto the street. That's where Spoon was discovered by Gerard Cosloy of Matador Records at SXSW 1994, when the line was too long to get into Emo's to see Johnny Cash.

At 900 Red River, Chances (1982–94) was that rare lesbian bar that booked indie rock bands, like Sixteen Deluxe, Glass Eye, Handful, and Sincola. That open-clientele policy continued at Cheer-Up Charlies in the same former second location of Don Politico's, one of *Statesman* columnist John Kelso's hangouts.

From El Charro to the Mohawk

The Mohawk has kept the Red River music scene strong since opening on September 15, 2006, with Ghostland Observatory, but the building at 912 Red River had quite a history before the 'hawk.

Built in the '20s to house an architectural firm, it was a popular Mexican restaurant El Charro from 1937–66. After a couple years as a boarding house, 912 became

Mrs. Fun plays Chances, Austin's low-rent lesbian version of Red Rocks, 1992. Photograph by Lisa Davis. Courtesy of Austin History Center.

the home of the Night Train restaurant, open until midnight from 1968–1971. It was perhaps affiliated with or inspired by NFL Hall-of-Famer Dick "Night Train" Lane, the Austin-born defensive back for the Detroit Lions.

After Night Train, it became Nick Kralj's private club for legislators and lobbyists called Quorum Club. Former board of regents chairman Frank Erwin, who became a lobbyist for UT in 1975, racked up such expenses picking up checks at the Quorum, money had to be raised to cover the bill without using university funds.

The most notorious tenant at 912 was the Caucus Club, also private in the beginning (1977) because they had high stakes poker in the back room. Building owner John Joseph was a convicted gambler, and the Caucus was investigated after the 1979 suicide of Triumph Motors owner Roy Burton, Jr., who defaulted on bank loans totaling $140,000 to cover gambling debts. The club came back with "new owner" Donald Sconci, Joseph's nephew.

While Red River currently has some stability with the Mohawk and Stubb's anchoring the strip like Nordstrom and Macy's, those blocks went through some serious changes in the twentieth century. The 1915 Waller Creek Flood washed away rows of houses, with a death toll of thirteen, but the Red River neighborhood was even more physically affected by acts of man. Early '70s wrecking balls wiped away everything from 10th St. to 19th St. (MLK today), and San Jacinto to I-35 as part of the Brackenridge Urban Renewal Project, which covered 144 square acres. Before that, Austin's racial dividing line was Waller Creek, not the freeway, with shotgun shacks lining the Eastern banks. They were all torn down. Waterloo Park opened in 1975 on land that had been home to dozens of Black families, which caused detractors to term the project "urban removal."

It would take years for Red River to bounce back in gritty glory.

ouis Armstrong could be the greatest musician America's ever produced, 1938.

V.

The Thirties and Forties: Satchmo's Inspiring Set, and Austin Rocks on the G.I. Bill

Louis Armstrong at the Driskill

Austin native Charles L. Black Jr. was a freshman at the University of Texas in 1931 when he saw a placard advertising "Louis Armstrong, King of the Trumpet, and His Orchestra" at the Driskill Hotel. He didn't know jazz from jehovah, but he bought a ticket. There would be girls and dancing, which was worth seventy-five cents admission.

Six bits changed his life. "It is impossible to overstate the significance of a sixteen-year-old Southern boy's seeing genius, for the first time, in a black," he wrote in 1979. "We literally never saw a black man, then, in any but a servant's capacity." Black's essay "My World with Louis Armstrong" was published in the *Yale Review* and quoted in Ken Burns's ten-hour *JAZZ* documentary.

The former UT student went on to become a noted civil rights attorney, who taught constitutional law at Columbia and then Yale for almost fifty years. In 1954, Black helped Thurgood Marshall draft the brief for the Supreme Court case known as *Brown v. Board of Education*, a victory which declared school segregation unlawful and galvanized the movement to end the racist white regime in the South.

Armstrong, perhaps the greatest musician America has ever produced, was forbidden to stay at the Driskill during his appearances October 12–14, 1931. The hotel did not allow Black guests until quietly desegregating in 1962.

Armstrong's hold never left Charles Black, who died in 2001 at age eighty-six. "All through those years, he was letting flow, from that inner space of music, things that had never before existed," the professor wrote forty-eight years after that show on Sixth Street. When they say the Driskill is haunted, they're right.

Satchmo had played Austin earlier in 1931 at the Cotton Club at 817 E. 11th St. (formerly Royal Auditorium). After hearing the hometown opening act, the Dixie Musicmakers, Armstrong asked Israel Fontaine, the band's trumpet player, if he wanted to join his touring band. "Of course I said yes," Fontaine said in 2001, when I visited him at his home in East Austin on the occasion of Armstrong's centennial. "I knew there was a lot I could learn from him. I'd never heard anyone play the horn like that before."

Austin High senior Tommy Hill remembered standing behind a rope at the Cotton Club with the handful of other white kids, amazed at the powerful performance. "He played 20 choruses of 'Tiger Rag,'" recalled the eighty-seven-year-old in 2001. "He was sweatin' like crazy, with a white towel across his back, but he just kept playing."

Fontaine, who did only one short tour with Armstrong and didn't play the Driskill shows, recalled an Austin club, the Blue Knight, taking up a collection to get the trumpet great to play. "'They wrote him a letter that said they could pay him $100, and he wrote back and said he'd play for $100, but they'd have to come up with a lot more money to also get the band."

Teen dance in a ballroom off Rosewood Avenue, 1944.
Courtesy of Austin History Center.

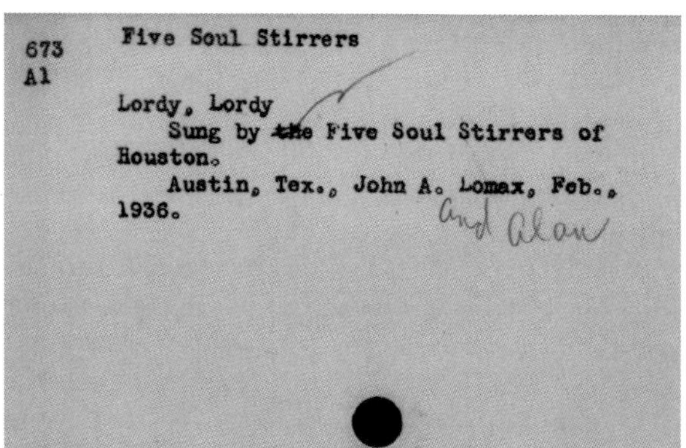

673 Five Soul Stirrers
A1

Lordy, Lordy
Sung by ~~the~~ Five Soul Stirrers of Houston.
Austin, Tex., John A. Lomax, and Alan Feb., 1936.

This historic recording was before Rebert Harris joined the Soul Stirrers. Courtesy of Library of Congress.

The grandson of former slave Jacob Fontaine, who published the first issue of the *Gold Dollar* at 2402 San Gabriel St. in 1876, Israel also went into the printing business. He gave up jazz in 1943 when he joined the ministry at the Mount Zion Baptist Church founded by his grandfather. "Preaching and publishing—that's in my blood," he said. Just as his father George put out the *Silver Messenger*, Israel started an African American newspaper in 1938 called the *Austin Express*.

The fifteen-hundred-capacity Cotton Club, which booked many of the hot swing bands, like Cab Calloway and Jimmy Lunceford, remained open off-and-on until 1944, when the two-story building was repurposed as a dormitory and dining hall for Samuel Huston College across the street. The "unique hepcat haven where all the dark and light folk meet" (*Daily Texan* 1942) was torn down in the '50s, when East Avenue was broadened into I-35, and became a parking lot.

Most Influential Austin Recording: Soul Stirrers, 1936

The Soul Stirrers are best known today as the Chicago gospel quartet that launched the career of Sam Cooke in 1951, but the group is actually from Trinity, Texas, by way of Houston. The Stirrers revolutionized gospel quartets by adding a fifth member—a second lead singer—which upped the intensity when the two leads traded verses, while keeping the four-part harmony intact. Before the Soul Stirrers, gospel quartets were mainly barbershop or jubilee groups doing old spirituals like "Down by the Riverside." But the Stirrers came out to "wreck a house" with their hard gospel style and, in the process, influenced every quartet to follow.

The Golden Gate Quartet are generally credited as the precursors to the heightened emotionalism of quartets, but the Soul Stirrers recorded a year before those Norfolk heavyweights. They made their recording debut in Austin with John and Alan Lomax for the Library of Congress. Billed The Five Soul Stirrers of Houston, the group recorded four songs on February 12, 1936, a performance Alan Lomax called "the most incredible polyrhythmic music you've ever heard."

Through the years, several national acts have made records in Austin that made an impact. The best-selling of those was 1996's self-titled *Sublime* by the SoCal ska punks that has sold over seven million copies and counting. Produced at Willie Nelson's Pedernales studio by Paul Leary of the Butthole Surfers, *Sublime* was released two months after the heroin overdose death of singer-guitarist Brad Nowell. The next best-seller made in Austin is the Dixie Chicks' 2003 LP *Home*, recorded without drums at Cedar Creek studio with producer Lloyd Maines, father of singer Natalie. It would've sold a lot more copies than six million if not for the backlash over Natalie Maines's criticism of the impending Iraq invasion. (She was right, by the way).

In influence, not sales, Uncle Tupelo's 1993 swan song *Anodyne*, which turned a younger generation onto special guest Doug Sahm, is another significant Austin recording from Cedar Creek. Jeff Tweedy's next band Wilco returned to Austin in 1998 to record *Summerteeth*, the album that left alt-country in the rearview mirror.

But in terms of historical importance, the Soul Stirrers' session for the Library of Congress, which signaled a transformative moment in the evolution of spiritual sound, is at the top. "No other recordings from that era are anywhere close in style," wrote gospel historian Ray Funk.

Usually, the Lomaxes went out looking for treasure in the blight, but this time it came to them.

Leadbelly and the Lomaxes

The Lomax family first gave Austin a reputation as a city of song in 1910 when patriarch John Avery Lomax created a national fascination for folk music with *Cowboy Songs and Other Frontier Ballads*. The UT administrator preserved such now-standards as "Home on the Range," "Streets of Laredo" (as "The Cowboy's Lament"), "Old Chisholm Trail," "Jack o' Diamonds," and "Git Along Little Doggies." Blind musician/teacher Henry Lebermann (the grandfather of future City Councilman Lowell) and wife Virginia were hired to transcribe those songs and twenty others into sheet music from crude field recordings on wax cylinders.

Based in Austin and curating the Archive of American Folk Song in DC, the Lomaxes lived to keep songs of the working-class people alive, road-tripping all over the country, then all over the world. Funded by grants from the Carnegie Corporation and the Rockefeller Foundation, John A. and/or son Alan found and recorded "House of the Rising Sun" in Kentucky, "Rock Island Line" in an Arkansas prison, "Sloop John B" in the Bahamas, and Muddy Waters at Stovall Plantation in Mississippi.

Their greatest find came in July 1933 at the Louisiana State Penitentiary with a prisoner called Lead Belly, who played a twelve-string guitar and sang in a powerful

Lead Belly at the National Press Club in Washington, DC, circa 1940. Photograph by William P. Gottlieb. Courtesy of Library of Congress.

baritone. If the Lomaxes hadn't hauled a 350-pound disk recorder, powered by two seventy-five-pound batteries, from Austin to Angola, LA., "Good Night, Irene" might've rotted behind bars or escaped into thin air. Instead, the recording was archived at the Library of Congress and in 1950 helped launch the folk music revival when the Weavers took it to #1 on the charts.

Lead Belly's recording of "Rock Island Line" would have an even greater impact, when covered by Lonnie Donegan in England in 1955. That sped-up and washboard-driven version gave birth to skiffle, which influenced an entire generation of British musicians who weren't yet musicians. "We all went out and bought guitars," said Paul McCartney, who formed the Quarrymen with John Lennon in 1957.

But neither John Lomax nor Ledbetter, whose professional association lasted less than a year due to monetary disagreements, would live to see the broadness of their influence. John Lomax died of a stroke in 1948 at age eighty. Lead Belly passed away the next year from ALS ("Lou Gehrig's Disease") at age sixty-one.

Lead Belly's final concert was June 15, 1949, at Hogg Auditorium on the University of Texas campus, in homage to his former mentor. Their collaboration had ended with a knife pulled, but Lead Belly couldn't forget what John A. Lomax had done for him, including helping him get out of prison. Plus, it was probably a good payday.

The concert was recorded live, though not released until 1973 on short-lived Playboy Records. KUT is credited with recording the music, but since that station wouldn't launch until 1958, it was most likely the Radio House mobile recording unit from the College of Fine Arts that got it down on transcription discs.

Clubland Paradise: The Skyline, 1946–89

Lead Belly isn't the only musical giant whose final concert was in Austin. Hank Williams sang at the Skyline Club twelve days before he was found dead in his Cadillac in Oak Hill, West Virginia on New Year's Day 1953.

Between the time it was built in July 1946 until its demolition in the expansion of Braker Lane in 1989, the Skyline held more musical history than any club in Austin. It's most remembered today as the site of not only Hank's swan song at age twenty-nine in December '52, but Johnny Horton's in November '60. The "Honky Tonk Man," at age thirty-five, was killed by a drunk driver on Hwy 79 in Milano, on his way back home to Shreveport. Both country singers being married to the former Billie Jean Jones at the times of their deaths was an eerie coincidence.

The five-hundred-capacity roadhouse on the old Dallas Highway (11306 N. Lamar) was also where Elvis Presley performed in 1955, and where noted Austin noise-punks Scratch Acid played their first show with singer David Yow in 1983. In the early '70s, a sheet metal worker from San Antonio named Moe Bandy brought his band of Mavericks to the Skyline weekly before conquering Nashville with his cheating songs.

During its honky-tonk heyday, such acts as Johnny Cash, Louvin Brothers, George Jones, Patsy Cline, Lefty Frizzell, Kitty Wells, Webb Pierce, Jim Reeves, and Marty Robbins played the Skyline, often backed by house band Jody Meredith and the Round-Up Boys. Bob Wills, Ernest Tubb, and Hank Thompson brought their own groups.

The Skyline was hardcore country, but such local acts as Dolores and the Blue Bonnet Boys and Grouchy and the Texans always threw in a couple polka numbers to get the Germans and Czechs on the dancefloor. Wednesday was ten-cent beer night, and every night was don't-

ABOVE: Marty Robbins at the Skyline, shown with Warren and Clara Stark. Courtesy of Cathy Stark Quick.

BOTTOM: The Skyline is perhaps Austin's most historical club. It was torn down in 1989. Courtesy of Stark family.

give-Maydell-Crumley-any-lip night. The waitress was as much the boss as was Warren Stark, who opened the club with his father Charles as a twenty-two-year-old just out of the service.

The Starks were similar to the Whites of the Broken Spoke in that they were personable and loved traditional country music. But Warren Stark drew the line at profanity, making it an offense worthy of ejection to shout "bullshit!" during "The Cotton-Eyed Joe." Groups knew to save that number until the end.

Warren was also not a fan of the counterculture, proudly helping the Dodge City Steakhouse next door hoist a bathtub on a pole outside "for flower children." On his boat at Lake Travis, he'd don his white coast guard uniform and get on the bullhorn near Hippie Hollow to tell everyone to put their damn clothes back on.

Raised on the Capitol View Dairy farm off far east Slaughter Lane, the three Stark siblings—Gerald, Margaret, and Warren—inherited the Skyline after their father died of a stroke in 1955. Oldest child Gerald, whose disability had the family move from Houston to Austin so he could attend the deaf school, lived behind the club and handled maintenance, while Margaret took money at the door and Warren booked and handled talent. The way he handled an increasingly erratic Hank Williams, was to drive up to Dallas to personally deliver him to his December 19, 1952, Skyline show.

According to brother and sister opening acts Tommie and Goldie Hill from San Antonio, the Skyline show was one of the best they'd played with Williams. Hank did two sets and, according to Chet Flippo's essential biography, threw in a few gospel songs, which was rare for Hank at a honky-tonk. He must've had an inkling he'd soon meet his maker.

Hank had spent the day with Austin country singer Jerry Green, who he knew from the Louisiana Hayride, and Ernest's son Justin Tubb, who was attending UT. They visited the Hays Record Shop at 916 E. First St., then dropped Williams off at the Stephen F. Austin Hotel. "He was trembling something fierce," said Green, "but when he played, he did a fine job." Ol' Hank did sing a few songs on guitar at a party for the musicians' union in Alabama a few days later, but the Skyline was his final public performance.

The Skyline closed in 1977 and became the second location of Soap Creek in 1979, for a couple years. The punks rented the barren Skyline for random concerts in 1983, but it otherwise sat vacant. Warren Stark passed away from a stroke in 1985 at age sixty-one. The historic club was bulldozed four years later and is a CVS drug store today.

Dolores and the Blue Bonnet Boys

In the first year after the end of WWII, more than half of the 17,108 students at UT attended on the G.I. Bill, according to campus magazine *Alcalde*. They were older, of drinking age, and had money. It was the first heyday of Austin nightlife.

A pair of war vets, R. D. Edwards and Joe Sanders, opened the swanky Club 81 on the San Antonio Highway (4700 S. Congress today) in March 1946, booking big bands of R&B (Jimmy Liggins, Johnnie Simmons) and Western swing. The *Statesman* called it "the costliest club ever built here," but less than two years later it burned to the ground. Another Club 81 opened several blocks south in 1955, but it wasn't affiliated. South Congress was US 81.

In the nine years before the advent of rock 'n' roll, the local music scene was dominated by Western swing and country bands including Jesse James and All the Boys, Doug and the Falstaff Swing Boys, Leon Hawkins and His Buckaroos, Hub Sutter and the Galvestonians (later Hub Cats), and Buck Roberts and the Rhythmaires (featuring Johnny Gimble). The Taylor-based Jimmy Heap and the Melody Masters recorded nascent versions of the classics "Wild Side of Life" and "Release Me," later made more famous by Hank Thompson and Ray Price, respectively.

But Dolores and the Blue Bonnet Boys stood out because it was that rare country band led by a woman who wasn't the main vocalist. Far from a novelty, Dolores Fariss wrote songs, chose outside material, played piano, and ruled her group of talented musicians like Bob Wills in a skirt.

Rule No. 1 was no drinking before or during a set. And Fariss was also clear that she didn't like her musicians showing off. "Dolores was very commercial-minded, and she called the shots as to what we played," said the band's fiddler, Bill Dessens, who joined the Blue Bonnet Boys in 1949 while still in college in San Marcos. "Her motto was 'Keep it simple, boys.' She'd say that whenever me and (twin fiddler) Joe Castle would take off on a crazy course. We used to get together in the basement of Joe's church and learn songs like 'Stompin' at the Savoy,' but Dolores didn't care for that hokum (jazz)."

The band had a big fan in Kenneth Threadgill, who often sat in at the Skyline. "Dolores and the Blue Bonnet Boys did more to teach me about music than anybody I've ever known," he told the *Statesman* in 1970.

Rather than tour the dancehalls and honky-tonks all over Texas, Oklahoma, and Louisiana, Dolores and the Boys rarely ventured outside Austin, where they played as often as three nights a week at the Skyline. The group also performed at Dessau Hall twice a month and the Buckholts SPJST Lodge in Milam County about four times a year. They knew how to make the people dance.

There was more money out on the road, but the Blue Bonnet gang stuck to Austin and environs because drummer Lee Fariss, Dolores's husband, had a successful home construction business with his wife's father, Alfred Hanson. They also had two young sons—James and Don.

Of Danish descent, the Hansons came from Hutto, where Alfred had a polka band featuring teenage daughter Dolores on piano. Lee Fariss also had a band at the time, Lee's Bees, in which he was the only member who wasn't blind. Lee and Dolores met at a Hansons polka gig in 1930 and married the next year.

KVET

The group publicized its shows by playing live on KVET (AM 1300), which signed on the air October 1, 1946, the same year Dolores put together her Blue Bonnet Boys. Before KVET, there were two stations in town—the Lady Bird Johnson-owned KTBC (AM 590), a CBS affiliate, and ABC-aligned KNOW (AM 1400), headquartered in Norwood Tower. KTBC featured Jesse James and All the Boys every day at 1 p.m. Dolores was KVET's answer.

Lyndon Johnson, then a rookie US congressman, encouraged several of his closest associates, including future Texas govenor John Connally and future US representative. Jake Pickle, to pool their resources and launch a third station, before NBC could enter the market. Better that competitors be friends than enemies. Because the new station owners and ten investors ($5000 each) were all veterans of World War II, they went with the KVET call letters.

In 1948, KVET expanded its market by hiring African American DJ Lavada Durst, and Lalo Campos to host Spanish-language music shows every day. Those popular programs—*Rosewood Ramble* and *Noche de Fiesta*, respectively—kept the local music scene from being lily white. As did a new stop on the "Chitlin' Circuit" that's still around today.

OPPOSITE (TOP): Dolores and the Blue Bonnet Boys at Dessau Hall, 1949. Courtesy of Texas Music Museum.

Johnny Holmes opened the Victory Grill so Black soldiers returning from WWII had a place to celebrate. After the club added a live music room in the early '50s, it became a stop on the "Chitlin' Circuit," hosting the likes of Ike and Tina Turner, Joe Tex, and a Fort Hood soldier who would call himself Bobby "Blue" Bland. Courtesy of Texas Historical Commision.

AVE SMITH, Program Director
"MIKE MYSTERIES"
Monday through Friday, 10:00 A.M.

"BIG BOY" JONES
"K-BAR ROUNDUP"
Monday through Friday, 4:00 P.M.

BOB GWYN
"WAKE UP AUSTIN"
Daily, 7:00 A.M.

JOHNNY ROARK
"THE UNIVERSITY HOUR"
Nightly, 11:15

GLENN BROWN
SPORTS DIRECTOR
PLAY-BY-PLAY ANNOUNCER

LALO CAMPOS
"SALUDOS AMIGOS," 6:30 A.M.
"NOCHE DE FIESTA," 7:00 P.M.

DR. HEPCAT
"ROSEWOOD RAMBLE"
NIGHTLY, 10:30

STUART LONG, News Editor
"CAPITOL NEWSROOM" M-F, 6:15 P.M
"TEXAS AT TEN" NIGHTLY, 10:00

ABOVE: The KVET lineup in 1949.
Courtesy of Texas Music Museum.

ABOVE: Opened in March 1946, Club 81 was called "the costliest club ever built here." It burned to the ground two years later. Courtesy of Austin History Center.

Female impersonation show on E. 12th, October 1955. Club not verified. Photograph by Neal Douglass. Courtesy of Austin History Center.

Clubland Paradise: The Victory Grill, 1945–Present

During the time of segregation (any time before 1964 in Texas), the Black community found havens in church, at the barber shop, and at the juke joint. Before they became mainstream acts, B. B. King, Ike & Tina Turner, Joe Tex and many more made their living playing clubs like the Victory Grill. The Grill also spawned a local blues scene that included Erbie Bowser and T. D. Bell, the Grey Ghost, Jean and the Rollettes, Major Burkes, W. C. Clark, Blues Boy Hubbard, and more. A singing soldier from Fort Hood named Bobby Bland came down every weekend in the early '50s to take top prize in the talent show.

Waco-born, Bastrop-raised Johnny Holmes moved to Austin to attend Samuel Huston College on a track scholarship (pole vault) and opened the Grill the day after V-J Day—August 15, 1945. He wanted a place where Blacks could also celebrate the end of the war. Originally a small icehouse and burger stand, the Victory moved a block two years later to the current building at 1104 E. 11th St. Holmes reopened it as a classy restaurant, with waitresses in starched maroon shirts. But when he built the Kovac Room (named after a club in Alaska from his travels) in 1951, Holmes created a near-perfect nightclub, with a nice stage and dancefloor, café-styled booths and a bar of glass bricks with red, green, and blues lights shining through. This was a 350-capacity place for Black touring acts to play between Houston and San Antonio. Segregation dictated they usually stay at the Deluxe Hotel (1101 Navasota St.), Austin's only lodging for Black travelers at the time, or in private homes.

East 11th Street, with Tony Von's Show Bar on the next block from the Victory, and Shorty's jazz club across the street, was The Stroll on the Eastside in the late '40s/early '50s. That Shorty's faced away from the sun in the afternoon, and had an awning for rain, made it where the prostitutes hung out. At night the strip lit up like someone dropped two blocks of Harlem in the middle of Texas. The Victory Grill and Charlie's Playhouse (which took over the Show Bar location) fought it out to be Austin's Apollo, and Charlie's won when it stole Blues Boy Hubbard and the Jets by paying twelve dollars a man instead of the ten dollars they were making with Holmes. When it came to food, the Victory got heavy competition from Southern Dinett, a soul food joint that opened a block away in 1947.

Holmes wasn't making any money at the Grill, so he leased it in the early '50s and moved to West Texas, where he worked as a cook and independent promoter. His best musician friend B. B. King had bemoaned that there was no place to play between San Antonio and El Paso, eight hours away, so Holmes helped open and booked the Cobra in Big Spring, which held eleven hundred people.

He returned to the Victory Grill in 1965, with Mary Wadsworth closing her club, Big Mary's on E. 12th Street, to help him run it. Richard Powell opened Good Daddy's Cafe in the old Mary's spot at 12th and Chicon, and with Sam's Showcase moving into the former Tasby's Tavern just a block west, "the Ends" (slang for 12th and Chicon from when the streetcar route ended there) was happening in the '60s. Sam Campbell continued one of the Tasby's weekly attractions—a cross-dressers revue called "Women of Tomorrow" on Tuesday nights.

Tough times in the '70s closed the Kovac Room first, then the cafe. The Grill sat boarded up for years, but through the efforts of Tary Owens of Catfish Records and others, the club reopened with Holmes in charge on Juneteenth 1987. In October '88, a fire was set by transients who'd been living in an abandoned building two doors down and the Grill suffered extensive damage. It was marked for the bulldozer in 1990, until Black community leaders stood up for East Austin history. Holmes family friends R. V. Adams and Eva Lindsey did their best to keep the Grill afloat.

Aged eighty-three and suffering from Alzheimer's, Holmes died of hypothermia in February 2001, when his daughter found him in his driveway. His family still owns the Victory Grill, which was included on the National Register of Historic Places in 1998.

OPPOSITE (TOP): The Driskill Hotel was home to Austin's first TV station. Courtesy of Austin History Center.

OPPOSITE: *Statesman* ad from the '70s.

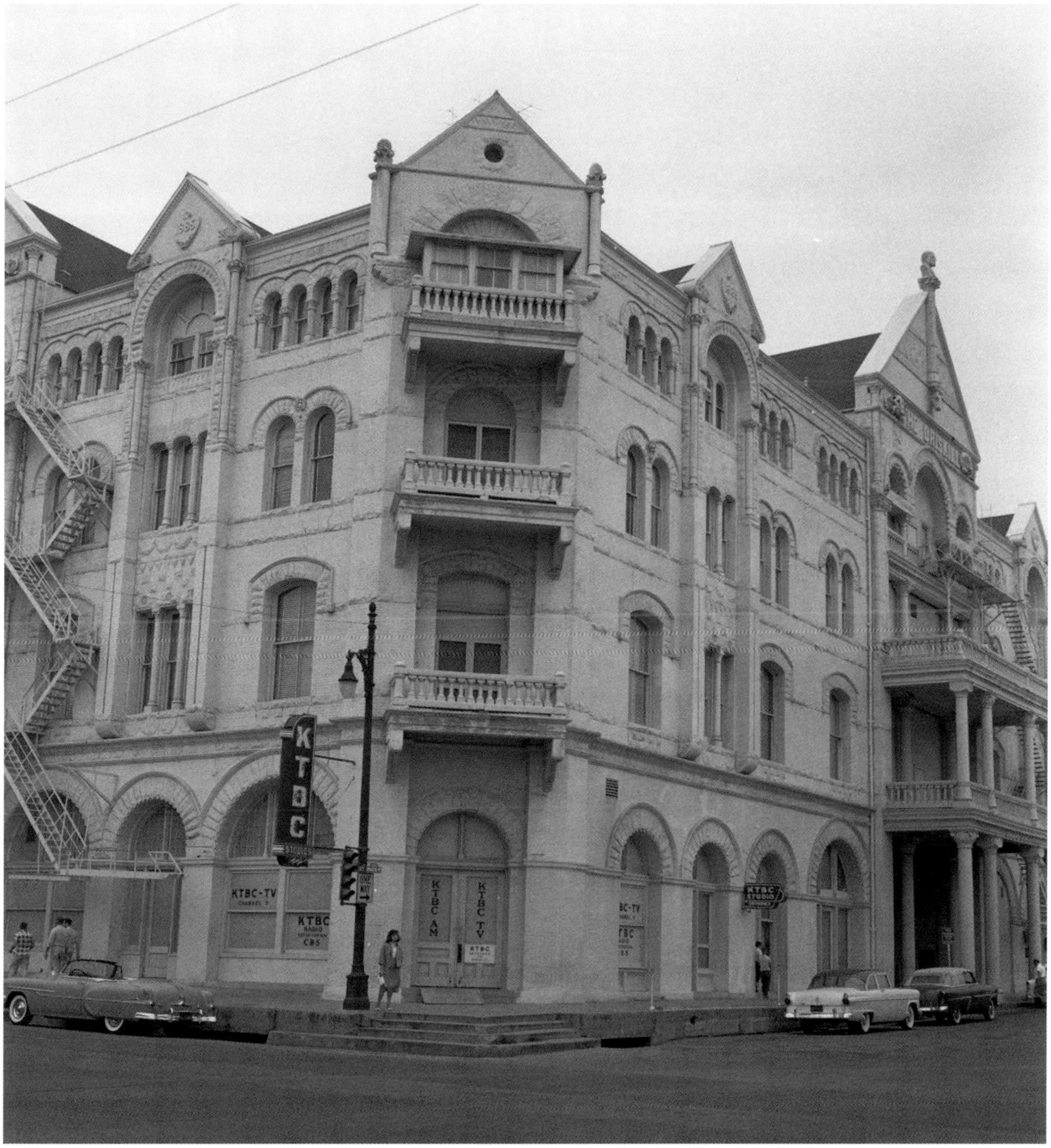
KTBC
KTBC-TV
KTBC AM
KTBC TV

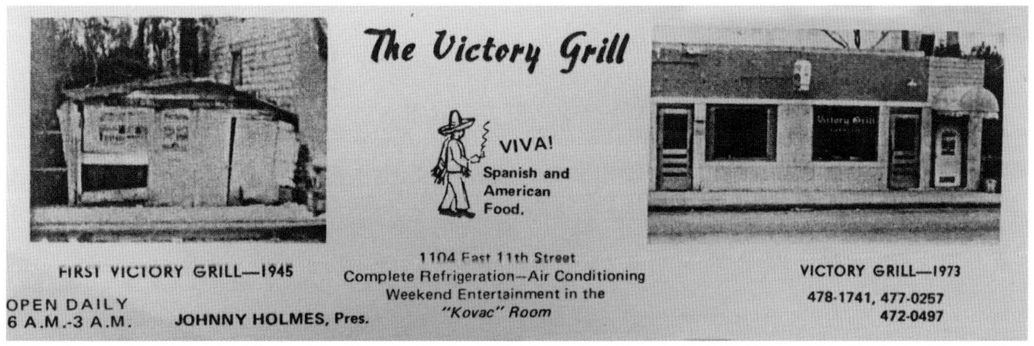

The Victory Grill
VIVA!
Spanish and
American
Food.
FIRST VICTORY GRILL—1945
1104 East 11th Street
Complete Refrigeration—Air Conditioning
Weekend Entertainment in the
"Kovac" Room
VICTORY GRILL—1973
478-1741, 477-0257
472-0497
OPEN DAILY
6 A.M.-3 A.M.
JOHNNY HOLMES, Pres.

Richard "Cactus" Pryor was nicknamed after his father, Skinny's Cactus Theater at 521 E. Sixth Street. A DJ, humor columnist, and TV announcer, Cactus hosted the popular local TV show *Now Dig This!* Photograph by Neal Douglass. Courtesy of Austin History Center.

VI.

The Fifties: "Now Dig This!"

Ray Campi: "The Town Was Hoppin"

Wild-eyed rockabilly veteran Ray Campi wrote his first song on the last day of 1949 and left Austin at the end of 1959. He was a man of the '50s in his hometown, so in his mind the Magnolia Café at 1920 S. Congress Ave. was still Flossie's Drive In, where country bands like Leon Carter and the Rolling Stones played.

While legions continue to mourn the December 31, 1980 swan song of the Armadillo World Headquarters on Barton Springs Road, Campi had fonder memories of the cavernous hall when it was the Sportcenter in the mid-1950s. On nights when there wasn't pro wrestling, he and such local acts as Betty Barnes, Irene Franklin, Chester Ayres and the Hungry Mountain Boys, and Buck Fowler and the Black Diamonds would play the Saturday Night Jamboree. Billed the "Folk Music Fireball" by Sportcenter promoter Owen Davis, Elvis Presley played the future hippie haven August 25, 1955—one of four Austin appearances that year before his January 28, 1956, TV debut on the Dorsey Brothers' *Stage Show* made him a national sensation.

"Some people talk like Austin became a music town in the '60s and '70s," said Campi, who lived primarily in Los Angeles for five decades until he passed away in March 2021. "But the town was hoppin' when I was coming up."

Most of the major Black acts, including Bo Diddley, Big Joe Turner, and Little Richard on one memorable night, played Doris Miller Auditorium on the Eastside. In the year it was open, the Sportcenter hosted an R&B bill in January 1956 starring the Platters, Earl King, Gatemouth Brown, and others, though it was billed "Rock 'n' Roll Dance and Show" for the white kids. Perhaps the greatest roster in Austin concert history was an October 7, 1957, package show at City Coliseum with Fats Domino, Buddy Holly and the Crickets, Chuck Berry, The Everly Brothers, The Drifters, Lavern Baker, Clyde McPhatter, and more. That talent makes the ACL Fest lineup look like, well, the ACL Fest lineup.

For Latinos, a weekly highlight in the '50s was the Nash Hernandez Orchestra's "Friday Frolics" at Zaragoza Park. Accordion master Camilo Cantu, meanwhile, had couples dancing at La Polkita, an open-air venue bounded by Christmas tree lights in Del Valle, and at Janie's Place on E. Seventh, owned by his first wife.

Manuel "Cowboy" Donley and Ruben Ramos

The nascent Austin Tejano scene was ruled by Manuel "Cowboy" Donley, who introduced electric guitar to the genre in 1955 with his six-piece Las Estrellas. With electric bassist Mike Amaro and drummer Emilio Villegas replacing brushes with sticks, Las Estrellas brought Tejano into the rock 'n' roll era. "They called me a monster," Donley told musica tejana scholar Evaliza Fuentes in 2018. But Las Estrellas would always win the Sunday "Mexican Night" battles at the Skyline Club—their sextet beating orchestras twice their size. Donley's Fender transformed traditional Mexican music, as honky-tonk did Western swing.

The son of violin-playing E. Sixth St. barber Ramon Donley (whose father was Irish, mother Mexican), Manuel learned to play at the barbershop afterhours, when

ABOVE: Ruben Ramos went from singing drummer in his family's band to "El Gato Negro," the smoothest crooner in Tejano. Courtesy of Texas Music Museum.

ABOVE (LEFT): Manuel "Cowboy" Donley brought electric guitar to Tejano music. "They called me a monster." Photograph by Clay Shorkey. Courtesy of Texas Music Museum.

LEFT: East Austin barber Ramon Donley, far left, was also a bandleader. Courtesy of Texas Music Museum.

there was a jam session almost every night. "Playing until daybreak with the old guys was my school," he said of the nightly lessons on how to play polkas, waltzes, foxtrots, rumbas, and more. He earned the nickname "Cowboy" because he stood at the front of the stage when he played, like country stars of the day, not seated on a bandstand. He roamed East Austin with a guitar, a Latino Gene Autry.

"I used to go to La Perla on East Sixth and Comal, and when I walked in with my guitar they unplugged the jukebox," Donley told the *Austin Chronicle*.

Also coming of age in the '50s Tejano scene was Ruben Ramos, a singing drummer in his older brother Alphonso Jr.'s orchestra who sounded a little more like Bobby "Blue" Bland than other Tejano singers.

Born in 1940, Ruben Ramos grew up in Utley, thirty miles east of Austin, in a family of musicians that, at first, played mainly for their own entertainment after a day of picking cotton. Mother Elvira (Perez) was a good guitarist and father Alfonso Sr. played fiddle. Ten of their brothers were musicians, as were Ruben's six brothers and sister Inez.

After returning from WWII, Elvira's brother formed Justin Perez and the Ex-G.I.'s, a popular dance band where the generations merged. Alfonso Ramos Jr. sang for that group before moving on to the Nash Hernandez Orchestra, and then the Ramos-Guerrero Band with Louie Guererro.

In 1969, Ruben and brother Roy cofounded the Mexican Revolution, a popular horn-driven dance hall band aligned with the Chicano rights movement. He was a singing drummer for a couple years, but he had such an impassioned tenor and great presence, bandleader Roy (who everyone called "Pia") moved him front and center. Ruben was now "El Gato Negro," the coolest crooner on the Tejano circuit and beyond.

Mexican Revolution became Texas Revolution in 1981, but went back to the original name in the 2000s and won a Grammy for best Tejano album in 2009.

Ray Campi at the Jade Room in 1959, when it was still on the Drag. Courtesy of Ray Campi.

Domino Records

Before Roy Poole opened Austin Recording Company on the second floor of the Littlefield Building at Sixth and Congress in the early '50s, the only studio in town was UT's Radio House, built in the former coach house and horse stables of the Littlefield House on campus in 1939. Campi recorded several tracks at Radio House from 1951–58. The Slades and Joyce Webb also recorded in that brick building that is still there at 24th and Whitis, though it's no longer a radio-television production studio.

Campi never became more than a local act, at least in his prime. Soon after recording "Caterpillar"/"Play It Cool" for San Antonio's TNT Records, he was signed to the Dot label, home of Pat Boone, in 1957. Although his single "It Ain't Me" went almost nowhere, it led to a lip-synced appearance on *American Bandstand*, which made Campi a bit of a star back home.

After being "one and done" at Dot, Campi was courted by Domino Records, Austin's first label of note, which made a little noise in the years between Elvis and the Beatles. Formed in 1957 as a night school project, Domino featured such acts as the Slades, Joyce Webb, Barney Tall, and Joyce Harris, a white singer from New Orleans whose backing band was a Black group from East Austin called the Daylighters. Their "No Way Out," featuring a spoken "I gotcha!" intro by Sonny Rhodes (then known as Clarence Smith), is a cult classic that most assumed featured a Black female singer. Joyce and the Daylighters never performed together live, which could've landed them in jail due to Jim Crow laws, but they sure cooked at Poole's place.

Campi's contribution to the Domino catalog was "My Screamin' Screamin' Mimi" in 1958, but that rocker didn't make it further than local record hops.

The $3 million Municipal Auditorium opened in January 1959 with Conway Twitty supporting Shirley Jones and Jack Cassidy in front of a crowd of four thousand. The next night Campi and others (Carolyn Hester, the Traits, the Slades, and more) opened for Gene Vincent—a show sponsored by the Civitan Teen Canteens, which provided safe, wholesome environments for young rock 'n' rollers at three locations: an armory at Camp Mabry, Doris Miller Auditorium, and Toomey Road in South Austin.

Geezinslaw Brothers

Melodramas were big in the '50s, with hillbilly comedy acts often opening the show. Campi was in a hayseed trio with Joe Bill Hogan and Betty Jo Gregory, performing such tunes as "Why Don't You Haul Off and Love Me" at Saengerrunde Hall before popular play *The Drunkard*.

"The crowd would throw peanuts at the villains," said Campi. "It was a lot of fun." Also usually on the bill were the Geezinslaw Brothers, who grew out of an Austin High talent show in 1955. Sammy Allred and Dewayne "Son" Smith were discovered in 1961 by Arthur Godfrey, who was visiting Cactus Pryor at the KTCB radio studio while the Geezinslaws were performing live on the air. Godfrey booked Austin's answer to Homer & Jethro for his nationally-syndicated radio show, and they were a big hit, which led to a record deal with Columbia and a move to New York City.

When they opened for the red-hot Tijuana Brass in Queens in '66, the *New York Times* wrote that the Geezinslaws "nearly eclipsed the stars of the evening," singling out Allred as "an owlish-looking Will Rogers type of rustic wit." The singing jester's musicianship was often a target of his self-deprecating humor, as when he recounted a young mandolin player approaching him after a set. "How long have you been playing?" Allred asked the kid, who answered "a year and a half." "Do you play like me?" Allred followed. "I used to."

ABOVE: The Radio House, an annex to the Littlefield Building at the University of Texas, was the first recording studio in Austin. Courtesy of Austin History Center.

LEFT: One of the top acts at Domino Records. Courtesy of Texas Music Museum.

Geezinslaws publicity shot circa 1963. Sam Allred and DeWayne "Son" Smith moved to New York after signing with Columbia Records. Courtesy of Rick Henson.

Left to right: Hub Sutter, Junior Burrows, Harold Horner, and William "Jesse" James. Courtesy of Austin History Center.

Superstar Glen Campbell took them out on a national tour in '69, with Allred flying home on off days to do his popular radio show on KVET. But Willie Nelson was probably the number-one Geezinslaws fan, booking them for every Fourth of July Picnic, and coproducing, with Bobby Bare, the '79 LP *If You Think I'm Crazy Now* on Willie's short-lived Lone Star Records. True Austin original Allred passed away in 2018, with Son, an underrated country singer, following the next year.

Jesse James and All the Boys

While a senior at St. Edward's High, Campi came under the musical spell of Jesse James and All the Boys, who he called "*the* western dance band in town." Cactus Pryor (who would later host the weekly *Now Dig This* TV show at the Driskill Hotel) emcee'd their daily set on KTCB, and sometimes sang parodies, like "Jackass Caravan" ("Mule Train"), backed by the James gang. Campi and his classmate, aspiring steel guitarist Bert Rivera, would sometimes skip school and go to the Brown Building for an hour of musical education. "Bert would watch Jim Grabowske on the steel and then go home and try to play like him." Rivera went on to an illustrious career as a steel guitarist, playing in Hank Thompson's band for almost a decade.

A featured guest of the James band was Cajun music pioneer Harry Choates ("Jole Blon"), who lived the last year of his life, his twenty-eighth, in Austin. Struggling with alcohol addiction since age twelve, Choates died in July 1951 in the Travis County Jail from injuries suffered when he couldn't control his DTs and banged around his cell. Grabowske said he and fiddler Junior Burrow visited Choates, jailed for failure to pay child support, a couple hours before he died and tried to get help but were met with indifference.

"Harry Choates would really light a fire," said Campi. "He was a showman for sure."

Whenever Campi returned to Austin he visited other musicians from the '50s, especially his former bassist Henry "Poochie" Hill. From a musical family, Poochie played everywhere, from orchestras to dives like Nero's Nook on Ben White. He backed Loretta Lynn at Dessau in 1962, and the singer, who'd just had her first hit with "Success (Has Made a Failure of Our Home)," was so impressed she offered a gig in the touring band she was putting together. But Poochie, raising a young family, declined. "I had a good job (as construction inspector) with the city," he said.

Poochie and his older brother Doug (who played bass for Willie Nelson in the '50s) owned the first electric Fender guitar and bass in town, preordered in 1952 from J.R. Reed music store on Congress Avenue. This made them particularly in high demand.

"When folks went out, they wanted to hear the songs the way they heard them on the radio, so when Billy Byrd (from Ernest Tubb's band) came out and honky tonk became the going thing, you had to have an electric guitar," said Hill, who passed away in 2018.

The Slades

Poochie was a link between country and pop in Austin when he replaced Bobby Doyle on bass in the Slades.

"The Slades were the only act on Domino that really sold any records," said Ed Nichols, who cofounded the label with Jane Bowers, Bob Williams, Lora Jane Richardson, Kathy Parker, and Ann Miller. (Nichols ended up as a US agriculture bigwig in DC during the Carter administration.) Signed to Domino after performing at a Girl Scouts event, the Slades were originally called the Spades, after a deck of cards, but had to change the name for racial connotations. ("The Spades" was also the name of Roky Erickson's first band, five years later.)

Led by Don Burch, the band was poised for a national breakout in 1958, with soulful doowop number "You Cheated" getting them booked on *American Bandstand*. Major labels were circling, but the fledgling Domino crew wanted to handle the single themselves and struck a distribution deal with a Los Angeles company.

It turned out the "one-stop" had oversold its capabilities, so while the Slades original waited to be pressed and distributed, an LA producer cheated, assembling a group of Black singers, including Texans Johnny "Guitar" Watson and Jesse Belvin, to copy the tune as the Shields. That version on Dot Records made it to #12 on the Billboard singles chart, while the Slades original stalled at #42.

"That was the mistake that killed Domino Records," said Campi. They were one hit record away from establishing themselves, but those night-schoolmates with almost no experience in the music business can be proud of preserving some of the great sounds made in Austin before it became known as a music mecca.

Campi's failed Dot 45 ended up blowing a big second wind behind his career during the '70s rockabilly revival. German-born Ronnie Weiser flipped over "It Ain't Me," which featured Doc Shyrock's finger-snapping rhythm, and signed Campi to his Rollin' Rock label. Besides

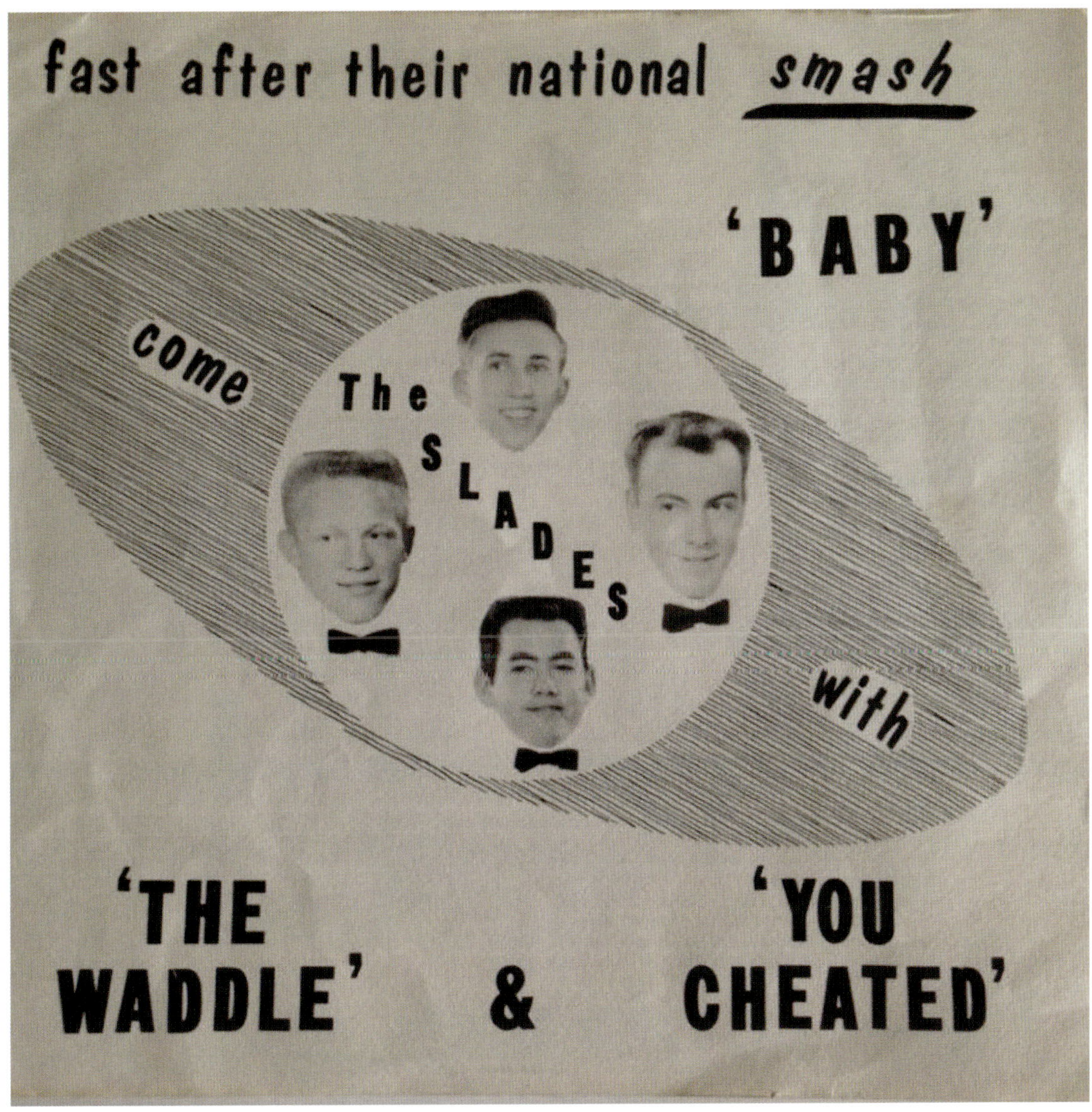

McCallum High grads the Slades were signed to Domino after playing a Girl Scout function.

reissuing most of Campi's forgotten 1950s recordings, Rollin' Rock released several highly regarded new Campi records, with Weiser producing the sessions in his living room. Campi was stunned to be hailed a rockabilly pioneer—the guy who kept double rhythm slap bass alive—on his first tour of Europe in 1977 with his band the Rockabilly Rebels. "I never had any hits, but those folks knew every one of my songs," he said. The Grand Marshal of Rockabilly continued to play festivals until his late seventies.

The song that best brought Campi back to the days of spot dances and necking in the hills above Barton Springs was "The Austin Waltz" by Dolores and the Blue Bonnet Boys. Recorded in 1948 by KVET program director Fred Caldwell for his Lasso label, Campi called it "the greatest song ever written about my hometown." He cut his own version in 1980 and let the words of Dolores Fariss flow through him:

"Why did I ever leave you?/ When I loved you so much/ Please let me come back to you, dear/And dance to the Austin Waltz."

CHARLIE'S
PLAYHOUSE

VII.

East Side Stories

Charlie's Paradise: The Playhouse and the Chicken Shack

A story of race in Austin in the late '50s comes from an unexpected angle. African Americans were protesting on E. 11th Street, but the picketing was *against* integration. White college kids had become crazy for rhythm & blues after listening to "Dr. Hepcat" on KVET and watching *Now Dig This* show on KTCB, and so they'd been flocking to Eastside hotspot Charlie's Playhouse. Which was fine except that the club's regular Black clientele was left outside if they didn't get there early enough.

"We couldn't go into any club on the west side, but yet we couldn't go to our own clubs on the east side on Friday and Saturday night," lamented *Villager* editor/publisher Tommy Wyatt.

Fraternities would reserve four or five tables each in the three-hundred-capacity joint. Double-dating couples showed up in Caucasian clusters. They had more disposable income than the Black clientele, so they were fine with Charlie Gildon, who owned the entire block of E. 1200, with a barber shop, a liquor store, and the Playhouse.

"Charlie's Playhouse is where we went to learn all the new dances," said Lucky Attal, the antique dealer who graduated from Austin High in 1959. Jim Crow segregation didn't limit where whites could go.

Gildon didn't allow the races to sit at the same tables, but they danced together to house band Hubbard and the Jets, as well as touring acts like Freddie King, Johnny Taylor, Albert Collins, Hank Ballard, Miss Lavelle, and Joe Tex. Guitarist Bill Campbell, a white man from Smithville, often sat in with the Black bands and even toured the South with Pigmeat Markham, leading the way for the Vaughan brothers, Denny Freeman, Paul Ray, Angela Strehli, and the like. If you wanted to learn how to cook Creole cuisine you went to New Orleans. If you wanted to play the blues, you went to the Eastside.

Gildon's initial consolation to picketers outside Charlie's Playhouse was to have "Soul Night" for Blacks only on Mondays, a school night. "So many of the students didn't think that was quite right," Wyatt said.

"Now, economically, you can understand that this man was in business, that's the way he was making his money. I mean he was making huge amounts of money on Friday and Saturday nights. But at the same time it was still offensive to the students over here."

The protest worked. Not wanting to cross the picket lines, and, no doubt, feeling unwanted, the white flock dwindled to the hardcore and eventually Charlie's became a Playhouse almost exclusively for African Americans again. "Charlie was a little upset," said Wyatt.

Integration ended up crippling the tight-knit East Austin community, especially when the hub—Black high school L.C. Anderson—was shut down in 1971. The federal government sued Austin Independent School District, which opposed crosstown busing, so it was a national story when AISD was forced to comply. The buses only went one way, with Anderson students sent to white high schools, amid rock-throwing and racial slurs, sullying Austin's reputation as a liberal city.

But let's remember that it was an Austinite, Lyndon B. Johnson, who signed into law the Civil Rights Act in 1964, which prohibited discrimination on the basis of race, gender, religion, or nationality.

With the African American clientele permitted to shop, eat, dance, whatever, all over Austin, the shops and clubs along East 11th and East 12th hit hard times.

Charlie's closed in early 1973 after a brief run as Twink's Playhouse, then became Mexican restaurant La Cucaracha. But the blues players wanted to keep the legendary room alive and bugged owner Rey Delgado until he booked Storm, Stevie Vaughan, Southern Feeling, and more. It was quite a scene at "La Kook" in '73 and '74, then the mostly white blues scene moved to Alexander's Place on Brodie Lane in the boonies, and the Lamplite Saloon on Sixth Street.

Charlie's building was torn down in the late '70s and remained an empty lot across the street and up a block from Nickel City (formerly Longbranch Inn) for decades.

But in 1960, Charlie's was so hoppin'—and nobody was ready to go home at midnight—that Gildon bought the padlocked (for liquor law violations) Cheryl Ann's nightclub at 1167 Webberville Road and turned it into Ernie's Chicken Shack. Besides the best fried bird in town, Ernie's served live music until 5 a.m. on weekends.

Until it closed in 1979, after Gildon died of a heart attack at age 57, this was the after-hours club in Austin. Whoever was playing at Charlie's that night would pack up at midnight and head straight over to the Chicken Shack. Gildon ran a gambling operation in the backroom, where UT football legend Bobby Layne was a regular.

Eastside, man. In the '50s and '60s, it was its own world with its own code. Some grease going around, for sure, but if it didn't impact life on the other side of the freeway, it didn't seem to matter much to the cops. Gildon packed heat at all times and had to shoot a couple customers who'd gotten out of line, but he was always back at the Shack by Friday.

People will argue about which era of Austin was the greatest. Was it the '70s during the Armadillo heyday? Was it the '80s when the Liberty Lunch/Beach/Continental Club axis put some euphoric jangle in your stride? To some, it was the '90s, when South by Southwest made Austin the live capital of cool every March.

Put me in a ripped vinyl booth at Ernie's Chicken Shack in the '60s. It's 3 a.m. and Freddie King just walked in with his big, red Gibson guitar. Bury me there if you can.

Tony Von *Was* Black Radio

"This is Tony Von, the only colored T.V. on the radio." The mellow, mesmerizing voice rolled out of the 1260 slot on the AM dial six days a week from 1954 until tragedy was a sad silencer twenty-five years later. His real name was Tony Von Walls, and his radio nickname was "the Master Blaster," but most everyone knew the irrepressible KTAE disc jockey and soul concert promoter as T. V. When Clifford Scott's sax on Bill Doggett's "Honky Tonk" came skronking out of the speakers at 4 p.m. weekdays and 2 p.m. Saturdays, a community gathered together.

Reflecting the neighborhood, he played gospel and blues side-by-side, but more significantly, at a time before cell phones and pagers and emails, Von was how Austin's Black community knew what was going on. He'd plug shows, give birthday greetings and announce events, often in free-form rhyme. "Tony was Black radio back in the day," said local blues artist Major Lee Burkes, whose regional hit "Break These Chains" got its earliest airplay on Von's show. "Communication was sometimes quite difficult back then, so I'd listen to T.V. to see where I'd be playing that night."

The Austin scene's reputation was built not just by the players and singers, but club owners, disc jockeys, journalists, and record store owners. Tony Von performed all those duties. Radio was his calling, plus he opened a couple of nightclubs—Show Bar and Club Exclusive—and a record shop on "the Cuts" (popular slang for East 11th Street) in the early '50s. After selling his share of the block to Charlie Gildon in 1958, Von moved full time to Taylor, where he opened another record shop that he could plug on the air. He also brought such acts as James Brown and Ike and Tina Turner to Doris Miller Auditorium (pronounced "Dorie" after a Black hero of Pearl Harbor who perished later in the war), and occasionally wrote for the Capital Argus. Von put a lot of miles on his car driving on Hwy 95 between Taylor and East Austin.

"Tony yielded a lot of power," Burkes recalled. "He had all the connections." He didn't make much money on KTAE, but used those airwaves to his advantage in business. Many of the biggest names in black music played for a pittance at Von-promoted shows (which translated into tons of airplay), while Von provided the backing band—usually Blues Boy Hubbard and the Jets, featuring Major Burkes, to keep the expense down. If you liked a song Tony played, you knew it was in stock at Von's record shop. He hustled to stay solvent.

On the air, however, he was the personification of laid-back. "Be cool, be back and remember one fact: We love you," is how TV signed off each day. "Austin truly was 'the live music capital of the world' back in the '60s," Burkes said. "And Tony Von had a lot to do with it."

A native of Dallas, Von joined the army in 1942 with no idea what he would do when he got out. While being treated for ulcers at a VA hospital in New Mexico in

Tony Von ends his radio shift in Taylor, 1977.
Photograph by Zach Ryall. Courtesy of *Austin American-Statesman* Photographic Morgue at the Austin History Center.

ABOVE: Lavada "Dr. Hepcat" Durst became the first Black DJ in Texas in 1948. Photograph by Dewey G. Mears. Courtesy of Austin History Center.

RIGHT: Robert Shaw recorded his first album at age fifty-four after being tracked down by Houston musicologist Mack McCormick. Photograph by Burton Wilson.

1948, a bored Von volunteered to be an announcer on the hospital's intercom system and found his husky vocal talent and natural delivery. He graduated from Huston-Tillotson in 1952, the year the two historically Black colleges in East Austin merged.

Back in Dallas, Von got his radio start at Top 40 pioneer KLIF, but it didn't work out because Von wouldn't embrace the corny, stereotypical "Jackson the Jiver" persona radio legend Gordon McClendon had devised for him. He was a veteran with a college degree, goddammit!

Von moved back to Austin, and his girlfriend, and got a job at KTXN, where his "Blues for Breakfast" show led to an offer by KTAE owner Gillis Conoley, up in Williamson County, who was looking for a replacement for retiring Jukebox Jackson in the afternoon. KTAE specialized in country and rockabilly, but the station also made time for R&B and Spanish music (Chicano DJ George Martinez followed Von's show at 5:30 p.m. for ten years).

In a 1977 interview with the *Austin American-Statesman*, Von laid out the inclusive philosophy that made his show a forerunner of community radio. "I have always believed in playing anything by everybody, anybody and nobody," he told writer Ronald Powell.

Two years after the *Statesman* story was published, Von met his tragic fate at the hands of ex-con James Earl Pullins. Von was working in his record shop on East Walnut Street ("The Line") the evening of June 20, 1979, when an intoxicated Pullins stood in the middle of the street and fired a shotgun in the air. Von came out with his pistol and told Pullins to put the shotgun away. Later, the Taylor garbage man shot Von in front of the Soul-Ful Club. The Black music entrepreneur was fifty-seven, the same age that Charlie Gildon died four months later.

Having served two prison terms for armed robbery, this third strike against Pullins ensured a life sentence, so prosecutors didn't try him for murder, thinking his guilty plea on an aggravated assault charge would put him away for good. But after only ten years in the joint, Pullins was paroled in 1990 because of prison overcrowding.

Ten years for taking the life of someone who brought such unity to his community, through the radio and concerts and records.

The Brooklyn band TV on the Radio doesn't even know about the original, having taken their name from British DJ Tommy Vance. But the catchphrase was born on the second floor of a building in downtown Taylor in 1954.

Piano Men Durst and Shaw

Tony Von didn't cross over like KVET's Lavada Durst, whose *Rosewood Ramble* was the top-rated music show in town for all races during the late 1940s to mid-1950s era when R&B was becoming rock 'n' roll. He also promoted R&B package shows like the one featuring Fats Domino, Little Richard, Ruth Brown, the Clovers, and Little Willie John at City Coliseum in March 1956.

Before radio, Durst colorfully announced Negro League games at Disch Field on Town Lake near the Coliseum. Calling a high pop fly, for instance, Durst would say the ball "asked the moon if it was really made of cheese." Dr. Hepcat was a natural, hired for KVET by co-owner John Connally, the future governor of Texas.

During the mid-'50s, Durst played exclusively Black artists with one exception—Elvis Presley—which is why the crowd was racially mixed at Presley's first show here—March 17, 1955, at Dessau Hall. Black listeners just assumed he was one of them.

Also a piano player of note, Durst wrote "Let's Talk about Jesus," the biggest gospel hit of 1951, for his fellow New Mount Olive Baptist Churchgoers, the Bells of Joy. But because he was a bluesman, he gave songwriting credit to singer A. C. Littlefield. You didn't mix secular and spiritual back then, though Ray Charles would three years later with his career-launching 1954 hit "I Got a Woman."

Durst (b. 1913) came of age during the boogie woogie craze of the 1930s with such Austin contemporaries as the Grey Ghost, Boots Walton, and Baby Dotson. But his greatest influence was the barrelhouse player Robert "Fud" Shaw who moved to Austin from Houston's Fourth Ward in 1935 to play juke joints and run numbers in the wake of Prohibition's repeal. "I could sit there and throw my hands down and make them gals do anything," Shaw said in a 1975 interview of those times when a piano was all the band you needed. "I told 'em when to shake it and when to hold back. That's what this music is for."

A second marriage in '39 demanded legitimate concerns, so instead of numbers, Shaw ended up running a popular BBQ/grocery joint, first on West Lynn in Clarksville, then at 1917 Manor Road. Everyone called it the Stop n' Swat, though the official name was Shaw's Food Market.

Rediscovered in 1963 by Houston musicologist Mack McCormick, who recorded *Texas Barrelhouse Piano* that year in Austin, a fifty-four-year-old Shaw started playing in public again. He teamed with Janis Joplin at the Texas Union Ballroom in May 1966, a month before she debuted in San Francisco as the singer for Big Brother and the Holding Company. Shaw played the Kerrville Folk Festival in its first fourteen years before a heart attack took him away in 1985 at age seventy-six.

Durst, who passed away ten years later, also had a life change in '63, quitting his radio show after a fifteen-year-run to join the Baptist ministry. He kept his job as athletic director for the Rosewood Rec Center until retirement age, and remained a preacher at Mount Olive the last thirty-two years of his life.

The radio support of Dr. Hepcat and Tony Von was a big reason touring R&B acts didn't skip Austin on their way from Houston to San Antonio. Those early Black DJs also provided an outlet, a connection, for Austin musicians who would otherwise be lost. The interest in Black music their radio shows cultivated continued to have impact on a music scene incubated in East Austin juke joints and carried all over the world.

Smokey Rhodes: "Like Playin' Piano with Your Feet"

At age eighty-two (or eighty-three—he's not sure) in 2002, Oscar "Smokey" Rhodes still had the moves that made him the favorite dancer of Austin musicians, including Stevie Ray Vaughan, who would often call him onstage. As one of the last of the great buck dancers (from "a buck and a wing"), Rhodes was often sought out by up-and-coming hoofers.

Visiting Rhodes on an afternoon at his apartment in the Rosewood Courts housing project in 2002 was to hear about a life that knew great camaraderie, but also tragedy. The highs and lows were reconciled in the marriage of clicks and thumps of the flat-footed buck dance, which is more syncopated and reliant on musical accompaniment than the standard tap dancing. When Smokey was dancing, he said, his mind was at peace.

This craft was handed down by his mother Mary, a rare female buck dancer, who toured the southern vaudeville circuit in the 1920s and 1930s. She also taught Smokey how to dance tap and the ol' soft shoe.

"I've missed my mother every single day since she passed," he said of the fun-loving disciplinarian who died of heart failure in the early '70s. "She taught me that when it's time to work, you work your tail to the bone. When it was time to play, well, go have yourself a ball."

Mary and Harvey Rhodes, who both grew up in Bastrop, but moved their family to East Austin in 1938, picked cotton when they weren't dancing. "They'd dance for a man from Kyle who sold a potion he called 'Getcha Ready.' Wasn't nothing but hackberry limbs all chopped up and boiled. My parents' job was to rouse up a crowd with their dancing, then the medicine man would step up and sell his bottles." Smokey and his brother Willie would sometimes play percussion.

Before he started taking dance seriously, Rhodes's first love was baseball. After attending Anderson High School, Smokey was a star left fielder for the Austin Black Senators, a minor league Negro League team that once featured future Hall-of-Famer Willie Wells. Calling the games at Disch Field was Smokey's best friend Lavada Durst.

Local 7-Up distributor Ed Knable was a big baseball fan who often gave jobs to players he liked, so he hired Smokey as a driver—a job he'd hold, during three different stints, for thirty-one years.

The first time he had to quit was when he was drafted into the Navy. Back in Texas after the war, Rhodes delivered ice for a Waco company. One stop on his route was the Harlem Club in Dallas, ruled by blues guitar pioneer T-Bone Walker. "He blew everybody away," Rhodes said with a big smile. "I got so excited I just hopped onstage and started dancing. That's how it started for me, dancing with bands."

Smokey especially liked to dance to the rhythms of barrelhouse piano, and in East Austin in the '50s and early '60s he teamed with such ivory thumpers as Robert "Fud" Shaw, Roosevelt "Grey Ghost" Williams, Erbie Bowser, and Lavada Durst. "The piano, man, that's the whole program with buck dancing. It's like playin' the piano with your feet."

When there wasn't a piano around, Durst would pound out rhythms on a barrel while Rhodes danced. In their teens, the pair used to do this routine from a raft in Barton Springs Pool. "They used to have this contest, where four guys would stand on the raft with one hand tied around their back and the other one with a boxing glove on it. They'd try to knock each other into the water and the winner would get five bucks. Well, when they were all done with that, me and Lavada would take over the raft."

By the mid-1960s the old scene had died down, after Dr. Hepcat became a preacher, the Ghost drove a school bus, and Smokey had his ice route.

An unlikely revival would come in the '80s, when Tary Owens and Jon Foose of Catfish Records got the lifelong friends back in the studio, and on tour as the Texas Piano Professors, featuring Rhodes as a dancer. Smokey's "Stop Time" routine with Bowser was a nightly crowd-pleaser.

ABOVE: Erbie Bowser was one of Smokey's favorite piano players. Photograph by La Zona Rosa. Courtesy of Marcia Ball.

ABOVE: *Left to right:* Tary Owens, Smokey Rhodes, Grey Ghost, Lavada Durst, Erbie Bowser, Marcia Ball, and Carol Fran, circa 1992. Courtesy of Marcia Ball.

Smokey Rhodes demonstrated buck dancing at La Zona Rosa, circa 1991. Courtesy of Marcia Ball.

A protege of noted UT folklorist Americo Paredes, Owens had recorded the Grey Ghost in 1965, but spent the next two decades in a fog of his own doing. One day, after getting sober in the mid-'80s, he heard his old Ghost recordings at a blues history exhibit at UT and set out to find the last of the original barrelhouse players. Owens worked as a drug counselor who often talked to inmates, usually ending a session by asking if any of the men had ever heard of an East Austin piano player they called the Grey Ghost.

Otis Bell's hand shot up. "Hell, I knew the Grey Ghost," said Bell, who was awaiting trial for murder. "He was out of his damn mind! So I called my grandma and she said he was still alive, still living on Juniper Street. The next week I told the drug counselor where to find him."

Thanks to his prison informant, Owens tracked down an eighty-four-year-old Ghost, who hadn't played in public for decades, and reissued the 1965 tapes on Catfish in 1987, as well as an album of new Ghost recordings. In 1991, Owens and Foose put out *It's About Time* by T. D. Bell and Erbie Bowzer, that took them from the Victory Grill to Carnegie Hall

"Those guys were my brothers," Smokey stated in 2002. "Lavada Durst, Grey Ghost, Erbie Bowser, T.D. Bell — man, we were all so tight." As he sat in the living room with the front door open on a hot afternoon, sadness passed over his face.

"They all died in a row. Like, one died on a Saturday and here comes Tuesday and another one passed. Now all my friends are gone."

Durst died in '95, with Grey Ghost and Bowser going the next year. Bell passed away in 1999. Smokey Rhodes was the last to go, dying of cancer in 2004, at age eighty-four (or eighty-five). To the very end, he honored his mother in the steps she taught him, and his friends in the moves their music inspired.

ABOVE: 13th Floor Elevators in Houston 1966. Photo by Bob Simmons.

Bob Dylan held a press conference at the Villa Capri
the day of his first concert in Texas, September 24, 1965.
Courtesy of *Austin American-Statesman*
Photographic Morgue at the Austin History Center

VIII.

The Sixties

Dylan and The Band's First Waltz

Though the British Invasion of '63 and '64 had a big impact on frat party bands like Sweetarts, Baby Cakes, and the Chevelles, "the Sixties" didn't really start in Austin until September 24, 1965, when Bob Dylan brought his new rock sound to Municipal Auditorium, backed by four Canadians and a drummer from Arkansas. Austin was the first city in which Rick Danko, Levon Helm, Robbie Robertson, Richard Manuel, and Garth Hudson—later known as The Band—shared a stage with a twenty-four-year-old Dylan, making his Texas debut.

The first set at Municipal was solo acoustic, including "Gates of Eden," "It's All Over Now, Baby Blue," "Desolation Row," and "Mr. Tambourine Man." After a short break, Bob returned with the band and launched into a loud, biting "Tombstone Blues," followed by "Baby Let Me Follow You Down," "It Ain't Me Babe," "Ballad of a Thin Man," "Maggie's Farm," "Just Like Tom Thumb's Blues," and the big hit at the time, "Like a Rolling Stone."

Those two sets were how Austin music segued in the '60s, when folk gave way to rock 'n' roll. In the audience, separately, were Roky Erickson and Tommy Hall, soon to be the voice and vision of the 13th Floor Elevators. Also on hand were the four men who would open the Vulcan Gas Company on Congress Avenue in October 1967.

"It was so in-your-face," show promoter Angus Wynne recalled of Dylan's electric segment. "You couldn't really understand the words—quality concert sound systems were nonexistent back then—but you could feel the energy. It was like being knocked over by this huge burst of sound."

On the cusp between the beatniks and the hippies, Dylan and The Band were playing a precursor to what would later be called punk rock.

Gilbert Shelton, the future Vulcan art director who was then a student at UT, met Dylan and the band, which he could tell "had recently joined Dylan because they still had their Canadian haircuts and clothes," at the Villa Capri Motor Hotel on Red River Street the night before the concert.

In an account printed in the November '65 edition of *Texas Ranger* magazine, Shelton describes a crazy scene of "go-go girls" from Dallas who just wanted to touch Dylan, a local beatnik turning up with cheap Mexican rum, and a late-night listening session to *Highway 61 Revisited*, Dylan's first all-electric album.

The next day a press conference was held at the Capri, with about eight reporters firing off questions that Dylan answered in his surreal, slapshot style. "Do you believe in God?" a student journalist from Baylor asked. "First of all, God's a woman," Dylan responded. "We all know that, and you can take it from there." Who's your favorite performer? "Charles De Gaulle." Jim Langdon from the *Statesman* brought some substance to the inanity when he asked Dylan about the change in style from Woody Guthrie-like ballads to a rock group sound. "It just came natural," said Dylan. "I wish I could still write like 'Girl From the North Country,' but I can't write like that anymore."

Twenty-one-year-old Wynne had decided to try to book Dylan in Austin and Dallas on consecutive nights after repeatedly hearing "Like a Rolling Stone" on the radio after its July 20, 1965 release. "I looked at the back of a Dylan album and it said he was managed by Albert

Grossman, so I called information in New York and got the number," Wynne recalled. "When I called and made my pitch, someone yelled to the other room, 'Hey, do you want to go play in Texas?' and someone yelled back 'Yeah, sure.'" That's how things went, back in the days before big-scale national tours.

Dylan had met the The Band when they were called the Hawks (from backing Ronnie Hawkins), through John Hammond Jr., whose father had signed Dylan to Columbia. He hired guitarist Robertson and drummer Helm to play concerts at Forest Hills Stadium, in Queens, NY, and the Hollywood Bowl that would showcase songs from the new album. Those shows were met with scattered boos from folk purists who felt Dylan was selling out, but they weren't as bad as at the Newport Folk Festival on July 25, 1965, when Dylan came out blazing, backed by the Paul Butterfield Blues Band. Those betrayed folkies weren't yelling "Bruce!"

Dylan flew up to Toronto on September 15, 1965, nine days before the Austin show, to rehearse with the Hawks. Three nights later he was back in New York. The band was ready.

So was Texas. In its review of Dylan's show at Southern Methodist University the night after Austin, the *Dallas Morning News* reported that as Dylan strode offstage at the end of the concert, he suddenly whirled around and said into the microphone, "I think Texas audiences—in Austin and Dallas—are the best." Those shows were the first Dylan electric sets without any booing.

In the audience at the Austin show was Dylan's Greenwich Village contemporary Carolyn Hester. "I don't think I've ever heard him do a better concert," she told John Bustin of the *Statesman*. The striking redhead from Austin also soon went electric, with less success, as the Carolyn Hester Coalition.

When Dylan toured again, almost eight years after his 1966 world tour ended with the famous concert at London's Royal Albert Hall, his backing group was The Band, no longer anonymous sidemen with Canadian haircuts, but artistic peers. They performed "The Weight" and "The Night They Drove Ol' Dixie Down" alongside Dylan classics no longer burdened with acoustic/electric distinctions.

OPPOSITE (TOP): Folk singer Allen Damron managed the 11th Door for Bill Simonson. Photograph by Bob Simmons.

OPPOSITE: Janis Joplin got back into music at the 11th Door in late 1965. Photograph by Bob Simmons.

Clubland Paradise: 11th Door, 1965–68

Bill Simonson is best remembered as the co-owner of Mother Blues (1971–81), which some consider the greatest rock club in Dallas history. Ray Wylie Hubbard sang about it on *Letterman* and folks are still talking about the aftershow jams with Led Zeppelin, Freddie King, Thin Lizzy, and the like.

But Simonson got his start in the club business in Austin as a twenty-one-year-old in 1964, running the id on W. 24th. "The basic decoration was darkness," Jerry Jeff Walker wrote about the coffeehouse in *Gypsy Songman*, his 1999 memoir.

The other popular beatnik hangout was the Ichthus coffeehouse, inside the surprisingly hip Methodist Student Center on the Drag. That building's auditorium was where Janis Joplin and the 13th Floor Elevators shared a stage for the only time in Austin, at a March '66 benefit for fiddler Teodar Jackson. Torn down in 1980, it's currently a parking lot on the 2500 block of Guadalupe.

Simonson's "folk shows early/jazz jams late" format moved to the 11th Door, at the former Jazz Room at 1101 Red River, in November 1965. That building dates to 1871 when formerly enslaved Jeremiah Hamilton, who was in the first group of Black Texas legislators, laid those stones.

Besides giving Janis Joplin her first paying gigs, the 11th Door once booked Lightnin' Hopkins for a ten-night stand in December '65 with Cleveland Chenier on rub board and Billy Bizor on harmonica. It was where Austin fell in love with Big Bill Moss, a powerfully-voiced Cleveland native with a twelve-string guitar, who claimed to be "an American Indian Negro of Spanish Jewish descent." Peppering his sets with edgy humor ("here's the white part" he'd say, slowing down a song), Moss had an occasional act with roomate Allen Damron—the first interracial duo.

Learning photography skills while in the army during Korea, Moss made more money taking pictures than singing and writing songs, so he stopped performing during the cosmic cowboy era, except for the occasional comeback show with Damron. Moss was also a constable for the Travis County sheriff's department.

The Door closed in early '68, replaced by Club Insomnia, which booked everything from jazz to a thirteen-year-old Eric Johnson's first band the Sounds of Life. In its last few months, Insomnia became a gay bar, managed by Marie Nohra. Patrons had to walk up exterior stairs and enter on the second floor. Then they walked downstairs to the groundfloor club. It was illegal for men

the
eleventh
door

The guru and the muse: Tommy and Clementine Hall pressed the Elevator buttons. Photograph by Russell Wheelock. Courtesy of Wittliff Collections.

to dance with each other back then, so if the cops came—also having to climb the stairs—Marie would stomp on the floor as a warning to act like you're waiting for the chicks to show up.

Simonson was busted in Laredo in September 1968 with two other men, charged with trying to smuggle 118 pounds of marijuana from Mexico. Hiring Roy Q. Minton as his attorney kept him from doing hard time, but he served a couple years before opening Mother Blues in Dallas in 1971. A cocaine charge put him back in prison in the late '70s. Maynard Delmar "Bill" Simonson Jr. died of brain cancer in 1990 at age forty-seven, unrecognized as a pioneer of the Austin club scene.

Elevation on San Jacinto

Roger Kynard ("Roky") Erickson's band of fellow Travis High students, the Spades, had been playing every Wednesday and Thursday at the Jade Room at 1501 San Jacinto St. for a month before the mind-shifting Dylan concert at Municipal Auditorium. In late November '65, Erickson was recruited to join the former Lingsmen, a skiffle/beach music group from Port Aransas, who were told, erroneously, that "Ling" meant crazy in Chinese. In Mandarin, it translates to "spiritual," which better fit the new band of guitarist Stacy Sutherland and drummer John Ike Walton, both originally from Kerrville, plus bassist Benny Thurman. These instinctive sound explorers fell under the spell of a charismatic philosophy student with a jug named Tommy Hall. What Roky supplied was James Brown-like intensity to the standard gtr/gtr/bs/drms format, plus the looks and charisma of a born front man. He also brought the band's signature tune "You're Gonna Miss Me," which he'd written and recorded with the Spades just a few months earlier.

Since the band's mission was to take the crowd higher with their psychedelic sounds, they were billed Roky and the Elevators when they first played the Jade on December 8 and 9, 1965. Hall's wife Clementine, a band muse if there ever was one, suggested "13th Floor," the missing flight of superstitious hotels. She also wrote some of the best lyrics ("Splash 1" and "I Had to Tell You").

Doc and Marge Funk were Austin nightclub veterans, opening the original Jade Room on the Drag in 1955 with the Benny Ray Trio playing cocktail jazz. The couple, who moved to Austin from Oklahoma in 1945 to take over the St. Elmo-tel, also owned the Flamingo Lounge on Lake Austin Boulevard with a similar Vegas-y format.

Folksingers Bill Moss and Allen Damron had an interracial duet act in 1966. Courtesy of *Austin American-Statesman* Photographic Morgue at the Austin History Center.

The Jade moved to San Jacinto on the southeast side of campus in 1962, with weeknight entertainment provided by jazz trios or cheesy vocal groups like the Four Maldehydes. Playing on weekends was "6-piece colored combo" the Rhythm Kings, a jazz/soul group of moonlighting Black high school band directors, who got the college kids and Bergstrom airmen dancing. Led by L. C. Anderson's Alvin Patterson on trumpet, his brother Roy on keyboards, and singing drummer LaRue Banks, the group featured sax player James Jordan, who taught at Columbus Colored High School before a move to New York to manage his cousin Ornette Coleman. The former Jade Room sideman was the director of music programs for the New York State Council on the Arts from 1976 until retiring in 2005.

Doc Funk died of a heart attack in 1964, so he didn't witness the club's rock 'n' roll heyday, which red-headed Marge, then fifty-two, lorded over with an authoritative manner that earned her the "Dragon Lady" nickname (to go with the club's Far East décor). The Spades were the club's biggest weekday draw, helped by KNOW-AM, the big Top 40 station in town, playing the "You're Gonna Miss Me" single. The hometown high school heroes also played Le Lollipop, a short-lived, Shindig-inspired club off Riverside, and Swingers A-Go-Go near North Loop.

They had a big supporter in *Statesman* "Nightbeat" columnist Jim Langdon, who reported, in October 1965, that Roky had been kicked out of Travis High for refusing to cut his hair. "Pity poor Samson had he tried to get through Travis High without a haircut," Langdon wrote.

The Lingsmen left singer Max Range, also from Kerrville, and his blonde beach boy persona in Port A when they came up to Austin and met Hall. The four mysterious dudes showed up at a Spades gig at the Jade looking like a band in search of a singer, and when Roky followed them to their practice space after the show, the rest of the Spades knew they'd lost him. Musically, creatively, Roky had graduated to a band that was strobe-light years ahead. He'd never heard anyone play guitar like Stacy Sutherland, who gave the band it's psychedelic identity.

Originally from Houston, Hall was a born huckster who sold Erickson on musical mind expansion in the last year LSD was legal. "Tommy wanted to get everyone high," Roky's mother Evelyn told me in 2010. "Well, Roky was already high," naturally so. "That's where the trouble started."

With only a week and a half of rehearsal, the Elevators took over where the Spades left off, packing the Jade with up to three hundred fans every Wednesday and Thursday night. After just a month of playing out, they trekked to Houston to recut "You're Gonna Miss Me" for Gordon Bynum's Contact Records.

They also recorded their first drug bust in January '66, with every member but bassist Thurman getting popped for marijuana possession at Hall's house at 403 E. 38th Street and the Bel Air Motel where Sutherland and Walton lived. "Turn On Tommy" had been under surveillance for a month. The ages of those arrested ranged from Roky, eighteen, to Clementine, twenty-six.

When the elevated "You're Gonna Miss Me" came out in February, it sold well, but KNOW wouldn't play it. DJ Lou House told the *Statesman*'s Langdon he made that call because he was annoyed that the band and their friends seemed to be flooding the request line. No local single could be that popular. But the banning could've also been due to pressure from advertisers after the drug bust. The Elevators packed a heavy antiestablishment vibe.

The staid Jade Room had a strict dress code, which didn't change fast enough for the times, so the Elevators moved to the more wide-open New Orleans Club in February '66.

These were the band's glory days, captured in live remotes by KAZZ that are cherished to this day by diehards. But the Elevators couldn't tour out of state until August '66 when the marijuana cases were thrown out due to sloppy police paperwork. They made their Bay Area debut in September '66, a month before the release of debut LP *The Psychedelic Sounds of the 13th Floor Elevators*, still wearing their courtroom haircuts. It didn't matter.

"They blew away all the famous San Francisco bands," said Houston White, a light show artist at the time. "Nobody wanted to follow them because nobody could." The Grateful Dead were astounded that a band could play a concert that well while tripping on LSD!

Back home, Austin's first psychedelic club Fred took over the Library Lounge/Clown's Den at 1809 San Jacinto in the fall of 1966. "Being unkempt was part of the scene at this club," former Conqueroo drummer Gerry Storm wrote of Fred in his self-published history of Austin music in the '60s. "Performers from Fred did not play at the Jade Room nor vice-versa. But there was talent at both places."

Fred was dead, however, after just ten weeks of operation. Owner Bill Simonson had taken the Liquor Control Board to court in late '65 and won the right to sell beer and wine at his 11th Door folk club. But the LCB (AKA "the Man") evened the score by shutting down Fred for serving alcohol to one minor.

When the Vulcan Gas Company debuted the next year, it didn't even try to sell beer—a license for constant hassles from the authorities. Besides, they wanted to keep it all ages.

Next at 1809 San Jacinto after Fred was Club Saracen, owned by Hester Nohra and run by daughter Marie, a notorious figure whose name was in the paper so often for the wrong reasons, another "Marie Nohra"—married into the prominent Joseph family—took out a classified ad to say it wasn't her. Opening with Jesse Lopez, Trini's brother, and boasting go-go dancers from LA (actually Dallas), Saracen tried to bring the Sunset Strip to those blocks of frat bars, but wasn't successful, financially at least. A move in '68 to 1418 Lavaca Street, across the street from the Chequered Flag, didn't change things,

ABOVE: Elevators September 1967, the *Easter Everywhere* sessions. *Front*: Hall, Sutherland, Erickson. *Back row*: Danny Galindo, Leland Rogers, Danny Thomas. Photograph by Russell Wheelock. Courtesy of Wittliff Collections.

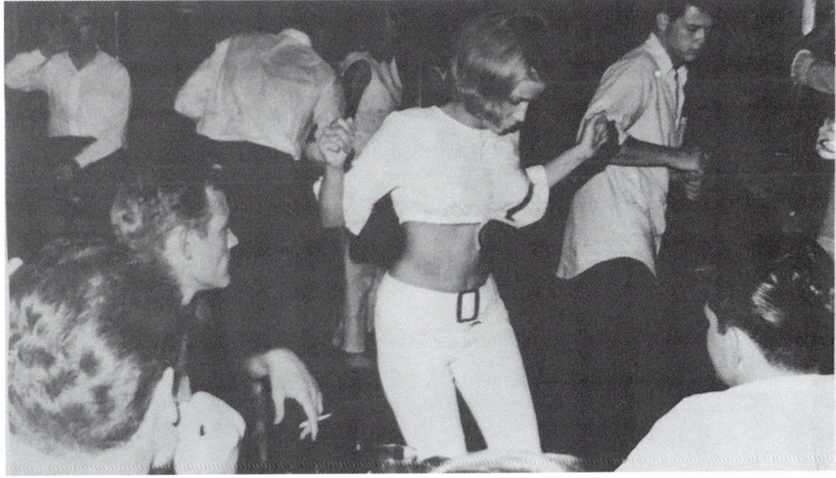

ABOVE: Austin's first "psychedelic" club was Fred, at 1809 San Jacinto in 1966. Photograph by Bob Simmons.

though Don Henley's Dallas band the Felicity packed the place a couple times a month. "Bad" Marie had more success three blocks north on Lavaca with the Pearl Street Warehouse gay bar in the early '70s. People still talk about that place.

Lavender Hill Express

Of the early Austin rock bands who survived by playing frat parties, the Wig and Baby Cakes probably came closest to the 13th Floor intensity. Featuring Johnny Richardson and Benny Rowe on guitars, the Wig's 1967 single "Crackin' Up" (written by drummer Rusty Wier) is crate-digger gold, chosen for the noted Pebbles compilation of '60s garage rock. Baby Cakes, with Bergstrom airman Don Lupo on bass, guitarists Layton DePenning and Leonard Arnold, and Chuck Bakondi on vocals, did spot-on covers of British Invasion bands. They were managed by KNOW disc jockey Dave Biondi, who dressed them in matching gold jackets with black pants and Beatle boots.

Members of the Wigs and Baby Cakes joined forces in 1968 to form Lavender Hill Express, the hottest rock band in town while the Elevators were in post-*Easter Everywhere* purgatory. Singing drummer Wier, keyboardist Gary P. Nunn (replacing Johnny Schwertner), bassist Jess Yaryan, and guitarists DePenning and Arnold, packed the Jade every Thursday night, and the New Orleans Club on weekends, for two years. Wier had the soul voice to sing all the Stax and Motown hits so big at the time.

Since Marge Funk gave the bands the door, the Lavenders were making good money. But some of the other groups were practically playing for free, so the local musicians union had their members boycott the club until Funk could guarantee thirty-five dollars per musician, per night. That hurt the Jade, as did a riot outside the club on "Soul Night," November 28, 1971, when police were pelted with debris when they tried to arrest two men fighting on the sidewalk. The billy clubs came out swinging, as two dozen cop cars screeched onto the scene. Officers hauled nineteen to jail amid charges of police overreaction from witnesses. The incident was in the news for days, with the NAACP getting involved.

The Brackenridge bulldozers finished the job on the Jade, turning it into a parking lot in early '72. Also shut down was the New Orleans at 1125 Red River, though the historic limestone building was moved and incorporated into Symphony Square.

Clubland Paradise: Vulcan Gas Company, 1967–70

The Electric Grandmother collective rented Doris Miller Auditorium on the Eastside in January '67 for the Elevators' return show from the West Coast—and first in Austin since their debut LP release. It was a madhouse, with nearly two thousand fans coming out, to also see opening act Conqueroo and the Jomo Disaster light show, which consisted of eight slide projectors, three overhead projectors, and strobe lights. But the acoustics were horrendous in that basketball gym, and the search was on to find a suitable large venue.

The Eastside welcomed longhairs, who generally drank more beer than the regulars, with the I.L. Club on E. 11th putting up a sign that said "Famous Beatnik Bands Nightly" (only "bands" was accurate). Conqueroo, which had an African American member in Ed Guinn, led the Eastern migration, though the I.L. billed them as "The Kangaroos."

Way on the other side of town was Lake Austin Inn, a boat deck club which opened with big bands in 1941 and changed with the times, musically. It leaned hippie down the stretch, with Leo and the Prophets and Mullet holding long residencies, until it was sold to developers (in a nine-acre lakefront tract for $300,000) in 1971.

West Campus got a rock club in late '66 when Simonson opened the Match Box at 2513 San Antonio, in what is now the back room of the Hole in the Wall. Future Vulcan/Dillo favorite Mance Lipscomb played there, as well as psych bands the Thingies (from Miami) and Human Factor. The Match Box also showed silent and experimental films, and eventually became a full-time movie house where you could drink beer. This was thirty years before Alamo Drafthouse launched in downtown Austin, at 409 Colorado.

Promoter Jimmy Moses tried to make a rock club out of the basement of Municipal Auditorium, which he called "A Place to Go." But even as Georgetown Medical Band (a better band than name) and Lavender Hill Express packed the Place in its September '67 debut, nobody besides Moses saw it as a viable venue.

With the addition of Don Hyde, just back from the Bay Area, where he and associates traded mescaline (extracted from peyote from the Rio Grand Valley) for the last two thousand hits of Owsley Stanley's "White Lightning" LSD, Electric Grandmother became the Vulcan Gas Company. The month after putting on the "Love-In at Zilker" in September 1967—Shiva's Head Band's de-

ABOVE: Members of Vulcan opening night bands Conqueroo *(left)* and Shiva's Head Band getting high, physically. Courtesy of Dolph Briscoe Center for American History.

RIGHT: Lavender Hill Express ruled the Jade Room in the late 1960s. Courtesy of Sonobeat Records.

Shiva's Head Band at practice 1969. *Left to right*: Spencer Perskin, Susan Perskin, Richard Finnell, Kenny Parker, and Shawn Siegel. Photograph by Burton Wilson. Courtesy of AusPop archives.

but—Hyde and his partners Houston White, Gary Scanlon, and Elevators soundman Sandy Lockett opened their Vulcan club in the Victorian building at 316 Congress that formerly housed Stein's men's clothing store. Hyde used proceeds from his share of Owsley's 2700-microgram-per-dose acid to fund the Vulcan, which he said wouldn't have stayed open more than a couple weeks, "if people in Austin had not enjoyed getting high and expanding their consciousness."

Congress Avenue was on the skids in the '60s, but neighboring businesses didn't want the druggies on their block, and brought their concerns to landlord Joe Dacy, from a locally prominent Lebanese American family. So Dacy showed up one night, unannounced, to see what was happening and walked away impressed with what the kids had done with the place. Just pay the $350 a month rent on time, he told Hyde, and everything's cool.

Hippies were generally not to be encouraged in the land of LBJ, whose escalation of the Vietnam War made him the most hated man in America. It was a tense situation between war-protesting longhairs and law enforcement in Austin (even though it was an ex-Marine with a crewcut who killed eleven people from the Tower on August 1, 1966). The Vulcan was seen as that club on Dragnet, where kids from good families lose their minds after buying drugs from diabolical guru-types.

An unairconditioned, no-frills rock box, with benches instead of tables and chairs, the Vulcan had competition just two months after opening when the plusher Pleasure Dome, yet another Simonson venture, debuted in December 1967 at 222 E. Sixth. But the Dome, with its Sacred Mushroom Bar and freaky light show, lasted only a few months at the former Yank Theater location. Same with the Ozone Forest "teen psychedelic club" at 3405 Guadalupe, which opened in July 1967, but didn't make it to cooler temps. Did those mind-expansion-themed clubs forget that Austin was in Texas?

What set the Vulcan apart were occasional national acts, like Moby Grape, Jimmy Reed, Canned Heat, Velvet Underground and the Fugs, and acoustics so good it was sometimes used as a recording studio. When KAZZ, the most progressive radio station in town, was sold to KOKE in '67, general manager Bill Josey Sr. and son Bill Jr. ("Rim Kelly" on the air) concentrated on the Sonobeat label, founded to record the best bands from their New Orleans Club remotes. After being blown away by Beaumont's Johnny Winter at the Vulcan, the Joseys signed him and had Sonobeat's only financial success when they sold *The Progressive Blues Experiment*—recorded live in '68 by Winter's trio in an otherwise empty Vulcan—to Imperial Records. Conqueroo and Shiva's also recorded live at the Vulcan during the day.

The Vulcan was continually under surveillance, not only from police but a "hippie watch" group of concerned parents, who patrolled the Vulcan as well as the Texas Union. "We're available to testify," head vigilante William Creamer told the *Statesman*.

But a much-greater threat came when Hyde was visited by a vice cop whose lawn he used to mow as a kid. Officer Spain told Hyde there was tremendous pressure on APD to shut the Vulcan down. "If you don't stop," he told Hyde, "half a pound of pot will be planted in your office and you'll do 15-20 years in Huntsville." Hyde put a for sale sign on his house and quietly slipped out of town.

This was soon after the Vulcan lost their asses booking Janis Joplin and Big Brother into the Hemisfair Theater in San Antonio on November 21, 1968. Both shows sold out, but all the money had to be refunded after the singer canceled due to illness. Questioning the excuse when Joplin fulfilled commitments in Dallas and Houston that week, a disgusted Hyde dumped three thousand posters he had made—one for each ticketholder—into the trash. "We never really recovered," Hyde said, estimating the Vulcan lost $3,500 in advertising and venue rental costs.

Johnny Winter, fresh from his stunning Columbia Records debut, came back to play a two-night benefit in March 1970. But the Vulcan held on only until May, which left a big void in the scene. At a Hub City Movers gig on June 13 at the Cactus Club on Barton Springs Road, Shiva's Head Band manager Eddie Wilson went out the back door to take a leak and before him was an abandoned Army Reserve Armory that was just about the size of the Fillmore in San Francisco.

Pianist Otis Spann and guitarist Muddy Waters at the Vulcan in August 1968. Photograph by Burton Wilson.

Johnny Winter trio at the Vulcan circa 1969. Photograph by Burton Wilson.

Vaunted Vulcan Night: When Muddy Met Johnny

Johnny Winter was instrumental in exposing the great Chicago bluesman Muddy Waters to '70s rock audiences, producing and playing guitar on the 1977 comeback album *Hard Again* and its crossover gem, "The Blues Had a Baby and They Named It Rock and Roll." But the duo had never met before playing on a bill together at the Vulcan Gas Company on August 2 and 3, 1968.

On the first night, a Friday, the Waters band didn't arrive at the club until after the Winter power trio finished. "They did a standard forty-five-minute set," Hyde recalled. Muddy's band wasn't even wearing their customary suits, as photos by Burton Wilson attest, with piano player Otis Spann's glare at the camera underlining the mood of the set. "It was only 10:45 (when they were done), so I asked Johnny if he would play for a couple hours more and he said sure."

Muddy was still in his dressing room when Winter came back out and blew the doors off the place, a scene captured by *Mother* magazine (Houston) publisher Larry Sepulvado in his review. Waters came out to the side of the stage and his jaw dropped at the albino's authentic blues style. He found a pay phone backstage and put in a collect call to King Curtis, the sax player who'd just signed Freddie King to Atlantic spinoff Cotillion. Hyde was standing next to Muddy when he held up the phone for about a minute during Winter's set and then returned to the receiver. "He white!" Waters exclaimed. "I mean, he really white! Can you believe this shit?"

The second night, Muddy and band were on fire, and called Johnny up for a couple songs to the delight of the sold-out crowd. The *Mother* review led to Jann Wenner assigning Sepulvado a December '68 cover story on Texas music (*Rolling Stone* #23, Doug Sahm cover), which along with Johnny's sensational jam with Mike Bloomfield at the Fillmore East in NYC, led to a crazy bidding war. The $600,000 record deal for Winter on Columbia, was the largest for any rock band up to that time.

Conqueroo. *Left to right:* Bob Brown, Gerry Storm, Ed Guinn, and Charlie Pritchard. Photograph by Russell Wheelock. Courtesy of Wittliff Collections.

The Other Two: Shiva's Head Band and Conqueroo

When Haight Ashbury disintegrated into a urine-stenched "kid row" for runaways and speed freaks, Capitol Records bet on Austin as the next new hip music scene. In 1969, Shiva's Head Band became the first Austin rock group to sign with a major label, with Capitol giving them an extra $10,000 to develop other acts from Austin. Shiva leader Spencer Perskin used some of that advance bump to open the Armadillo World Headquarters with his manager and former North Texas State classmate Eddie Wilson.

Conqueroo was Shiva's main cohorts in the local rock scene, but they left Austin too soon, moving to an overplayed Bay Area in early '69 and having to get straight jobs because gigs were few. Drummer Gerry Storm headed home immediately, creating empty drumseat syndrome, a malady that persisted to the point that the band hired a Black soul drummer, Alvin Sykes, who made them too good. Finally, they got their big break, opening for the Grateful Dead at Golden Gate Park. When they came onstage in SF and looked out onto a crowd of thousands, the band dug in to kick ass. They hated always being compared to the Dead, a band they didn't get, so they were ready to show what Conqueroo was really about.

But the PA died during the first song and they had to play an abbreviated all-instrumental set. Magically, the sound system was restored in time for the Dead. "I'm sure it wasn't intentional," Bob Brown, Conqueroo's singer/guitarist/songwriter, said in an interview, sounding not entirely convinced. "But it was an omen for our whole San Francisco experience."

By the time Conqueroo came back to Austin in '73 (without guitarist Prichard, who joined Cat Mother and the All-Night Newsboys in Mendocino), everything had changed. Psychedelic was out, cosmic cowboy was in,

ABOVE: Early stages of the Vulcan.

RIGHT: Spencer Perskin of Shiva's, the first Austin rock band to sign with a major label in 1969. Photograph by Van Brooks. Courtesy of AusPop Archives.

Shiva's Head Band plays Wooldridge Park in 1969. Photograph by Burton Wilson.

and they couldn't get booked at the Armadillo. One plum gig was Soap Creek's packed opening night on March 24, 1973. But when the group returned three weeks later, only a handful were in attendance.

"All the practicing and moving equipment for fifteen dollars a night sucked when there wasn't the fan base that had sustained us earlier," Brown said of the eminent breakup in a 2018 interview.

Originally called Powell St. John and the Conqueroo (a play on the St. John the Conqueror Root, a mojo potion for sexual prowess), they played old-timey, acoustic folk-blues at first, with Tommy Hall blowing bass lines on a jug. But harmonica player St. John, who wrote several songs for the 13th Floor Elevators and "Bye, Bye Baby" for Janis, was freaked out by the tower sniper, and decided to follow Joplin to the Bay Area. There, Powell started Mother Earth with singer Tracy Nelson and Fort Worth drummer George Rains.

After St. John split, so did Hall to start 13th Floor Elevators. Conqueroo went electric, with Guinn switching from clarinet to bass and lead guitarist Pritchard dictating a psychedelic R&B feel on twelve-minute covers of "Midnight Hour" and "Yonder Wall." On originals like "1 to 3," the band's first and only single on Sonobeat, Brown brought an edge of esoterica to the mix.

Shiva's and Conqueroo played opening night of the Vulcan and remained the club's unofficial house bands. The Bubble Puppy, which moved from San Antonio to Austin in '67, were also popular Vulcan regulars with their twin-lead guitar psych sound. But they were off to Houston the next year, recording for International Artists, and having the label's biggest hit with "Hot Smoke and Sasafrass" (#14, 1969). "You're Gonna Miss Me" by the Elevators stalled at #55 in 1967.

"Liberal" Austin wasn't safe for longhairs in the '60s, which is one reason so many moved to San Francisco. "The average person (in Austin) then was totally conformist, conservative, intolerant, and hated us on sight," Brown said. "I could be walking down the street and a car full of frat boys or just normal good ole boys would pull alongside and taunt me, or all pile out with the intent of beating the shit out of a freak."

Conqueroo left town before the Texas International Pop Festival, just two weeks after Woodstock, so Shiva's was Austin's lone representative at that landmark event near Dallas, featuring Janis, Led Zeppelin, Sly and the Family Stone, and the breakout of Grand Funk Railroad.

Born in Brooklyn, the son of a traveling salesman, Spencer Perskin eventually ended up with his family in Dallas. The violin prodigy enrolled at North Texas State in Denton in the early '60s, where he joined the folk music club headed by English professor Stan Alexander, whom student Michael Murphey credited with instilling in him a love of country music. Steve Fromholz was also a folk club regular, as were Travis Holland and harmonica great Donnie Brooks (Waylon Jennings). Alexander used to sing old country ballads at Threadgill's Wednesday night hootenannies in the late '50s when he was getting his PhD at UT. That was the scene he tried to recreate in Denton.

Perskin eventually ended up in Austin, living at the Jewish Student Center where he met pianist Shawn Siegel. Perskin played him "Kaleidoscopic," a song he'd written on an acid trip in San Francisco, which would become the band's debut single on Ignite Records in 1968. Drummer Jerry Barnett, guitarist Bob Tom Reed, and bassist Kenny Parker were suitably adventurous. Spencer's wife Susan Perskin was then brought on for additional vocals.

During live performances, the Head Band (billed "Headband" by Capitol for less druggie connotation) ended their show by repeating the word "Yes" for several minutes. But Capitol said no to the second LP after *Take Me to the Mountains* didn't sell. *Coming to a Head* came out on the band's Armadillo label.

The reason folks gush about Shiva's and Conqueroo is not their recorded work. An objective listener can hear why neither band really made it. The magic was in the connection with a live audience, creating a community in a whole new world.

James Brown at Municipal Auditorium (8/1/66)

If that date looks familiar that's because it was the day UT engineering student Charles Whitman killed eleven people from the observation deck of the UT Tower, after killing three on the way up.

JAMES BROWN PLAYED AUSTIN ON THE NIGHT OF THE SNIPER MASS MURDER!

You would think that would be an infamous musical event, except, until a few years ago, hardly anybody had even known about it. This wasn't like the night Martin Luther King Jr. was assassinated and the James Brown show went on to quell rioting in Boston. There had been absolutely no trace of this concert in Austin lore until 2013 when Tim Hamblin, a video archivist for the Austin History Center, was going through some old footage from 1982 at Club Foot and found an interview with James Brown. Asked if he'd ever played Austin before, the Godfather of Soul said, "Yeah, I played here the night that guy went crazy up there on the tower!"

Ads in the *Statesman* confirm the date, and we know the show went on because the *Capital City Argus*, Austin's Black newspaper of the time, covered the concert. Credited to "Roving Eyes," the review had James Brown sitting in with the eighteen-piece band on organ before taking the spotlight. Nowhere in the review did it mention the day of terror, which began just eleven blocks from Municipal Auditorium at the Bouldin Creek house at 906 Jewel Street, where Whitman stabbed his wife to death while she slept. He then went to the Penthouse Apartments at 901 Guadalupe St. and killed his mother in similar fashion.

Austin was pretty much segregated in 1966 and what happened over at the white college didn't affect the goings on in the Black community. So, although it's a tad surprising the review didn't mention sixteen murders in town that day, it's not a shock.

Austin was in shock, but the show must go on.

Smoke from Charles Whitman's rifle, August 1966. Courtesy of Austin History Center.

Rod Kennedy was Mr. Kerrville in the mid-1980s, but he also promoted other shows. Photograph by Niles J. Fuller. Courtesy of Dolph Briscoe Center for American History.

IX.

Field General Rod Kennedy

From KHFI to Kerrville

One afternoon at the Kerrville Folk Festival, Rod Kennedy, who founded the epic event in 1972, was seen standing in front of the empty main stage at Quiet Valley Ranch. "He didn't know anyone was watching," said Lloyd Maines, who was sitting under a tree, waiting to teach a songwriting class. "He just stopped and stood there looking toward the stage for a long while."

In the silence, the veteran promoter no doubt heard music. Kennedy could look back on his five-plus decades in the entertainment business, during which he produced thousands of shows in every genre, with great satisfaction. In a town full of talkers, Kennedy, who passed away in 2014 at age eighty-four, got things done for Austin.

When the *Batman* TV series with Adam West was a national phenomenon in 1966, leading to a quick cash-in movie, Kennedy flew out to LA to convince executive producer William Dozier to have the film's world premiere in Austin at the Paramount Theater. Austin's Glastron Boat Co. built Batman's speedboat for the movie, so the tie-in with Aquafest, which Kennedy helmed that year, was a natural. On July 30, 1966, West and Catwoman Lee Meriwether led a parade down Congress Avenue, lined with thirty thousand exuberant fans. The event was covered by the national press.

But Austin was in the news two days later for tragic reasons. That the tower killer was an ex-Marine especially saddened Kennedy, a proud jarhead who fought in the Korean War.

Austin soared one day, and came crashing down the next, like the up-and-down concert promotion business. Kennedy learned to accept the losses—and go on to the next thing—in a chosen profession celebrated with a three-hour tribute concert at the Paramount Theater on his eightieth birthday. Such Kerrville favorites as Robert Earl Keen, Ruthie Foster, the Flatlanders, Eliza Gilkyson, Bobby Bridger, Randy Rogers, Terri Hendrix, and more performed for "the Rodfather" one more time.

Kennedy's career began as a sixteen-year-old "boy singer" for the Bill Creighton Orchestra in Buffalo, NY. Kennedy didn't have to haul an instrument, so he was drafted to handle stagehand chores, and within a matter of months was booking the band.

"I was hooked from that point on," said Kennedy, who loved to sing, especially in barbershop quartets, but found his place behind the scenes. He moved to Texas in the late 1940s with his mother Dorne when she got a job as a buyer for Palais Royal, an upscale clothier based in Houston.

After his time in the Marines, Kennedy moved to Austin to attend the University of Texas. He stayed, first as a radio station owner-manager, and then a tireless promoter of jazz, gospel, country, classical, rock, Broadway shows, ballets, in addition to the singer-songwriters in Kerrville, where the main stage bears his name.

Carolyn Hester

The first concert under the auspices of "Rod Kennedy Presents" was the May 1962 hometown return of Carolyn Hester at Austin Civic Theater Playhouse at Fifth and Lavaca. Growing up at 38th and Duval, Hester had attended University Junior High, an experimental teaching school on the UT campus, and Austin High.

Her self-titled Columbia Records debut, which came out two weeks after her Playhouse shows, is especially noteworthy because Bob Dylan made his recording studio debut on harmonica.

Hester was the only rising star of the Greenwich Village folk scene who could introduce a song with "Buddy Holly taught me this one," having recorded 1958 debut LP *Scarlet Ribbons* (Coral) at Norman Petty's studio in Clovis, New Mexico. She didn't play in Austin for three years before the Civic Theater shows, which featured brother Dean Hester as opening act, so they easily sold out. But with all the family and friends, the guest list was a bitch and Kennedy lost thirty-five dollars. He would get better at saying no.

Under Kennedy's stewardship, the Kerrville Folk Festival grew from an indoor event that attracted twenty-eight hundred people over three days into an eighteen-day event that annually draws more than thirty thousand "Kerrverts." That is, when it doesn't rain. Downpours limited seven of the first nineteen outdoor festivals, leading to the "Kerrville Flood Fest" nickname.

Kennedy was well-established as an Austin promoter in 1972 when organizers of the Kerrville-based Texas State Arts & Crafts Fair asked him to put on a music festival at night to keep the crowds in town. Attendance at Kerrville Municipal Auditorium doubled to fifty-six hundred after the first year, and the folk festival moved outdoors in 1974, on sixty-three acres Kennedy bought nine miles from Kerrville for about $47,000.

Kennedy's career impacted not only live music, but radio in Central Texas. As a twenty-four-year-old freshman at UT in 1954, Kennedy used a school project to spearhead efforts to raise money for a campus radio station that would become a reality four years later when KUT-FM went on the air. Weeks after graduating, Kennedy and his new bride Nancylee (the great-granddaughter of former UT president William Prather) bought the KHFI classical music station he had managed while in college for $21,000. Austin's first FM station, KHFI switched to an adult contemporary format in 1965 and donated all its classical records to KMFA-FM, which went on the air in 1967. When KHFI went into the TV market with UHF channel 42, Kennedy produced *The Younger Set*, a half-hour live music program that aired at 6 p.m. Tuesdays for twenty-two weeks, debuting in October '66 with the Wig. Allen Damron was host, with Tim Lively and the Profits serving as house band. It went nowhere, but at least it tried.

The roots of Kerrville were planted at the Zilker Hillside Theater in 1964, when Kennedy began booking and hosting the KHFI-FM Summer Music Festival over six nights in July. Monday was Folk Night and featured Carolyn Hester two months after she was on the cover of the *Saturday Evening Post*. Also on the bill that first year were John Lomax Jr., Lightnin' Hopkins, Mance Lipscomb, Segel Fry, and Dallas folk/comedy duo Mickey and Marty.

Longhorn Jazz Fest

Teaming up with Newport Jazz and Folk Festivals founder George Wein, Kennedy copromoted the Longhorn Jazz Festival at Disch Field in 1966. The jaw-dropping first-year lineup included Dizzy Gillespie, Sonny Stitt, Dave Brubeck, Stan Getz, Gerry Mulligan, Gary Burton, Pete Fountain, Maynard Ferguson, Bud Freeman, and an unbilled Coleman Hawkins (he jammed with Getz and Freeman on "Body and Soul"), plus homecoming sets from Austin-born piano great Teddy Wilson and former Anderson High Yellowjacket Kenny Dorham. John Coltrane was booked for the first LJF but had to cancel due to ongoing gum problems. The Miles Davis Quintet, with Herbie Hancock on piano and Tony Williams on drums, was not a bad last-minute replacement.

Over eleven thousand tickets were sold over two days, and it would've been more if the LJF hadn't been booked the same weekend as UT's Roundup, which snapped up most of the hotel rooms. Next year would be different.

Next year would rain like hell (Kennedy's reputation as "the Drought Killer" begins), with the fest, featuring Thelonious Monk, Nina Simone, Illinois Jacquet, Arnett Cobb, and two of the all-time greatest drummers, Jo Jones and Buddy Rich, moving indoors to Municipal Auditorium.

The acts stayed at the Downtowner Hotel at 11th and Trinity, so there was lotsa afterhours jamming in the Wee Hours, the basement jazz club of the Iron Gate Inn across the street. It got crazy and Kennedy got his first call about damages as a promoter. "Thelonious Monk trashed his hotel room," said Kennedy, who made the jazz legend reimburse $400 after he admitted swinging from the chandelier.

Lightnin' Hopkins played the 1966 Longhorn Jazz Festival. Courtesy of *Austin American-Statesman* Photographic Morgue at the Austin History Center.

David and daughter Carrie Rodriguez at Kerrville in 1995. Photograph by John Carrico.

The Longhorn Jazz Fest lost about $20,000 in its first year, but Kennedy was great at lining up sponsors—twenty-five Austinites pledged $1000 ($9,400 in today's money) each to bring to town an event that would showcase the live music potential of the capital city.

The fest lasted until 1970, with pop acts Dionne Warwick, Blood, Sweat & Tears, and Roberta Flack headlining the last three years. "The good ones lost money and the pop ones made money," bemoaned jazz purist Wein, an old friend of Kennedy's who'd actually played a jazz piano set at the '65 KHFI-FM Summer Music Festival.

Clubland Paradise: The Chequered Flag, 1967–71

Enamored with folk singer Allen Damron, a native of Raymondville ("Gateway to the Rio Grande Valley") who shared his passion for sports cars, Kennedy thought about buying the struggling 11th Door in '67. But after token negotiations with Simonson, he decided to build his own folk club at the former Bureau of Water Engineers offices at 1411 Lavaca St.

The Chequered Flag debuted in September 1967 with a car racing décor and dipped roast beef sandwiches on kummelweck rolls, modeled after Meyer's Tavern in Buffalo. Kennedy put the Texas Speed Museum next door to display his collection of vintage Porsches, Ferraris, and Maseratis, plus other cars on loan. Kennedy drove competitively, and even won a couple races.

Damron managed the Flag, which was planted in the name of folk authenticity when Woody Guthrie died just two weeks after it opened, and Woodyphile Segel Fry threw together a brilliant tribute concert. A six-set run by Ramblin' Jack Elliott in February '68 solidified the one-hundred-capacity club's stature. The 11th Door closed that month.

Besides Hester, who packed it five consecutive nights, the Flag featured regular appearances by Jim Schulman, who had a wide repertoire of Israeli folk songs, and Frummox, the duo of Steven Fromholz and Dan McCrimmon who workshopped the classic "Texas Trilogy" before recording it on 1969's *From Here to There* (ABC).

"A marine doesn't fail" was Kennedy's motto, but the Chequered Flag was becoming as expensive a hobby as the fast cars, so it was announced that the club would close in September 1970. Instead, Damron and Fry bought the business from Kennedy and extended the run to June 1971. One of the last nights featured a screening of Tobe Hooper's Peter, Paul & Mary doc *The Song Is Love*, which the Austinite directed right before *Texas Chainsaw Massacre*. Talk about range.

Kerrville Folk Festival

A politically conservative owner of sports cars running a folk club in the '60s may seem incongruous, but Kennedy had long looked at life from both sides. He could be "a crusty old bird," as musician Bob Livingston led a memorial piece, but he also helped nurture hundreds of singer-songwriters in his organic setting. His best friend of forty years was the liberal singer Peter Yarrow of Peter Paul & Mary, yet, until switching parties in 2008 to back Barack Obama, Kennedy was an avowed bootstraps Republican.

But this right winger kept an open mind. Yarrow convinced Kennedy to add a New Folk songwriter competition to Kerrville, a new concept for music festivals in 1972. Winners through the years have included Eric Taylor, Lucinda Williams, Steve Earle, Slaid Cleaves, Hal Ketchum, BettySoo, Tom Russell, Adrianne Lenker of Big Thief, and future political consultant Mark MacKinnon. The New Folk winners concert is always a highlight of Kerrville.

Michelle Shocked publicity photo 1992. Photograph by Mercury Records.

Three Faces West at the Chequered Flag, 1971. *Left to right:* Rick Fowler, Wayne Kidd, Ray Wylie Hubbard. Photograph by Burton Wilson.

"Rod is that sensitive listener who has the determination to just plow through when things get tough," summated Gary Hartman, former director of Texas State University's Center for Texas Music History.

Kennedy laid down the rules that kept Kerrville unique: no talking in the audience during a performance, no recorded music between sets, and get that drum circle the fuck out of the campgrounds! There was a "no star" system, where each act got paid the same and the lineup was listed without headliner.

Kerrville has stayed alive over five decades because the biggest draw is the people who paid to get in. Now, that's a failsafe business model! The camaraderie of song freaks has the people coming back year after year, and you never know who you might discover. In 1986, a former punk squatter named Michelle Johnston thumbed her way into a career when a British label owner recorded her impromptu set—crickets and all—with a Walkman. *The Texas Campire Tapes* made Michelle Shocked a star in Europe and led to her signing with Mercury Records. But ye olde campfires of Kerrville have been put out by yearly burn bans, replaced by often-resplendent compounds that would rent for $5,000 a month if they were in Austin.

Attending the fiftieth anniversary festival in 2022, I wondered if Hardline Rod would approve of the psychedelic afterhours blowout Kerrville has become. If you're tripping, it's a heavenly scene. What's better than a lusty "Ooh La La" singalong at 5 a.m.? I was thinking sleep but didn't have that option.

Kennedy would love the heartfelt endurance of "Welcome Home" as the Kerrville salute that sets the festival's tone. As uptight as the head Kerr-ator could be, he believed in the spirit of music to connect.

Kennedy worked hard and expected the same of those in his employ, even the unpaid. (There's no more dedicated group of volunteers than those who run Kerrville.) He also demanded respect for musicians. There was that infamous night at emmajoe's in the early '80s when Kennedy flattened a drunk Blaze Foley, who was causing a ruckus during a folksinger's set. There had already been bad blood between the two, with Kennedy banning Foley from Kerrville for liberal use of profanity onstage. The six-feet-four-inch singer-songwriter crashed the festival in drag the next year.

"I was pretty intimidated by Rod when I met him in 1981," said Robert Earl Keen. "Not just because of his reputation, but because he ran something that I very much wanted to be a part of." Keen said that when he was one of five New Folk winners in 1983, "it validated music as a career choice for me." Many more can say the same.

Kennedy retired from Kerrville in 2002, leaving the producer's seat to his longtime protégé Dalis Allen, who passed it on to Mary Muse in 2015. He still got a check every month from the Kerrville nonprofit ("My title is consultant, but nobody listens to me anymore") and sold Enlyten dietary supplements for extra cash. Above all, though, he still listened for great songs until the very end. "Music changed my life," said Kennedy. "When I was in the Marines, I had a mission that had nothing to do with feelings. You're just not aware of anything else. But I've heard songs that made me cry."

When Kennedy was in hospice in 2014, among those who came to visit was Yarrow, who led a singalong of "Give Yourself to Love," Kennedy's favorite song by Kate Wolf, a Kerrville regular who died in '86 at age forty-four. "Love has made a circle that holds us all inside," sang the gathered. "Where strangers are as family, loneliness can't hide."

Austin became known as a town of good music and cheap living in the '70s and '80s, but it took a lot of hard work on the ground floor from folks like Rod Kennedy to build the Groover's Paradise that became the Slacker's Playground.

This is how 1966 Austin announced a jazz fest featuring Miles Davis, Dizzy Gillespie, Coleman Hawkins, and many more greats. Courtesy of *Austin American-Statesman* Photographic Morgue at the Austin History Center.

Mr. King with Leon Russell, in "the house that Freddie built," 1972.
Photograph by Van Brooks. Courtesy of AusPop archives.

X.

The Seventies: "Goodnight Austin, Texas, Wherever You Are"

Armadillo World Headquarters in Four Shows

The Satin '70s of disco and Styx and Helen Reddy has been a much-maligned musical decade, but in Austin those were the glory years of live music, centered around the freewheeling Armadillo World Headquarters. With a capacity of sixteen hundred, it felt like both the world's largest nightclub and smallest arena, hosting the likes of Bruce Springsteen, Van Morrison, Bette Midler, and Ray Charles, but also incubating a local scene that went national on *Austin City Limits* and with the "progressive country" radio format.

Before the shuttered Army Reserve headquarters reopened as the Armadillo in August 1970, Austin was not known for music, but for the reigning NCAA national football champion Texas Longhorns, still an all-white team in 1969.

Cofounder Eddie Wilson called the structure that housed the venue "the coldest, ugliest building in town," but because of the spirit of people working together, the Dillo had a big soul within its bare bones. As the reputation of this funky Austin concert hall spread and acts went out of their way to play there, the Armadillo became that rare and wonderful case where the crowds sometimes drew the acts.

But for all its glory, the Armadillo lost money, or barely broke even, every year. Creditors got in line behind KLBJ, which took the club to court in 1973 for $4,000 in unpaid advertising. More understanding was landlord M. K. Hage, whose lost nineteen-year-old son found his tribe with the Dillo crew. When Mitre Kahlil Hage III, or "Three" to the hippies, died of an allergic reaction to pharmaceutical cocaine in 1975, the venue lost its most valuable ally.

That the bumpy ride lasted more than a decade was only because so many people wanted it to, from the unpaid workers who considered it the best job ever, to Hank Aldrich, whose inheritance kept the club going after Wilson left in the mid-'70s. The venue truly understood the power and thrift of "plus one," using the guest list as a barter system for goods and services.

The final night of the AWHQ was December 31, 1980, ending with a cast of hundreds singing "Goodnight Irene" at 4 a.m on New Year's morning. The last line of the Armadillo's swan song goes, "I'll see you in my dreams," a fitting summary for all the great clubs we've lost. The reason they call them haunts when they're open is because it's hard to get them out of your mind after they're gone.

Don't feel too bad for those left out of the sold-out Dillo finale, with Commander Cody and Asleep at the Wheel. Other options in town that night included Townes

Van Zandt and Blaze Foley at Spellman's, Stevie Ray Vaughan at the Austin Opera House, Joe Ely at Club Foot, Marcia Ball at Hondo's Saloon, Fabulous Thunderbirds at Antone's, and Jimmie Gilmore at the Alamo Lounge.

The first band to play the Dillo was Tracy Nelson and Mother Earth, with former Austinites Powell St. John and Toad Andrews, on July 7, 1970. Unadvertised because the venue wasn't yet up to code, that was more like a rehearsal with people. The venue officially opened a month later with Shiva's Head Band and Hub City Movers (featuring Gilmore). Whistler was booked to be the first act, but they broke up that week, so bassist Bill Dorman's other band Ramon Ramon and the 4 Daddios had the honors of being the first act to officially play the most legendary of all Austin venues.

The national acts in the Dillo's first year (when the stage was on the south end, not the north), included Fats Domino, Ravi Shankar, ZZ Top, New Riders of the Purple Sage, Flying Burrito Brothers, and especially Freddie King, with Leon Russell on piano. Built in 1955 to host pro wrestling matches, the concert hall became known as "The House That Freddie Built" because the guitarist-singer was the first to sell out the expanded configuration in '72, thrilling a crowd of flower children who didn't know how much they loved the blues.

But all styles of music flew high at 525 ½ Barton Springs Road. A landmark local band bill—"the Punk Prom"—saw the live debut of the Dicks on May 16, 1980, and also featured the Next, Big Boys, Reactors, and Sharon Tate's Baby. For a local punk bill to play the Armadillo—and draw a big crowd—legitimized the Raul's scene.

The funky venue was also home to touring punk bands. Talking Heads played there six times in four years! The Dillo's most significant footnote, however, was that it's where AC/DC played their first show on American soil, opening for Moxy in July '76.

Books have been written about the Armadillo, but let's cook the experience and legacy down to four shows:

Michael Priest poster for the first Willie show at the Armadillo.

Willie Nelson in his 1972 Armadillo debut, the "Big Bang of Austin music." Courtesy of AusPop archives.

WILLIE NELSON – AUG. 12, 1972

With Vietnam still raging, the cultural chasm in Texas was wide as the Brazos River. Longhairs weren't welcome in honky-tonks, and cowboys didn't mingle with "peaceniks." It was jocks vs. nerds, Jesus vs. Jimi, bullies against the passive, but five words built a bridge.

"Ladies and gentlemen, Willie Nelson!"

A short-haired, clean-shaven Nelson stepped onto the stage of a counterculture haven and, with a three-hour show that nobody left early, expanded country music.

Talent booker Bobby Hedderman lived on the roof of the Dillo for sixty-nine days in 1976 to break a world record for billboard sitting that didn't exist, it turned out. But the venue did get a lot of publicity for its sixth anniversary. Photograph by Nancy E. Goldfarb LeNoir.

Leon Russell and Jerry Garcia confer with Doug Sahm at the Thanksgiving jam. Photograph by Scott Newton.

Willie Nelson, Michael Martin Murphy, and Eddie Wilson in the Armadillo Beergarden, 1974. Photograph by Prissy Mays.

That night, the Vulcan Gas Company merged with the Broken Spoke, as Austin became the city where kickers and freaks were starting to understand each other's culture. If we can both love Willie, and show pride for Texas, maybe we're not that far apart.

After years of wearing a suit, trying to get Nashville to accept him, Willie said screw it and moved to where his true audience was. His first Austin friend Leon Russell was a fashion mentor.

When Eddie Wilson heard that Willie, wife Connie, and the kids had moved to the Riverwalk apartments on Riverside Drive in July '72, he made it his mission to book Nelson into his hippie beer barn. It wasn't hard. Willie stopped by the Armadillo not long after his utilities had been turned on. "I've been looking for you," said Eddie. "Well, you found me," said Willie.

Willie Nelson's first show at the Dillo was the Big Bang of Austin as a renowned music mecca. Chet Flippo, a grad student attending UT on the G.I. Bill, was there and wrote a big feature on Austin's groovy longhaired cowboy scene in *Rolling Stone* in Oct. '72. "Musicians from all over were flocking to Austin to see what the fuss was about," said guit-steel master Junior Brown, who was one of them in early 1973. There was something special happening in the capital of Texas, but the '70s was when the supply of musicians started surpassing the demand. As more bands moved to Austin with Dillo dreams and Soap hopes, gigs were harder to come by. It was a groover's market.

THANKSGIVING JAM – NOV. 23, 1972

Austin has long been the site of memorable jam sessions, but the most famous (sorry, U2 and SRV at Antone's in '87) was on Thanksgiving 1972. The Grateful Dead had a gig at Municipal Auditorium the night before and they worked up a deal with the nearby Armadillo to cater the preshow meal for band, crew, and entourage. Jerry Garcia looked around the nice-sized hall, and said, "I'd love to play this place." Within earshot was Eddie W., who said to tell him when. "Well, we're not doing anything tomorrow," said Garcia. The Dead had a day off, but only Garcia and bassist Phil Lesh were gonna be in Austin, as the rest of the band was headed to a Thanksgiving feast in Corpus with top tier Deadhead Frances Carr, whose family was prominent there.

Garcia's good friend Doug Sahm said, "Let's have a jam session, man, and let everyone in for free!" Later that night, Leon Russell was backstage at the Dead show when Garcia asked if he wanted to stop by tomorrow and play some piano. It would be a Thanksgiving jam to beat 'em all.

The next morning, Eddie Wilson called up radio station KRMH ("Good Karma Radio") and said that the Dillo, which was scheduled to be closed on Thanksgiving, would be open after all for a free show. "A bunch of friends got nowhere else to go today, so they're gonna be jamming," Wilson said. Since the Dead had played the night before, it didn't take folks long to figure out they'd be involved. The surprise guest was Leon, who had the #2 album in the country in '72 with *Carney*. Wilson was tight-lipped about his appearance lest a bunch of townies show up and yell requests for "Tight Rope."

Garcia, Lesh, and Russell got there at about 3 p.m., but wouldn't start until Sahm arrived about half an hour later. "Doug knows a thousand songs," Jerry told Leon. They seemed to play most of them that night.

Soon after the Thanksgiving jam started, a torrential downpour bore down, so one of the first songs played was "Stormy Monday" by T-Bone Walker. Leon, who played more guitar than piano, later kicked everybody in on "A Hard Rain's Gonna Fall." But Sahm was clearly the leader. Garcia played pedal steel all night, with Sweet Mary Egan from Greezy Wheels a standout on fiddle on the first set, which was heavy with country songs, while the second set was more blues and rock. Jerry Barnett of Shiva's Head Band warmed the drum seat most of that magical day, which ended early eve with an all-hands-on-deck medley of Chuck Berry's "Roll Over Beethoven" and Little Richard's "Good Golly Miss Molly." About one thousand lucky fans had reason to be thankful that night.

It was not a day to be starstruck. After the jam, Jerry Garcia approached adventurous violinist Benny Thurman and asked if he'd consider going on tour with his band. "You're a starling and I'm a crow, so I must decline," said Thurman, the former 13th Floor Elevators bassist, whose mind was often in a faraway zip code. "You don't want to be in the Grateful Dead?" someone asked the violinist after Garcia, the guy he'd been playing with for two hours, walked away. "Oh, shit," said Thurman. "Is that who that was?"

FRANK ZAPPA AND CAPTAIN BEEFHEART – MAY 20 & 21, 1975

Next to Willie, Freddie, and Commander Cody, the musician with the deepest connection to the world's grooviest party barn was Frank Zappa, who never smoked dope and often satirized the counterculture in his songs. But he had an affinity for the Dillo tribe, even writing a verse about Big Rikke, the Guacamole Queen, in his 1975

Infamous hippie-hater Frank Zappa loved the Armadillo.
Photograph by Ken Hoge. Courtesy of AusPop archives.

song "Inca Roads," from *One Size Fits All*. "He played so often that we had to rotate the artists who did the posters, and they all seemed to get a crack at Zappa," said Eddie Wilson. The second time rock's weirdo composer (and great guitarist) played the hip hangar in '74, there was a bomb scare in the middle of a song. After the evacuated fans were returned to the hall an hour later, Zappa struck up the band at the exact point in the song where the concert had paused.

But none of Zappa's shows on Barton Springs Road stand out this many years later like the two nights in May 1975 that were recorded for *Bongo Fury*, the last Zappa album with the Mothers of Invention as his band's name. Released five months after the Armadillo shows, *Bongo* teamed Zappa with his former Antelope Valley High School (Lancaster, CA) classmate Don Van Vliet, better known as Captain Beefheart. The two avant-guardians of the hippie era had huge influences on each other growing up, and Zappa produced the Beefheart masterpiece *Trout Mask Replica* (1969). But the *Bongo Fury* tour was the only time Beefheart went on the road with Zappa. The album also marked the first appearance of drummer Terry Bozzio, who later moved to Austin, as original Mothers skinsmith Jimmy Carl Black had done.

"Zappa was a compulsive perfectionist," recalled Wilson. "Our crew worked their asses off for him. I think that's one of the main reasons he liked the Armadillo." But Zappa was also able to adapt on the fly. For one show his contract stipulated that he'd have four hours to rehearse and a full hour soundcheck before the doors opened at 7 p.m. Except Zappa's equipment trucks didn't arrive until 5:30 p.m. and he had only fifteen minutes to soundcheck. "Zappa was really pissed off and I said, 'I know the last thing in the world you want to do right now is meet anybody, but you've got a blind, crippled guy opening for you and I'll take you over to meet him if you'd like.'" Zappa and Blind George McLain hit it off and Zappa took the Split Rail regular out on the road with him to open a couple more Texas shows.

Of the nine tracks on *Bongo Fury*, six were recorded at the Armadillo, including the Van Vliet poem/songs "Sam with the Showing Scalp Flat Top" (the title *Bongo Fury* comes from the lyrics) and "Man with the Woman Head." Three tracks were recorded in the studio. The concert ends with Zappa (who passed away from prostate cancer in 1993), saying "Goodnight Austin, Texas, wherever you are," a catchphrase that speaks to the moveable spirit of those shows.

THE CLASH WITH JOE ELY - OCT. 4, 1979

Someone described this October 1979 show as Ely and his band pouring gasoline all over the stage and then the Clash coming out and lighting a match. "There was such an explosive feeling in the air," said Ely. "I felt it. The Clash felt it. Our attitude was 'it's Saturday night at the honky tonk and someone just shot a gun into the ceiling.' It was one of those dangerous nights where anything can happen."

A few punks threw cups and stuff on stage during Ely's set, but by the end of the night Joe was onstage singing "Fingernails" with the Clash. It's always great when a local favorite is embraced by a bigtime act, as Bruce Springsteen would later do with our Joe E.

The modern singing cowboys from Lubbock met the Clash five months earlier in London, when the punk explorers showed up at an Ely gig at the Venue, and then guided the band around London for a week. "I said, 'if you ever come to Texas, we'd like to return the favor,'" recalled Ely. "They were all fascinated with Texas." Joe Strummer called Ely a few weeks later and rattled off the cities the Clash wanted to play: Laredo, El Paso, San Antone, the cities of cowboy movies and Marty Robbins songs. But first was the show at the Armadillo: the Clash's Texas debut.

The band had recently recorded *London Calling* before the '79 US tour, but it wasn't out yet, so the Armadillo audience was hearing "Spanish Bombs" and "Clamptown" and "London Calling" for the first time. When the Clash ended with "White Riot" they almost caused one. Afterwards everyone followed opening act the Skunks to the Continental Club.

The Dillo was known among fans for its ñachos (a fairly new culinary concept), but touring acts loved the quality of chef Jan Beeman's preshow catering. Van Morrison once booked a show there on short notice because he wanted to try the shrimp enchiladas Jerry Garcia had been raving about. But the Clash's only meal request was for a toaster, a loaf of white bread, and a big can of baked beans. "Beans on toast is all they ever ate," said Ely. That diet seemed to work.

ABOVE: Joe Ely joins the Clash for an encore of "Fingernails" at the Armadillo. Photograph by Mark Ely.

RIGHT: The Armadillo billboard after the club closed down on the first day of 1981. Photograph by Kevin Vandivier. Courtesy of Dolph Briscoe Center for American History.

L-R: Micael Priest, Artly Snuff of Uranium Savages, Guy Juke, Jim Franklin. The bumper sticker was for Franklin's campaign to paint a yellow rose on the watertower off Lake Austin Boulevard. That project fizzled when fundraising fell way short of the $30,000 needed. Photograph by Bill Leissner, 1987.

Posterfarians

Though the accepted chronology has Austin artists following San Francisco's lead, the first '60s underground comic book was actually produced in Austin by artist and historian Jack "Jaxon" Jackson in 1964. Jaxon's forty-two-page *God Nose*, xeroxed in the state capitol print shop after hours, came out four years before the first *Zap Comix* hit the streets of San Francisco. Gilbert Shelton started drawing the *Wonder Wart-Hog* superhero spoof in UT's *Texas Ranger* humor magazine around 1963.

Jackson and Shelton, with fellow Austinites Dave Moriaty and Fred Todd, started Rip Off Press, home of the wildly-popular *Fabulous Furry Freak Brothers*, in SF in January 1969. Shelton's Freak Brothers introduced a motto for the times: "Dope will get you through times of no money better than money will get you through times of no dope." OK, boomers, how many times did you say that when you were broke and high?

Images of armadillos set Austin apart from the Haight-Ashbury scene of national obsession. Cartooning for the *Texas Ranger* in the mid-'60s, Glenn Whitehead was the first in town to artistically obsess on that possum with aluminum siding. But Jim Franklin turned it into the mascot for Austin's hippie-slacker weirdness. In 1968, he was hired to draw a poster for a "love-in" concert at Wooldridge Park and was thumbing through a zoological guidebook when he came across the critter that scared the life out him at age ten, when one ran between his legs on a hunting trip with his dad. Franklin drew a 'dillo smoking a joint, giving Austin's poster scene it's whimsical, surreal identity. The armadillo slept during the day, coming out at night, and it always had its nose in the grass.

Spencer Perskin of Shiva's Head Band was inspired to name his label Armadillo Records and hired Franklin to draw the logo, as well as the cover of Shiva's 1969 debut LP on Capitol. Was there any doubt what the new hippie music hall on Barton Springs Road would be called? (Actually, Wilson lobbied for Uncle Zeke's Rock Emporium.)

The image was what mattered for Franklin and the others of the Art Squad (including Micael Priest, Sam Yeates, Henry Gonzales, Guy Juke, Danny Garrett, Kerry Awn, Gary McIhenny, and rising star Ken Featherston). Details of time and place were often placed at the poster's bottom or edge. "The music was the castle, separated by a moat," Franklin said. "Then came the village, the marketplace. Every time I drew a poster, it was made so that the information could be cut out and the rest could stand alone as a work of art."

ABOVE: Henry Gonzales was a poster artist who held various other duties at the Armadillo. Ralph Barrera, UT Student Publications. Courtesy of the Dolph Briscoe Center for American History.

RIGHT: Micael Priest, the most prolific of the Armadillo Art Squad, passed away in 2018. Photograph by Nancy E. Goldfarb LeNoir.

The star artist of LaMarque High School, near Galveston Bay, Franklin attended the Kansas City Art Institute between his junior and senior years. His studies continued at the San Francisco Art Institute before moving to New York City in the early '60s. That's where you went to become a famous artist. But it was a chance meeting in Galveston with musician/beatniks Ed Guinn and Travis Rivers, and the promise of psychedelics, that lured Franklin to the capital city in 1965.

LSD caused a bit of trouble when, while tripping, Franklin presented his penis to a cop who asked for ID. The court ordered Franklin to undergo therapy, including electroshock treatments. He and Roky and Townes had that in common.

People have made a lot of money off the art of Franklin, from his posters to his paintings, yet not much came back to him, as he's maintained the spartan existence of an artiste. He's not mansion-trained, some art dealer remarked. JFLKNs lived at the Vulcan, the Ritz, the Armadillo, and even an old Albertson's—home is just a place to sleep when you're not making art.

One of Franklin's most valuable contributions was not visual, but with words. In 1974, he was hired to do a painting promoting Lone Star Beer, and he needed a tag. Addressing the buzz that Lone Star was going to do away with bottles and go can-only, Franklin wrote "Long Live Long Necks" on the bottom of the painting, a stroke of cultural branding printed on thousands of bumper stickers, and solidifying Lone Star as *the* beer of the cosmic cowboy lifestyle. The next year Lone Star signed on to sponsor a new live music TV show called *Austin City Limits*.

Artist Ken Featherston was murdered in the Armadillo parking lot in November 1975. Courtesy of AusPop archives.

Tragedy in Eden: Murder of Ken Featherston

Ken Featherston was just twenty-three on November 10, 1975, when he was shot to death in the Armadillo parking lot by a drunk customer who had earlier been prevented from leaving with a bottle of booze he'd brought in with him. Just three months earlier, Featherston landed his first major label album cover design—Marshall Tucker Band's platinum-selling *Searching for a Rainbow*. That cover was based on a poster Featherston made for the Tucker Band's Armadillo show in June '74.

As a team player and former UT football recruit from Corpus Christi, Featherston worked as a bouncer at the venue because the muscular half-Filipino was an imposing figure. But a sweeter, more gentle soul never walked through that door. The murder was not only senseless, but cruel. There was sobbing at the Dillo for days.

Who killed Ken? The shooter had vowed to come back and do what he did, but nobody had seen him before. Wait a second, Dillo security chief Dub Rose thought. About a year earlier he had a scuffle with a man who fit the killer's description and turned him in to police. Earlier that night, house photographer Burton Wilson had taken a picture of Rose in his new cowboy hat, which he remembered removing before the physical encounter. If the date of that photo could be found, there would be a mug shot from that night. Wilson's organization was so precise, he easily found the dated contact sheet, and the twenty-two-year-old killer John Randolph Bingham, who lived on W. 33rd St., "Hippie Row," with his mother, was identified through his police mug shot. Bingham escaped out the back door and hopped on his bicycle when the cops came banging on the front door.

Both incidents with Bingham at the Armadillo were on nights the Pointer Sisters performed. Featherston did the poster for the first show on November 10, 1974, and was gunned down exactly a year later.

While Bingham was on the lam, Jim Franklin visited mother Grace Bingham, a Dillo semiregular nicknamed "Duchess," who told him more than she told police. Her son had close relatives in Waco, she said, writing down a phone number. Franklin called it and told the person who answered that Duchess was worried about her son. "Tell her that her baby boy is OK," said the man, and that was when Franklin knew he had the killer on the line. He gave the number to Waco police, who arrested Bingham three days after the murder. Grace Bingham testified at the May '76 trial that her son was having serious mental problems and begged for psychiatric help, but her calls were met with indifference. "Something was going to explode, was the feeling I had."

It's believed that Bingham was shooting at Henry Gonzales, the artist-bouncer he'd had the run-in with earlier. Also a Corpus native, Gonzales was walking with his best friend Featherston when the fatal shot rang out.

Declared unfit for trial due to his mental state, plus "amphetamine intoxication," Bingham was sent to Rusk State Hospital for the criminally insane. But what was really insane was that the man who pierced the armory of trust and innocence on Barton Springs Road was back on the streets of Austin just sixteen months later! Aside from a 1994 conviction for indecency with a child, which sent him to prison for a two-year term, Bingham lived in Austin until 1999, when he died at age forty-six. He lived twice as long as the kind, brilliant, beautiful man he murdered.

Does Ernest Tubb even know those other two guys?
Photograph by Rick Henson.

XI.

"The Great Progressive Country Scare": The Scene That Defined Austin and Defied Nashville

Murph, Jacky Jack, and the Road to *Terlingua*

Michael Murphey gave it a name with his 1973 album *Cosmic Cowboy Souvenir* (A&M), but Jerry Jeff Walker gave it a sound and an attitude—frisky and organic—later that year with *¡Viva Terlingua!* (MCA). Both albums were recorded with the same band—Bob Livingston on bass, Gary P. Nunn on keyboards, Craig Hillis on guitar, Mike McGeary on drums, and Herb Steiner on pedal steel.

The Austin Interchangeable Dance Band, as Steve Fromholz dubbed them, also backed Walker and Murphey when they played the Armadillo on a co-bill in August 1972, ten days before Willie Nelson legendarily officiated the wedding of hippies and rednecks. Murphey teamed with Willie a month later on the semidisastrous Armadillo Country Music Review, a six-city Texas tour which greatly overestimated the number of cowboy freaks in Abilene, Wichita Falls, Arlington, Lubbock, and Bryan.

Oneonta, NY, native Walker and Murphey, from Oak Cliff, had been mutual admirers since playing Dallas folk club the Rubiyat in the '60s. But two major label acts can share a band like they can a spouse, so sides were chosen, with Hillis and Steiner hitching a ride in "Geronimo's Cadillac," while the others became Jerry Jeff's Lost Gonzo Band. John Inmon, who had been in Austin rock band Genessee with Nunn, replaced Hillis on guitar, and McGeary's friend from California, Kelly Dunn, came sliding in with his B3 organ to make the Gonzos Austin's version of The Band.

Murphey, who lived in Austin only two years, had accomplished producer Bob Johnston (Bob Dylan, Johnny Cash, Simon & Garfunkel) in his corner. Hillsboro, TX, native Johnston also managed the singer, who would add his middle name to the marquee to distinguish himself from the actor Michael Murphy (*Manhattan, An Unmarried Woman*).

It hurt Murphey most to lose from his band the versatile Nunn, also a bass player, who he took with him to London for a month in early '73 while the others toured with Jerry Jeff. The duo did some gigs to publicize Murphey signing a European deal with EMI, plus the singer and then-wife Diana, a Brit, took their two-year-old son Ryan all around the UK to visit relatives. Nunn was left alone in cold, rainy London for much of the month.

That ended up being why Gary P. threw in with Walker. Not because he'd felt abandoned, but because he wrote "London Homesick Blues" in his loneliness, penning a classic "missing Texas" song (and the theme for *Austin City Limits* for twenty-eight years.) Nunn debuted the number at the August *'73 Terlingua* concert in Luckenbach and, hearing all those people singing "I wanna go home with the Armadillo" so loudly the first time they

Rare photo of the *Viva Terlingua* sessions.
Courtesy of Bob Livingston and Wittliff Collections.

heard it, made Gary P. realize he was in the right band. "That was Gary P. Nunn!" Livingston shouted at the end of the song, and Walker let it stay on the record. "All my friends are making this album for me," Walker said in one hot mic moment.

Jerry Jeff, who passed away in October 2020 at age seventy-eight, was a frequent flier by the seat of his pants.

He hated recording studios, found their precision soul-zapping. "When anyone mentioned 'studio,' I bought another round and looked for a hole to disappear into," Walker told Townsend Miller of the *Statesman* in 1973. He had no interest in becoming a bigger name if it meant changing. "Someone said they round you off so smooth nobody can pick you up," he told an interviewer.

His first album as an Austin resident—the self-titled one with Guy Clark's "L.A. Freeway"—was recorded in 1972 in the former Rapp Cleaners at 310 W. Sixth St. The General Audio Services studio of Steve Shields and Jay Aaron Podolnick was in the process of expanding into the cleaners' space next door with gear they'd just bought from Wally Heider in LA. Once the console had been installed, the renamed Odyssey Sound would be the first sixteen-track studio in Austin. "Jerry Jeff didn't want to wait," recalled Podolnick. "He said he'd rather record without any interference," so the mics fed straight into the tape machine. This was unheard of in 1972, but raw and unfiltered suited Jerry Jeff just fine. The title on the masters sent to New York said *Live from Rapp Cleaners*, but MCA changed it to *Jerry Jeff Walker* and had the album mixed at Electric Ladyland. One for them, one for you. It was ol' Scamp Walker's turn next.

Jerry Jeff's close friend Hondo Crouch, a rancher/humorist twenty-six years his senior, bought an old German/Comanche trading post outside Fredericksburg for $30,000 in 1971, also the year Jerry Jeff finally settled in Austin from Key West. He wanted to record there at the Luckenbach dancehall the first time he visited.

Virtuoso storyteller Crouch became a father figure to J. J., who felt free to create magic from that good, thin air in the wooden hamlet "where everybody is somebody." Established in 1849, Luckenbach offered a connection to the history and culture of Texas that would stamp the project with authenticity. In return, Walker and his band put Luckenbach on the map in a big way.

In August 1973, the New Jersey-based Dale Ashby and Father mobile recording unit set up outside the dancehall and taped Walker and the band for a week. Walker brought only two finished songs, his "Little Bird" and Guy Clark's "Desperados Waiting for a Train," to the sessions, with the rest of the album coming together on the fly. That MCA president Mike Maitland was uneasy about financing such a "let's see what happens" project was addressed in opening track "Gettin' By," when Walker sang, "Ah, Mike, don't you worry, something's bound to come out."

ABOVE: Jerry Jeff Walker at the Austin Opera House, circa 1980. Photograph by Ken Hogue. Courtesy of the AusPop archives.

ABOVE: Cover of *Viva Terlingua* LP, 1973. That's the hand of Hondo Crouch. Courtesy of MCA Records.

LEFT: Passport photos, 1973. *Top:* Murphey, Hillis, Livingston. *Bottom:* Nunn, McGeary. Courtesy of Craig Hillis.

The entirety of *¡Viva Terlingua!* was recorded live, with bales of sound-baffling hay the only audience the first five days. Saturday night called for the energy of a crowd, and the place packed out at one dollar a ticket. Audience interaction was one of the things that set the cosmic cowboys apart from the Nashville mainstream, but the crowd was over the top at the *VT* live taping.

Townsend Miller was there and wrote "seldom have I seen a crowd more boisterously enthusiastic," but he wondered if producer Michael Brovsky could get any useable tape from the pandemonium. Oh, he got tape. That was also the night Ray Wylie Hubbard's "Up Against the Wall, Redneck Mother" became an immortal singalong.

¡Viva Terlingua! is a black box recording of what was going down in Austin the year "outlaw country" became a national infatuation. "*Terlingua* just captured what seemed like the crazy Texas '70s in a way that was beyond real," says singer-songwriter Bruce Robison, who was seven when the album came out. "It was more like a John Ford western—better than the truth."

Inserting six minutes of poignancy to the Hill Country romp was "Wheel," which considers the unpredictability of life and the inevitability of death through a tragic memory. Fifteen-year-old Ron Crosby—Jerry Jeff's real name—witnessed the death of his beloved grandfather, when a tractor he was driving on his farm in upstate New York flipped over on him. "The rollin' wheels, rollin' on/ Takin' back all that they gave/ Takin' us all on our way," Walker sings wearily.

¡Viva Terlingua! ends in unbridled jubilation, with the band and three hundred backup singers nailing "London Homesick Blues" on the first take. But Brovsky came out of the control room with bad news—the tape ran out halfway through the song, and so they'd have to redo it.

"I've gotta put myself back in that place again," said Nunn of the headspace that guided his impromptu lead vocal to delirium. But the second take was even wilder. Those present could hardly wait until November when the album came out to put them back in that place.

Why was it not called *Viva Luckenbach*? Too obvious. Photographer Jim McGuire took a picture of Hondo pointing to the humble flier that brought the crowd, and Jerry Jeff declared, "That's the cover!" Stuck on the wall next to the flyer was the bumper sticker from a spiritual sister ghost town four hundred and twenty miles away that said *¡Viva Terlingua!*

Recorded as if the music industry didn't exist, it's an album that makes you feel like you were there even if you weren't, and you can't get that in a studio recording.

Before and after "Bojangles"

Jerry Jeff first drifted into Austin around 1964 when he played West Campus coffeehouse the id. The people, sitting on a rug, "were telling me with their eyes that I was connecting with them," he wrote in his *Gypsy Songman* memoir. Austin listens. Jerry Jeff took note.

Walker would debut his most famous song at the next Bill Simonson venue, the 11th Door, in late '66. Hitching a ride with an opening act from Kansas City, Jerry Jeff crashed at Allen Damron's apartment near the club. There, one night, "Mr. Bojangles" came tumbling out, "just one straight shot down the length of that yellow pad," Walker wrote. "On a night when the rest of the country was listening to the Beatles, I was writing a six-eight waltz about an old man and hope." Damron was the first to record "Bojangles," live to reel-to-reel, on the opening night of the Chequered Flag in September '67.

Mr. Bojangles was the title of Walker's 1968 album on Atco, but the big hit on the single was by Nitty Gritty Dirt Band in 1970. Even though the song was a Sammy Davis Jr. showstopper for years, it was charged with "dance for us, boy" racism. It wasn't about Bill "Bojangles" Robinson, however, but an itinerant white street-dancer in New Orleans, arrested, as Walker had been, for public intoxication.

Jerry Jeff's alcohol consumption was mythical. His friend, writer Bud Shrake, compared a Walker concert circa 1975 to a NASCAR race, "so full of thrills and suspense" and the possibility that he "might tumble off the stage and hurt himself." Whiskey made him fearless, which can also sometimes be a good thing.

After the Chequered Flag reached its finish line in '71, Walker found his new home club at the same location in Castle Creek. "One night Jerry Jeff asked me if a friend of his from Florida could play for five or ten minutes and it turned out to be Jimmy Buffett," co-owner Tim O'Connor recalled. "He came back and played many times and just loved the place." Attendance was so sparse in the beginning Buffett once took the audience, all eight of them, to dinner at the Capitol Oyster Bar between sets. After he got too big to play clubs, Buffett mentioned Castle Creek from the stage whenever he came to Austin.

After the dawn of the Parrotheads it was easy to dismiss Jerry Jeff as a Texas version of Buffett, but it was actually the other way around. Walker introduced Alabama native Buffett to the Florida Keys, and showed by example how to create an escapist lifestyle around your music.

Lung's Cocina del Sur restaurant on Anderson Lane had an even bigger impact on Buffett's career, introduc-

Greezy Wheels first made a splash with new fiddler Mary Egan at Hungry Horse on San Jacinto, 1971. Photograph by Burton Wilson.

ing him to a frozen drink of tequila, triple sec, and lime juice called the margarita in 1976. Before Jimmy could afford hotels, let alone build them, interior designer Victoria Reed put up him and some of his Coral Reefer band members at the six-bedroom house in Northwest Austin she shared with two other women. After dinner at Lung's one night, Reed watched Buffett sitting on the deck of her house, strumming a guitar, and messing around with some now-familiar words about flip-flops, pop-tops and a lost shaker of salt. He finished the song back home in Florida.

"Margaritaville" joined "Mr. Bojangles" as classics written in Austin while crashing at somebody's place.

"The mid-'70s in Austin were the busiest, the craziest, the most vivid and intense and productive period of my life," Walker wrote in *Gypsy Songman*. He cut nine albums from '72–'78, but he also cut up a lot of white powder and looked up at whiskey bottles upside down. "Jacky Jack" was not only burning candles at both ends, he wrote, he was finding new ends to light.

Tired of their Oak Hill house being party central for druggies and hangers-on, wife/manager Susan left him for a few months.

"Don't let your music kill you," someone had told Jerry Jeff years earlier and he brushed it off. But in the late '70s, he took that advice to heart. The 1979 LP *Too Old to Change* was ironically titled, as JJW gave up drugs, whiskey, cigarettes, and red meat the day he walked out of the studio and into an obsessively healthy lifestyle. In 1999, Shrake marveled that ol' Scamp Walker was in his prime when everyone thought he'd be in his grave.

"We're not in the music business," Jerry Jeff Walker once said when asked what attracted him to Austin. "We're in the business of having a life."

Greezy Wheels Keep On Rollin'

Before Michael Murphey and Jerry Jeff Walker moved to town, there was Greezy Wheels, Austin's first "progressive country" band.

Cleve Hattersley started a country rock band in the fall of 1970 because his more profitable line of work had been taken away by Harvey Gann of APD's vice and narcotics division. Busted with a suitcase full of marijuana at Mueller Airport, Cleve had to support his wife and newborn baby while out on appeal. Plus, the charismatic front man thought, well, maybe if he made his name with music during the coming period of legal limbo, the system might go easier on him.

By the time he took that last train to Huntsville in February '73, Cleve's Greezy Wheels were the biggest Austin band, taking in as much as $2,000 a night when they packed the Armadillo. For local acts, only Balcones Fault, that rare comedic jazz band, and straight-rockin' Too Smooth could occasionally make that kind of money. Major labels were circling, but none wanted to commit until Hattersley's situation was resolved.

A twenty-two-year-old Cleve was sentenced to seven years in prison, but a lack of probable cause—Gann lied and said the suitcase came open—was the main point of appeal that kept Greezy Wheels going for twenty-eight months.

By the time Cleve had to face the music—a minimum of two and a half years before the possibility of parole—he'd become an upstanding leader of a music scene that brought pride to Texas. (He admits to one last, forty-pound marijuana run.) After a mountain of letters to the parole board and an intercession from Texas State Rep. Ronnie Earle, Hattersley served eleven months.

Greezy Wheels started as a four-piece band about two months after the bust, with Hattersley and Pat Pankratz on guitar/vocals, Mike Pugh on bass, and drummer Tony Laier. With "Skiffle Group" added to their name in the wake of Mungo Jerry, they quickly learned fifteen songs and debuted at the One Knite.

Wednesday nights, everyone would go to an old barbecue shack in East Austin called Bonnie's Place, where Whistler cultivated quite a scene in 1970. The modern jug band would set out two cases of beer with a pay-what-you-can sign, while the broke and hungry would sometimes find a chopped beef sandwich in their hands, and pay for someone else's the next week. Miss Bonnie, an old woman with a walker, would kick off the second-set jam with "Will the Circle Be Unbroken." There was nothing like Bonnie's Place, where Hattersley, a native of the Finger Lakes area of New York, learned about fusing country/gospel/bluegrass/rock.

One night, Hattersley went to see Kenneth Threadgill at Bevo's Westside Tap Room and was mesmerized by a sit-in fiddler named Mary Egan. He asked her if she wanted to join his band and she said, "That's what I came to Austin for." She had moved here with third husband John Egan from Las Cruces, where her father conducted the New Horizons Symphony Orchestra at New Mexico State.

Classically trained Egan could play bluegrass fiddle like her daddy worked in a coal mine. "I give her credit for getting the ball rolling in this town," Gary P. Nunn told the *Statesman*, when asked about the roots of long-haired country in Austin. "She'd play that 'Orange Blossom Special' at the Hungry Horse on San Jacinto and the hippies would get off so bad. Until that time, most of the country music was confined to clubs surrounding the city, but never in the city itself." The rootsedelic playing of "Sweet Mary," as Cleve dubbed his future and current wife, reshaped country standards, causing fans to do a dance James White of the Broken Spoke called "the Hippie Hop."

Greezy Wheel's first big gig was opening for the Flying Burrito Brothers at the Dillo in June 1971. The word spread about a sensational hippie chick fiddler in Austin, who kicked when she played a hoedown.

"Everybody tried to steal Mary," laughed Hattersley. "Doug Kershaw wanted to turn her into the Queen of Cajun. Jerry Jeff Walker used her on his first two albums in Austin ('72's *Jerry Jeff Walker* and '73's *¡Viva Terlingua!*), but when I prevented her from playing on his third album, he tried to make my life a living hell." Walker often showed up at Greezy gigs, loud and buzzed to heckle Hattersley.

Outlaw Country's Walter Winchell

As progressive country became the rage in Austin, Townsend Miller was always quick to credit Greezy Wheels as the instigators. They opened the landmark Willie Nelson concert August '72 at the Armadillo to guarantee a crowd.

A stockbroker by day, Townsend wrote his influential *Statesman* column from 1972–83. He'd come home from Merrill Lynch, take a three-hour nap, and then hit the clubs, dapper and refreshed, at least five nights a week. In one pocket was that night's itinerary on an index card. In another was a flask of vodka, with a touch of creme de menthe for his breath. He'd hit as many as five clubs nightly, in "the capital of cosmic strum and twang."

Everybody loved the everywhere man, who wrote his column for the *Statesman* pro bono. "I think what he enjoyed most was seeing the renewed interest of youth in country music and how it brought young and old together," son Kent Miller told the *Statesman* in his father's April '89 obituary. He was sixty-nine and lived as full a life as imaginable.

Born in Gainesville, TX, in 1919, Miller grew up with two great passions—country music and fishing. As a

Townsend Miller and Willie Nelson before a fun run.
Photograph by Scott Newton.

Kenneth Threadgill and Townsend Miller.
Photograph by Rick Henson.

boy he heard the Light Crust Doughboys of Bob Wills and Milton Brown daily on WBAP, but seeing Jimmie Rodgers play a tent show in Gainesville in 1930 was a life-changing experience. That's something he had in common with Kenneth Threadgill, the other older gentleman of the scene. Well, that and sweetened liquor—Threadgill favored peppermint Schnapp's.

Miller rode a journalism degree from North Texas State to Austin in 1952 as editor of *Texas Fish & Game*. As an angler he made the pages of *Sports Illustrated* in 1954 by reeling in the biggest longnose garfish up to that time. Miller had become obsessed with that long slender fish with the distinctive snout since one sprung out of a lake to bite him in the stomach when he was twelve.

As an older man, his attention shifted to country music. Where he once defended the gar from its "trash fish" reputation, he used his music column to hoist the hippies who were resuscitating country and bluegrass.

"Townsend's support meant everything to us," said Cleve Hattersley, who watched the crowds swell after Miller raved. TM had other pets—Plum Nelly, Cooder Browne, and, especially Dottsy Brodt, the former Meadow Muffin singer from Seguin who had a couple moderate hits on RCA. Townsend never wrote a bad word about anyone, though he would sometimes convert criticism to backstage advice.

Cleveless

Nineteen-seventy-three was a big year for the Austin music scene. The Armadillo was in its prime, Soap Creek opened, Bobbie Nelson joined brother Willie's band, which sponsored its first Fourth of July Picnic, and Roky Erickson came home from Rusk. But it was not a good year for Cleve Hattersley, the only white player on the Huntsville prison basketball team. While Sweet Mary was being called to the stage by Frank Zappa to play "Orange Blossom Special" with Jean-Luc Ponty, Cleve was learning the hard way that they don't call fouls in the big house.

Lissa Hattersley emerged that year as the band's main songwriter, and new guitar player Tony Airoldi took the Wheel to new places with his extended solo at the end of Willie Nelson's "I Never Cared for You." On his release in January 1974, Cleve agreed that Airoldi should stay. That year a widowed Mary Egan, whose husband died in a motorcycle accident, became the newest "Mad Hattersley."

An original by Pat Pankratz (Dave Alvin drummer Lisa's uncle) called "Country Music and Friends" became a theme song and was used on commercials for Lone Star Beer, though they edited the singalong chorus: "Here's to cocaine, country music, and good ol' Lone Star Beer." Greezy Wheels would often follow that with a gospel song, like Lissa's "Standing in the Light," the band's "test" single on major label London Records in 1974.

Recording two albums for London meant Greezy had to hit the road constantly, and that's where they lost Airoldi, a vegetarian focused on a healthy lifestyle. "A lot of times we had to eat at McDonald's," said Cleve, and they didn't have salads back then. The band picked up a pretty good drummer in Chris Layton from Corpus late in their run. "When he left us to play with Stevie, who was sleeping on couches, we thought he was crazy," Hattersley said.

It was the same old story of a great live band unable to capture the magic on record. Greezy Wheels' albums didn't translate, and they broke up in 1978. Cleve and Sweet Mary moved to New York, where he managed the Lone Star Cafe and she played with Kinky Friedman and the Texas Jewboys, another Armadillo refugee, who had the distinction of being the only act whose *Austin City Limits* taping never aired due to off-color material. There were occasional Greezy reunion shows after the couple returned to Austin in 1985, but the "progressive construction" of Austin drove them to cash out and move to Mary's hometown of Las Cruces, New Mexico, in 2021.

Townsend Miller kept going out, even after he stopped writing his column. All the country acts, big and small, got a kick out of seeing him at their shows and afforded him the same access. He stopped by Raven's Garage (later Emo's) on the last night of his life, complaining to a loading-out Gary P. Nunn of the recurring hiccups he'd been having for six months. In the early hours of April 1, 1989, Miller was found on the ground outside his car, which was in flames. He had parked on dry grass near Fiesta Gardens, and it's believed that his catalytic converter started a fire. He died from smoke inhalation, survived by wife Rita and four kids.

History holds gratitude for Townsend Miller and Armadillo house photographer Burton Wilson, the old guys who got it all down when the youngsters were getting down.

"I was a huge fan of the early years of New Orleans jazz, but there was almost no visual documentation of that era," Wilson told me in 2007. "I knew that if I ever discovered a magical music scene, it would be my calling to document it. The hippies were doing something that had never been done before and I was smart enough to realize that it was something special."

Joe Gracey and daughter Jolie watch wife/mother Kimmie Rhodes's soundcheck at Liberty Lunch. Photograph by Bill Leissner.

Joe Gracey, KOKE-FM, and the Willie Effect

Joe Gracey had been invited to play golf with Willie Nelson and Ray Benson circa 1980. They ran into Coach Darrell Royal, and as they were chatting, Willie said by introduction, "Do you know Joe Gracey?" Of course he knew Ol' Blues Eyes, Coach said, using Gracey's radio nickname. "I just didn't recognize him without his voice."

Gracey made money with his deep, rich baritone since he was a sixteen-year-old weekend DJ on KXOL in his native Fort Worth. He was also a singer, and an inventor of radio characters. But at age twenty-seven he was stricken with "permanent laryngitis," as he called it. Cancer of the tongue and larynx was a cruel twist to a rising radio career that didn't even take a break during college.

Gracey was an announcer on all-hits KNOW while attending UT. After graduation, he worked at soft rock station KRMH as a DJ and program director. He started throwing in some Willie Nelson, who'd just performed at the Armadillo, so why not also mix it up on the radio? The phones lit up, but not in a good way. "What is this shit?" was the consensus. Neil Young fans didn't like Willie Nelson back then. But Gracey thought they should.

"Texas has always been a musical melting pot, and Austin is its cultural center of energy, so if anything big was going to happen, it had to be here," Gracey told Ed Ward in 1978, before he lost his voice completely.

Willie Nelson, Kris Kristofferson, and Rita Coolidge, at the KOKE-FM studios before the first Willie Picnic. Austin 1973. Courtesy of AusPop archives.

When a twenty-two-year-old Gracey was fired in a regime change at KRMH in the summer of '73, he went across the street to KOKE-FM which was in the process of switching from country-Western to "progressive country." Since that sounded a little stuffy, station manager Ken Moyer and program director Rusty Bell tagged the format "Super Roper." Gracey was initially hired for the 10 a.m. to 2 p.m. slot—hippie drive time. He played almost as many Austin musicians—counting former Adamson High School (Oak Cliff) classmates B. W. Stevenson, Ray Wylie Hubbard, and Michael Murphey as locals—as he did national acts.

Austin didn't invent longhaired country—Gram Parsons and the Byrds put out *Sweetheart of the Rodeo* in 1968. But it was the headquarters for a simple reason: Willie moved here in the summer of '72. He was the Bob Marley, the galvanizer, the human hub, of the scene.

Even as a rock fan growing up in Fort Worth and playing bass in the Loose Ends with T Bone Burnett and Stephen Bruton, Gracey was a big fan of Willie Nelson. "Willie struck me as someone special even when I was ambivalent about country music in general," Gracey wrote in his *Radio Dreams* memoir. "He was just somehow different. Once I realized he wrote those great classic songs ("Crazy," "Hello Walls," "Night Life," etc.), and saw him a couple times at Panther Hall, I was a confirmed Willie Nelson fan forever."

Even after Willie and Waylon and the boys became a national sensation circa 1976, KOKE-FM never got more than an eight share in the Arbitrons. Bohos don't keep listening journals. But if ratings were based on lifestyle influence, from food to fashion to beer to record collections, Super Roper 95.5 would've been #1 in the market. "Country music is essentially indigenous to Texas," Gracey said in '78, "and people here were rediscovering their roots." Longhairs loved to wear those crushed straw Western hats and cowboy boots with cutoffs. They were proud that Lefty Frizzell, George Jones, and Ernest Tubb were from Texas.

Many in the sixties Jade cover band scene ended up in progressive country bands, but nobody made the transition better than Rusty Wier, whose "Don't It Make You Wanna Dance" was 1975's party song of the summer.

After the Lavender Hill Express derailed, Rusty Wier quit playing drums and started woodshedding on guitar. "He locked himself in a room and practiced and practiced," said John Inmon, who played with Wier in the folk-rock trio of Rusty, Layton, and John. "He was a natural entertainer, so he could get his music across, but it took him awhile to get good." Rusty established himself in the 1970s as an outlaw folk singer with rock 'n' roll eyes and a trademark black riverboat gambler hat.

"There's this myth about the hippies and the rednecks meeting at the Armadillo and passing joints and Lone Stars to each other," said Inmon. "But the rednecks and hippies were the same people. That was Rusty Wier. He was a redneck son of Central Texas, but he was also a hippie."

Ray Benson's Asleep at the Wheel moved to Austin from Oakland in January 1974, in part, because no one in the audience here yelled out requests for Creedence; they wanted to dance to traditional Western swing. With a revolving door of topflight musicians (including pianist Floyd Domino, longtime Dylan bassist Tony Garnier, and Van Morrison's lap steel choice Cindy Cashdollar), the Wheel played the same songs for the hardcore two-steppers at the Skyline and Big G's in Round Rock as they did at the Armadillo and Cherry Street Inn (upstairs from what is now the Clay Pit restaurant).

There was no denying that something special was happening in Austin. "What makes us alike is that we're different," Willie said about himself, Murphey, Jerry Jeff, and the rest. "All of us are being what we were meant to be."

For the first time there was some legitimate music business in town, with manager Michael Brovsky following Jerry Jeff Walker down from New York, and Larry Watkins's Moon Hill providing full service (management, booking, publishing) to Murphey, B. W. Stevenson, Steve Fromholz, Greezy Wheels, and more.

A country voice for the counterculture, Gracey did all the radio ads for the Armadillo, wrote the rock music column for the *Statesman*, and was also the talent coordinator the first full year of *Austin City Limits* in 1976. Gracey was proud to reunite Bob Wills's living Texas Playboys and to book that great Ry Cooder and Flaco Jimenez show, but some of the other *ACL* acts were not favorites.

Gracey (no one called him Joe) clashed with producer Paul Bosner and was not brought back for the second season. "He would go out and get all pumped up over an act I thought was utterly banal and I'd tell (Bosner) that, so he disliked me more and more as the year went on," Gracey recalled in *Radio Dreams*. The opinionated Gracey went against the fawn patrol in 1974 when he reviewed Bruce Springsteen at the Armadillo. "I can't help but think he's highly derivative, highly repetitive, and I would like his music better if it wasn't for the pretension," Gracey wrote. "Springsteen rises up out of the '60s like the ghost of every high school band on earth and slams those teenage licks down like they're new and interesting."

KOKE-FM was born in 1967 when country station KOKE-AM bought KAZZ from restauranteur Monroe Lopez. After a block programming rotation of country and Spanish music for a couple years, KOKE-FM went straight country in the early '70s. It didn't officially identify as "progressive country" until August 1973, when the station broadcast live from Castle Creek for three weeks. In 1974, *Billboard* named KOKE-FM its Trendsetter of the Year.

The peak of "the great progressive country scare" (Fromholz) was 1976, with *Wanted: The Outlaws* giving the movement a marketing angle and selling a million copies in two weeks. Willie and Waylon, whose 1969 cowrite "Good Hearted Woman" was the smash of this "greatest misses" package, shared the album with Jessi Colter (Mrs. Jennings) and Tompall Glaser. Billy Joe Shaver was the intended fourth Outlaw, but his wife Brenda shot that down because she didn't get how that could be a good image.

Willie's old Nashville label RCA, which put out *Wanted*, finally made some money off their red-headed sinkhole, recycling "Yesterday's Wine" and "Me and Paul" from 1971. But when the outlaw movement became a trend it was given an expiration date, to be replaced by another. The urban cowboys of the late '70s even got their own hit movie.

Doug Sahm compared 1976 in Austin to '69 in San Francisco, the beginning of the end. "It was still there, but it showed signs of going down," he told the *Statesman* in 1979.

"We've just gotten over the stage when we were excited by the mere fact that we had something here. That was fun, like being a teenager with your own car. But you can't keep up that crazed pace forever," Gracey summed up the coming end. "The only thing that's changed, is the ratio of hard work to hot air." After the pioneers come the grifters.

Just a year after being promoted to program director, Gracey quit KOKE in June 1977 when the station went back to Blandrell country. A couple months later he was diagnosed with cancer, and eventually his tongue and vocal cords were removed. Unable to speak, he communicated with a Magic Slate children's toy, and rudimentary sign language.

But life gave him another thirty-four years, and Gracey made the most of them, falling in love and marrying singer-songwriter Kimmie Rhodes. She became his musical voice, while he wrote songs and played guitar in her backing band, the Jackalope Brothers.

Radio Dreams details the painful and difficult battle with cancer that took Gracey's life in 2011 at age sixty-one. Written with Rhodes as a "duet memoir" of alternating chapters, the 2017 book also chronicles a life of purpose and music.

Rhodes met Gracey in 1980 when T. J. McFarland took her to the Electric Graceyland studio in the basement of the KOKE building to record some demos. They courted through work and married in 1984.

Gracey was determined to find his way back on the radio through records he produced. Among his credits were albums by Billy Joe Shaver, Calvin Russell, the Skunks, and Kimmie's *West Texas Heaven*. Gracey was also among the first to record Stevie Ray Vaughan, in Austin and at his mentor Cowboy Jack Clement's home studio in Nashville. After Stevie got famous he didn't want those tapes floating around so he asked for them back—and Gracey complied, though he kicked himself later for not making a copy.

Gracey was honored with a "Thanks, Joe Gracey" benefit at the Armadillo on Thanksgiving 1978. Over $10,000 was raised towards medical expenses, but even greater was the spiritual lift in seeing seventeen hundred people, the largest attendance ever at the Dillo, come out in support.

Townsend Miller had praised Armadillo audiences, who "can spot a musical phony from here to New York, but they're also trigger-quick in recognizing—and appreciating—talent no matter what the brand." Joe Gracey, Austin's ear, can take some of the credit for that.

Gracey's career highlights, he wrote, were engineering three albums featuring Willie Nelson, his hero from high school. In 1996, Gracey worked the console on *Spirit*, Willie's spare masterpiece that changed the way he made music live. Seven years later, Gracey did the knobs for a pair of Willie duet albums, *Run That by Me One More Time*, with Ray Price, and *Picture in a Frame*, with Kimmie Rhodes. That last one was especially gratifying.

A radio announcer lost his voice forever, but found brilliant new ways to be heard. As tagged in the poster for his '78 benefit, Gracey played a huge role in "the music that made Austin famous."

OPPOSITE: Rusty Wier became a country rocker after he switched from drums to guitar. Photo shot upstairs at the original Alliance Wagonyard. Photograph by Nancy E. Goldfarb LeNoir.

The belly of the One Knite.
Courtesy of Roger Collins.

XII.

Clubland Paradise: Seven Great '70's Venues That Weren't the Dillo

One Knite, 1968–76

Her friends in Manhattan told her to be careful, the club was a hellhole and the clientele was pretty rough. Even the cab driver gave her a warning on the way to CBGB, the New York City club that spawned punk rock. When Rebecca Kohout looked around the graffiti-covered club full of black leather and ripped shirts that night in 1977, she had to laugh. "I thought, man this place isn't scary at all. I hung out at the One Knite!"

CBGB was the Copa compared with Austin's most notorious dive, located at 801 Red River St. where a much-expanded Stubb's currently sits.

From 1970, when a trio of pals bought the business for just under $2,000, until it closed on July 4, 1976, the One Knite was known for its illegal after-hours parties that often raged until dawn.

But the most lasting legacy of the counterculture speakeasy is the musicians who started out there and went on to bigger things. Long before Clifford Antone opened his first namesake blues club on Sixth Street in 1975, the One Knite hosted the likes of Stevie Ray Vaughan, Jimmie Dale Gilmore, Marcia Ball, Angela Strehli, Paul Ray and the Cobras, Joe Ely and many, many more. They all played for tips. "The first time I ever saw an all-white blues band was the Storm at the One Knite," said W. C. Clark, who would start Southern Feeling with Strehli, who would become his girlfriend.

Jimmie Vaughan and Doyle Bramhall's band Storm played every Monday night for five years. They called it "Stormy Monday," but Tuesday was just as nuts. The three-day weekend of the '70s was Sunday at Split Rail to see Freda, Monday at the Knite for Storm, and Tuesday at Soap Creek for the Cobras. Every week without fail.

Cleve Hattersley of Greezy Wheels remembers the crowd being right on top of the stage. "They were in your face, and pretty rowdy sometimes, but they would be cheering you on. It was a great feeling."

It was a time when there was no "Ray" in the middle of "Stevie Vaughan," who Ray Hennig drove to the One Knite almost every night after his Heart of Texas Music store closed up for the evening. "He'd play every guitar in the shop all day long, then go to the One Knite to jam," said Hennig.

"No club west of I-35 had such a funky East Austin feel like the One Knite," said Hattersley. With a craps game often breaking out on the pool table, "anything goes" was anything but an empty cliché at the One Knite.

The antithesis of the "cosmic cowboy" scene that was about to explode, the One Knite's interior was painted as black as bassist Keith Ferguson's fingernails. And with a fleet of Harleys usually parked out front, the aroma of danger was almost as strong as the stench of spilt beer.

This outlaw dive was where Bandidos sat next to former President Lyndon Johnson's Secret Service de-tail, who sat next to big-eyed flower children, who sat next to East Side bluesmen, and law students. They all sat under such objects as lawn mowers, tricycles, bed springs, shoulder pads, and typewriters, which hung from the ceiling from the room's years as a junk store.

Although the origins of the One Knite name, inherited from the previous owners, are unclear, it fits this many years later because remembrances of the dive almost always begin with the words "One night . . ." One night the Bandidos decided to have a little fun with the band Dirty Leg. In order to be admitted back into the club after a break, each band member had to allow a gnarly, teeth-missing, biker mama to give them a big wet kiss. One night a touring British band came in during a Storm set and asked if they could jam, but when they said they weren't a blues band, the members of Pink Floyd were denied the stage and sulked off to the dark side of the bar.

While clubs had to close at midnight in the early '70s, owners Roger Collins, Roddy Howard, and Gary Oliver merely padlocked the front door from the inside and let the revelry continue. We're not talking about just sneaking a beer after closing time.

When someone pulled out a couple of machetes and a bag of marijuana, the cheers would go up for a Hot Knife Party. "The knives were heated red hot on the kitchen stove," recalled T. J. McFarland, who played drums with D. K. Little at the time. "Then a handful of pot was spread along the length of one knife. The other hot machete was laid on top of the first and the knives screamed and spewed smoke like a rocket. The room would fill up with pot smoke and people got so stoned so fast . . ."

There had to be rules amid such chaos. "After midnight, we'd unlock the door only once an hour," said Collins, who slept in a broom closet in the ladies' room. "We'd pick up all the beer and clean up all the evidence, then let out whoever wanted to go."

The men in blue often were waiting to corral the OK gang, once hauling fourteen employees and customers off to jail in a paddy wagon. It was a one-block drive. "They were trying to run us out of business," said Collins. Sometimes the cops would barge in two or three times a night, checking IDs and looking for drugs. They couldn't stand those longhaired lowlifes flaunting their radical ideas right across the street. Collins kept a log in 1973 that showed his club was raided 150 times over a three-month period.

It would be the IRS that finally put out "the dive that wouldn't die." Well behind on back taxes, the club held a benefit in late '75 starring a red-hot Willie Nelson. Tickets were $2.50 each. Even though the club was jammed more than triple the legal capacity of 150 people, proceeds were limited because nobody could get to the bar.

As one could imagine, given the ability of Hot Knife Parties to slice and dice memory cells, there are several versions of how the One Knite was transformed from a hangout for University of Texas law students to a den of divine debauchery.

The story we like to believe is that the Velvet Underground christened the One Knite in cool. The New York City band was in town to play three nights at the Vulcan Gas Company in October 1969. After the Saturday night show, UT's hip English professor Joe Kruppa (whose class Reed spoke to the previous day) steered the band to the downtown dive that would most remind them of home.

The East Village People apparently went all out to show Austin a thing about decadence, and stories circulated about drag queens, and needles in the bathroom, and rock stars falling down drunk at a bar with a coffin-shaped front door called the One Knite.

Austin's most eccentric bar was opened in March 1967 by four UT law students: Jerry Loftin, Joe Mermis, Ernie Johnson, and Byron Kirby. There was no stage and they very rarely had live music.

After hearing about the VU takeover, UT student Gary Oliver, a budding cartoonist though legally blind, started hanging out at the One Knite, eventually tending bar. When one of the law students graduated and moved on, Oliver bought his share for $600. Two other newly minted lawyers also sold their shares—to Oliver's friends, fellow UT students Roddy Howard and Roger Collins, who met through a psilocybin mushroom transaction circa 1968.

"In the beginning we had only acoustic acts, like Jimmie Gilmore, Blind George, Little & Crow, and Cody Hubach," said Oliver. The first stage was four tabletops nailed together. "Then one night in 1971, the guys in Storm came in and said, 'This is the best blues dive we've ever seen. When can we play?' We didn't have a real stage, especially for a band with drums, so they just set up on the floor. They were incredible and the place was packed." The next day, a proper stage was built.

"After Storm, even the folk acts were turning up with full bands," Oliver said. One of those was the Flatlanders, featuring Ely, Gilmore and Butch Hancock, backed by Lubbock cohorts McFarland and guitarist John X. Reed.

"Those were some of our best shows," Ely recalled. "At the One Knite it never felt like a real gig." A June 8, 1972, set recorded by Oliver without the band's notice was found four decades later and released as *Live at the One Knite* to show the laid back vibe in that scary-looking joint.

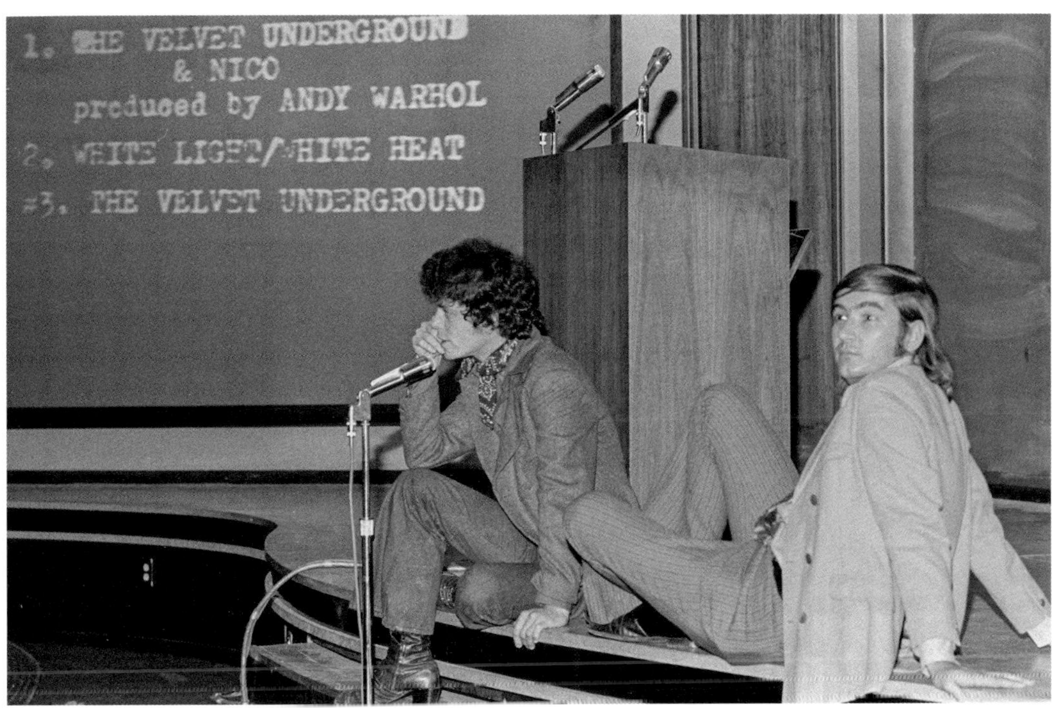

Lou Reed spoke to the class of English professor Joe Kruppa during the Velvet Underground three-night stint at the Vulcan. Courtesy of Dolph Briscoe Center for American History.

Rare stage shot from the One Knite with Denny Freeman and BooBoo Watson of the Cobras 1974. Photograph by Diana Ray.

Local blues luminaries have a garage sale in South Austin circa 1974. Do you see the Vaughan brothers? Photograph by Diana Ray.

Saxon Pub (The Original), 1971–74

The original Saxon Pub was an A-frame restaurant on the Interstate 35 frontage road near 38th Street taken over by top flight singer-songwriters. When it opened in 1971 at the former Canary Hut, the ads touted the steaks and seafood, with the after-dinner music labeled "Folk Entertainment." But it didn't take long for the Saxon to become "where the songs, attitudes, and creative interplay between songwriters and pickers went down," said Craig Hillis, who played guitar for various Saxon acts. Texas Fever was the first act to be named in the ad, to let folks know they were formerly Ray Wylie Hubbard's Three Faces West.

The Chequered Flag had closed in June '71 and Castle Creek wouldn't be open until the next year, giving the Saxon a nice window to be *the* listening room in town. It was booked by Jess Yaryan III, former bassist of Lavender Hill Express, so he knew the talent that was out there. The only competition was token, with the aptly named Other Place following a similar restaurant/folk club format from '71–'73, and booking some of the same acts, but it was in Dobie Mall.

The singer songwriter to become known as Michael Martin Murphey made his big splash in Austin with a three-night stand at the Saxon in Jan. '72. He soon moved here from California, with bassist Bob Livingston, a Lubbock native. Other regulars included Uncle Walt's Band, Bobby Bridger, Big Bill Moss, John Vandiver, Bill and Bonnie Hearne, and Billy Callery. "It wasn't the only bohemian salon in town," said Hillis, "but it was significant."

Manager Doug Burant and investors bought the club in February '74 and shortened the name to The Pub. But by the end of that year it was out of business and replaced by the short-lived Red Dog Saloon. The building, housing Hornitos Mexican restaurant, remained until 2024, when it was torn down in the I-35 expansion.

The original Saxon was where Steven Fromholz established himself solo after the breakup of Frummox. After playing guitar with the Stephen Stills Band in 1971, Fromholz came off the cocaine highway and put together the comedic Captain Duck and the Farmer's Electric Co-op Boys with Hillis on guitar, Travis Holland on bass, and drummer David Fore (Bubble Puppy).

Hillis opened the second Saxon Pub on South Lamar with Joe Ables in 1990, and found continuity by tapping Fromholz to christen the new joint, which eventually made its own legend.

Michael Murphey announced his arrival in Austin with three sellout shows at the Saxon Pub in early 1971. This photo taken later. Photograph by Nancy E. Goldfarb LeNoir. Courtesy of AusPop archives.

Castle Creek, 1972–76

The 1411 Lavaca Street address holds a lot of unforgettable memories, from the Chequered Flag to the '80s Comedy Workshop of Bill Hicks, Sam Kinison, and more. In between it was Castle Creek, a 285-capacity listening room that rocked. There was a strict "no talking" rule when an acoustic act was playing, but all hell was known to occasionally break loose, as when an up-and-coming Little Feat wrecked the club in March 1973. Six months later, Lowell George and company filled the Armadillo, which had six times the capacity.

That was the way Doug Moyes had planned it. He was a twenty-year-old piano player with some money, whose idea was to open a farm club to the big hall, but he needed a partner with club experience. That was Tim O'Connor,

Soap Creek was the Elm Grove Lodge in the 1940s.
Photograph by Sam Yeates.

Castle Creek. Photograph by
Nancy E. Goldfarb LeNoir.

Prime Cobras 1975. *L-R:* Paul Ray, Denny Freeman, Stevie Vaughan, Alex Napier, Joe Sublett, Rodney Craig. Photograph by Van Brooks. Courtesy of AusPop archives.

George, Ross, and Carlyne Majer.
Courtesy of AusPop archives.

in his mid-20s, who had been running a small venue (and pounds of pot) in Colorado. Castle Creek was named after an area near Aspen where Moyes had camped a couple years earlier. Soap Creek would not open for another year, so there was no name confusion in the beginning.

Between the Chequered Flag and Castle Creek, the location was home to short-lived rock/soul club Muther's, which had knocked down the wall between the listening room and Kennedy's sports car museum, doubling the capacity.

Opening on a shoestring with Lightnin' Hopkins, who played so often in Austin he was cheap, Moyes and O'Connor scraped together just enough money to pay a $1,500 deposit for banjo legend Earl Scruggs, then sold out all four nights. They were off! John Prine also played early in the club's run and told Steve Goodman. Or maybe it was the other way around. Word got out. Castle Creek was Austin's Troubadour, its Bottom Line. But the club struggled to pay the bills, as all the live music venues did, with all that overhead.

O'Connor opened a nonmusic venue on 19th St. near Guadalupe called Squeeze Inn, where everything, from pool to beer to the jukebox was twenty-five cents. It was a musician's hangout, where Jerry Jeff Walker recruited Gary P. Nunn, just back from London with Murphey, to play keyboards on an album he was going to record at Luckenbach.

O'Connor left Castle Creek in 1974 to work fulltime for Willie Nelson as his promoter and business partner. Moyes sold the Castle in '75 to Country Sunshine bandleader Jim Cannon, who moved it to a pair of Houston jazz fans the next year, and that didn't work at all. Singer-songwriters were the bread-and-butter.

The alley next to the club was the inspiration for the Michael Martin Murphey song "Alleys of Austin," while Guy Clark had his first of many mad dog margaritas at the Texas Chili Parlor next door, waiting for someone to come by and tell him "five minutes." Enough history was made in just a couple years, that Castle Creek has earned the "legendary" tag.

Soap Creek, 1973–85

In the '40s and '50s, when Westlake was out in the country, the bunkhouse-looking building a quarter mile up Bee Cave Road was the Elm Grove Lodge, home to Western swing bands led by Cotton Collins, Steve Lightsey, Aubrey Cox, and others. There was an infamous murder there in 1947, when the crazy Wright brothers, Blondie and Curley, beat to death Arnold Barrier, who managed the Windmill Club on far South Congress (the San Antonio Highway).

Owned in the early '70s by bassist Alex Napier, who came down from Dallas around the same time as fellow Cobras Denny Freeman and Paul Ray, the lodge became a party barn for young, white blues fanatics new to town. The Rolling Hills was the first club in Austin where seventeen-year-old Stevie Ray Vaughan played guitar—in October 1971.

The place needed a lot of work that Napier had neither time nor money for, so he put it out there that Rolling Hills' business/lease was for sale. Just so happened a young married couple heavy in the scene—she was an Armadillo "Sweathog," who cleaned up after shows for free admission, and he co-owned Oat Willie's with Doug Brown—were looking to open a club. Carlyne and George Majewski got married in 1971, became parents in '72, and gave birth to Soap Creek Saloon the next year.

Might not have moved so fast if Carlyne hadn't felt snubbed by the Dillo, which had plans to use a cabaret configuration—a club within the club—for some shows. Carlyne applied for the general manager job, but was not taken seriously, she said. So she and George decided to fill the cozier indoor venue void. There was no time for a maternity break, as the couple went to work on opening Soap Creek Saloon. Both the legal drinking and voting ages had just been lowered to eighteen, and Austin's "progressive country" scene was in its euphoric young love phase. Soap Creek provided the necessary intimacy. "If the Armadillo was the heart of the Austin music scene, Soap Creek was the soul," wrote Margaret Moser.

Born in 1947, the former Carlyne Gough grew up in College Station, where her mother was head nurse at Texas A&M Hospital, where you went for your bonfire and hazing injuries. Carlyne's twin brother Carl Merl went full Maroonatic, even playing football for the Aggies, but Carlyne bolted to our counterculture haven after only a semester at A&M. Austin had been a city of escape during her high school years, when she would buy peyote at "the Ghetto" beatnik flop.

She met George, a Tenafly, NJ, native, in her first of six years at UT. After he graduated with a business degree, ending his college deferment, Majewski was drafted in '67 and shipped off to Vietnam. Carlyne bought an Indian motorcycle from Jack O'Leary's on South Lamar, moved to San Antonio to work at O'Leary's motorcycle rental shop, and raced against men in motorbike enduro competitions. Both occupations prepared the soon-to-be couple for the obstacle course—a dirt road with potholes the size of artillery strikes—that led club goers to their "Honky Tonk in the Hills."

ABOVE: Doug Sahm and band at his house next to Soap Creek, 1975. *Left to right*: Louis Terrazas, Link Davis Jr., John X. Reed, Doug Sahm, Johnny Perez, Jimmy Stallings, Harry Hess. Photograph by Van Brooks. Courtesy of AusPop archives.

RIGHT: The second location of Soap Creek was the old Skyline. Photograph by Ken Hoge. Courtesy of AusPop archives.

Other live music clubs in town when Soap Creek opened, besides the Armadillo, included Castle Creek, Split Rail, One Knite, Black Queen, Alliance Wagonyard, Broken Spoke, South Door, Eli's Club, Saxon Pub, River City Inn, Toad Hall, Bevo's Westside Tap Room, La Cucaracha, and Mother Earth. Why would anyone drive the hell out to West Lake Hills to party?

But being isolated was one of the things that made Soap Creek special. You had to want to be there, which made the people feel safer with each other.

DWI wasn't much of a concern in the pre-Mothers Against Drunk Driving '70s, when the legal limit to drive was 0.15 blood alcohol content, almost twice what it is today. But wrapping your car around a tree was a concern, especially on Tequila Tuesdays (thirty-five cents a shot!), so Soap Creek looked like they served breakfast on Wednesday mornings because of all the cars in the parking lot from the night before.

"When Soap Creek opened, the Armadillo was king, but they only served beer over there, whereas Soap Creek served liquor, so you had a slightly more mature crowd," said Kerry Awn, who designed the club's posters and packed the joint with the satirical Uranium Savages. "Plus, that was where all the musicians hung out. The Armadillo had a lot of tourists and frat boys."

When Herbie Hancock played Municipal Auditorium, two blocks from the Armadillo, in 1974, he came five miles out to Soap Creek to jam with Doug and Augie. Or maybe he was looking for Willie Nelson, who lived a mile from Soap Creek at the time and was a club regular, though he played more dominoes than guitar. "Willie was my mentor in the music business," said fellow domin-eer Carlyne, who used "Majer" as her business surname.

Nelson's *Shotgun Willie*, whose cover unveiled his longhaired, bearded look, came out three months after Soap opened. Willie's deal with Atlantic Records gave him the creative control denied him in Nashville, and he made full use of it on the 1974 follow-up *Phases and Stages*, a concept album about a marriage breakup that many consider his masterpiece. But neither record sold, so Willie was dropped by Atlantic. All this was going on when he was hanging out at "Dope Creek."

Doug Sahm (who played guitar on *Shotgun Willie*) could empathize, as he was also two-and-through at Atlantic. His 1972 dream project *Doug Sahm and Band* (featuring Bob Dylan, Dr. John, Flaco Jimenez and others), and the *Texas Tornado* follow-up, registered lukewarm sales. After a token European tour in early '73, Sahm came back to Texas thinking nobody got him. But then he packed Soap Creek on successive nights with people who *really* got him. He had found his "Groover's Paradise."

"If more people had a stable place to come back to, more brotherhood," Sahm told the *Statesman* in '73, "it might've saved people like Jimi Hendrix."

Soap Creek Saloon was a place to get lost and to be found. Delbert McClinton didn't really know what he had until he played that stomp palace. Same with Joe Ely. This was an "outlaw" joint that held benefits for Raymond Frank, "the Sheriff who shoots straight," who also served as rules enforcer at the Spamarama potted meat cookoff.

The "Home of the Stars" had a great sense of humor, sponsoring yearly George Majewski look-a-like contests (usually won by a barnyard animal), and the Eddy Awards, hosted by the Uranium Savages, which basically went to whoever showed up to accept. All that played into the spiritual escape that Soap Creek offered.

Sahm rented a big limestone house a couple hundred yards away and became Soap Creek's self-appointed (unanimously approved) musical adviser. He turned the scene onto Freddy Fender when his Sir Douglas Quintet covered "Wasted Days and Wasted Nights" on 1971's *The Return of Doug Saldaña*. "This is for Freddy Fender, wherever you are," was Sahm's intro dedication. Carlyne made it her mission to find the Latino Aaron Neville, who had semiretired from music after prison for a low-level marijuana bust. She found him in '74 working as an auto mechanic in Corpus and wired him $200 to get to Austin. With Sahm opening, the club sold out and "El Bebop Kid" had a nice payday. The next year Freddy Fender was the hottest thing on the charts with "Til the Next Teardrop Falls." And it wouldn't have happened without Doug Sahm, Soap Creek, and Sahm producer Huey P. Meaux.

NASHVILLE MEETS AUSTIN AT SOAP CREEK

With 1975's *Red Headed Stranger*, Willie finally conquered the country music world, as he and his Sundance Kid, Waylon Jennings, brandished anti-Nashville sentiments all the way to #1. The "outlaw country" movement had Music Row shaking in its Luccheses, so the Country Music Association decided to make peace by moving its annual board meeting from Nashville to Austin in April 1976. Willie told them to stick that olive branch, um, over there in the vase. Outlaw, hell. Willie wanted as many people as possible to hear his music. He and Charley

The Country Music Association comes to Soap Creek, April 1976. *L-R:* Bonnie Garner of CBS Records, songwriter Pam Rose, Carlyne Majer, Marcia Ball. Courtesy of AusPop archives.

Pride would play a private concert for Nash Vegas bigwigs at the two-hundred-capacity Soap Creek, so they could really understand what's goin' down in Austin.

The "Home of the Stars" went all out for the CMA, with Big Rikke Moursand, an Armadillo legend as "the Guacamole Queen," cooking those famous shrimp enchiladas before the show. Anybody who wanted to, met legendary Coach Darrell Royal, country music's biggest fan. "Everybody had the time of their lives," said Carlyne, who also got Marcia Ball, Floyd Tillman, Pee Wee King, and Milton Carroll on stage that unforgettable Tuesday night. "Next time you come to Nashville," WSM/Grand Ole Opry CEO Bud Wendell told Carlyne, "let me show you around." When she took him up on the offer a few months later, Wendell took Carlyne to meet her idol Dolly Parton.

Majer's fledgling Austin Tejas Sounds (ATS) artist management business would benefit greatly from the door-opening CMA event, having a great '80s by signing Lone Justice (Geffen), Kelly Willis (MCA) and the Wagoneers (A&M) to major label deals.

ATS was formed in '76 to manage Marcia Ball, the former Freda of the Firedogs, the first hippie band to play the Broken Spoke. In June '77, Ball signed to Capitol Records, where she made *Circuit Queen* with Guy Clark producer Neil Wilburn. The next ATS clients were LA *cowpunk* pioneers Rank and File, who moved to Austin in '81. Highlight of that yearlong association was when Carlyne's subpublishing deal with a European company got the Everly Brothers to cover "Amanda Ruth." That's as good as any award.

With a hard Texas accent on the fog-cutter spectrum, Carlyne was a tough negotiator with southern charm, a sharp hayseed with a gold-star-encrusted tooth. "You want fair?" she'd tell whiners in her midst. "Fair's in Dallas." Her stage was the record label office, where she was an alt-country Texas Guinan, brightening up the room with her brass. She wasn't like the other artist managers.

Through Rank, Majer met Lone Justice, also from LA's alternative country scene, whose self-titled 1985 debut on Geffen Records heralded Maria McKee as the new Linda Ronstadt, but sold like Karla Bonoff. David Geffen (a UT student for a semester in '61) asked Carlyne what she was going to do to turn it around, so on New Year's Day 1986, Carlyne brought black-eyed peas and cornbread to Willie Nelson. "I said 'I know you don't usually use opening acts, but you've got a show coming up at Universal Amphitheater in L.A. and I'm wondering if my new client can open.' So Willie got on the phone to (manager) Mark Rothbaum and asked if he could put another act on the bill in L.A. Then he turned to me and asked, 'What's the name of the band?'"

BACK TO 707 BEE CAVE ROAD

Aside from Paul Ray and the Cobras, and Stevie Vaughan's new band Triple Threat Revue, redneck rock ruled the Saloon, with twice-weekly plugs from Townsend Miller. Alvin Crow and the Pleasant Valley Boys, Asleep at the Wheel, Lost Gonzo Band, Doak Sneed Band, and Plum Nelly always brought the crowd. When Peter Fonda's *Outlaw Blues* filmed a scene at Soap Creek, the band was Greezy Wheels (Rolling Hills Club veterans).

Soap Creek also kept a strong Louisiana pipeline, filling the void when Castle Creek dried up in '76, with Professor Longhair, the Meters, Rockin' Dopsie, Clifton Chenier, and Gatemouth Brown as calendar regulars. Marcia Ball, meanwhile, was transforming from country singer to the queen of Gulf Coast piano.

Listen to the musicians. That was a Soap Creek rule, except when they wanted to be slid a beer after midnight on weekdays or 1 a.m. on Saturday. The folks of Westlake couldn't have been too happy with all those dope-smoking longhairs in their hot real estate market. And the best way to flush 'em out would be to catch 'em serving underage or after hours. "We never had a single TABC violation," Majer said.

One night, police thought they had 'em, barging in at 4 a.m., when the club was still rockin', with a Johnny Winter/Doug Sahm jam session. "George and Carlyne were always really good about picking up all the bottles and glasses. Nobody was drinking, but we were all tripping," said Awn. "Roadies from the Grateful Dead had been in that night and dosed everybody. The cops had to leave empty-handed." Cancel the paddy wagon. There are no laws against melting faces.

Majer's mothering/managing instincts were honed at Soap Creek, which fostered a family environment amidst all the loud music, dope smoke, and tequila shots. The Majewskis raised their own kids there, as well as those Sexton boys, Ian and Cheney Moore, and Doug Sahm's kids. Who needs babysitters or summer camp? They all turned out pretty damn good!

A condo project knocked Soap Creek #1 out of the Eanes school district in January '79, but thanks to Townsend Miller, who introduced the Majewskis to Warren Stark, they found a new home at the old Skyline club on far North Lamar. They signed the lease, at $1,000 a month, and opened in February 1979, but they ruffled the Starks when two major motion pictures—*Honeysuckle Rose* and *Roadie*—filmed their nightclub scenes there. That was not in the lease! A subsequent rental agreement would stipulate that the Starks share in any Hollywood money.

Written by the *Austin Sun's* Big Boy Medlin and Michael Ventura, *Roadie*, starring Meatloaf as Travis W. Redfish and Debbie Harry as herself, shot some scenes at Crazy Bob's (soon to become Club Foot), but the most memorable footage in the forgotten flick was from Soap Creek. A duet with Roy Orbison and Hank Williams Jr. on "The Eyes of Texas," could not save the Alan Rudolph-directed film, however.

The Skyline building was sold in April 1981 to Jack Holford, a realtor and country music historian, and the Majewski's were on the move again. In August 1982, Soap Creek relocated into the former Backstage Bar, but George and Carlyne were soon burnt out by the 7-24-365 commitment that responsible club ownership requires. He took a job managing the Austin Opera House, she concentrated on ATS Management, and their friend Ed Bennett, from the old Split Rail, took over Soap Creek #3. When the lease ended in August '85, Willie and Tim's Southern Commotion company sold that block to a developer of high-end apartments. It's where the younger cast members of *Friday Night Lights* stayed during filming (2006–11).

All three locations had some great shows, but when folks talk about the original Soap Creek they get, well, misty is only halfway there. *Austin Chronicle* editor Louis Black recalled his first visit to the Bee Cavern Club on Thanksgiving 1974 to see Doug Sahm: "Glory Hallelujah! I was born at 24 because when I walked through those doors, paid my cover to the man mountain there, and came inside, the black and white movie of my life went technicolor. It was the truest Bar Mitzvah! On that day, in that moment, I became a man living in a community of adults."

Rome Inn, 1975–80

Antone's is Austin's internationally renowned "Home of the Blues," but from 1977 until its final blowout on April 24, 1980, the Rome Inn had the hottest blues scene in town. Stevie Vaughan and Lou Ann Barton played every Sunday, and Paul Ray's Cobras with Denny Freeman had Tuesdays, but the hottest night was "Blue Monday" with the Fabulous Thunderbirds.

The T-Birds had only one album during their Rome run, but it was a great one. *The Fabulous Thunderbirds* (also known as *Girls Go Wild*) brought the Louisiana swamp to their Texas blues romp, making fans out of the Rolling Stones and Eric Clapton, who hired the band to open shows. Kim Wilson, Jimmie Vaughan, Keith Ferguson, and Mike Buck: These white boys from Austin knew how to play the blues!

Rome was built as an Italian restaurant in 1958, at the former Shipwash Grocery on 29th Street at Rio Grande. The club didn't start hosting live music until 1976, with a progressive country lean. Everybody was trying to ride that wave. Manager Jack Davis booked the likes of David Allan Coe, Denim, Milton Carroll, Willis Alan Ramsey, Vassar Clements, Asleep at the Wheel, Mother of Pearl, and Doug Sahm (Bob Dylan and Joni Mitchell stopped by to see Sahm on a day off from the Rolling Thunder tour). The music was so successful that beer sales topped food receipts, which put the Rome Inn in violation of its restaurant zoning. Citing proximity to campus, and a rash of noise complaints, the city denied a zoning change, so Rome Inn owners Tom and Mike Watson brought in the Armadillo kitchen in November '76, with Bruce Willensik as chef, to see if they could sell more food. And they did for a while.

But when the Watsons, brothers from Denver, added booker to cook Louis Charles "C-Boy" Parks's duties in '77, the blues took over and it was only a matter of time before the city pulled the plug. So let's keep rockin' till they do!

"Nobody would go down to Antone's on Sixth Street to see the T-Birds," said former club owner Steve Dean, whose AusTex Lounge on South Congress was a hub for roots rock from '78–'82. "But when C-Boy gave them

ABOVE: The Fabulous Thunderbirds had quite a scene at the Rome Inn in 1978. That's C-Boy Parks behind singer Kim Wilson. Photograph by Kathy Cable for the *Daily Texan*. Courtesy of Briscoe Center.

RIGHT: Louis "C-Boy" Parks.
Photograph by Nancy E. Goldfarb LeNoir.

Mondays, they built it up to the point that if you didn't get there by 8 o'clock, you might not get in."

Billy Gibbons took a busload of friends from Houston about once a month, but he was forbidden to jam by manager Bill Ham (the penalty was $25,000), who didn't want to give that ZZ Top guitar sound away for free. Gibbons took a seat and watched the "fiend scene" he wrote about on "Lowdown in the Street" from ZZ Top's 1979 album *Degüello*: "So roam on in, it ain't no sin to get low down in the street." That same year, the T-Birds paid tribute to the lovable man in the sweat-stained blue T-shirt with slow harp instrumental "C-Boy's Blues."

A hard-working cook with a love in his heart for people, C-Boy made the Rome Inn special. He came to work in the kitchen in 1967, the year after a fire gutted the dining room. "C-Boy would crack you up, like how he'd cover his crotch with his hands whenever he passed a microwave," said his unlikely protégé Steve Wertheimer, an accounting student who lived in the neighborhood. "He was just always having fun, and just always working."

The blues scene integrated Austin before the Civil Rights Act, with white musicians seeking out the old Black bluesman who looked and talked like C-Boy, which gave the Rome a lift of authenticity. There was no race there, just mutual respect.

Parks died in 1991 at age sixty-six, but not before he saw his student flourish in the club business at the Continental. Then, in 2014, Wertheimer fulfilled a longtime promise to himself by opening a soul-themed bar seven blocks up South Congress from the Continental. It's called "C-Boy's Heart and Soul," after the man who worked two fulltime jobs a day (including fry cook at the Nighthawk), but always came from back behind the bar, no matter how busy he was, to dance to "Mathilda."

After the Rome Inn closed in '80, the club on 29th Street had a brief resurrection as punk dive Studio 29. It was also a bookstore for a couple years, but since 1987 it's been Texas French Bread.

Austin Opera House, 1977–88

It's sad to lose a beloved music venue, but another one usually takes its scorched place to reset the ecosystem. But has anything replaced the Austin Opera House as a midsized indoor venue with major league talent—and free parking?!?

Liberty Lunch, the Continental Club, and the Mohawk gave and give you raw, powerful, in-your-face experiences, but for pure music appreciation, wouldn't you rather listen to Randy Newman, R.E.M., Tom Waits, Patti Smith, Tina Turner, Dire Straits, Tom Petty, Lou Reed, Warren Zevon, and even AC/DC and Iggy Pop in a venue where you could sit unobstructed, or stand in front of the stage if so moved?

The Armadillo had nachos, the Austin Opera House had theater popcorn—and air conditioning! That was the concept—a more comfortable auditorium for a slightly aging fanbase.

Willie Nelson bought the entire Terrace Motor Hotel and Convention Center, with three hundred rooms and two swimming pools, from developer L. L. "Dude" McCandless in 1977 by assuming a million dollar note and handing over $5,000 in cash. This is the same "Music Lane" parcel that sold for $55 million not long ago. Ace Lumber owner McCandless built the Terrace in 1951 (and the Villa Capri in '57), then converted the convention center's main ballroom into the private Terrace Club for jazz and big band dancing in 1965. But business hit hard times in the '70s. He rented the low-ceilinged Terrace Club space to the Texas Opry House in 1974, but after eight months of great shows, co-owner Bronson Evans bounced a $10,000 rent check and "the greatest club in country music history" (Townsend Miller) didn't make it to '75.

SPIRIT OF '74

The year Richard Nixon resigned as president was also when the Ramones first played CBGB and South Bronx DJ Kool Herc was making his name with a new style of music that didn't have one yet. But while punk and hiphop would take years to crawl out of the Big Apple underground, the era of the *Cosmic Cowboy* hit fast. Austin became the place where traditional country music took peyote, buttons bought legally from Hudson's Cactus Nursery.

The gas crisis of '73–'74, whose rationing caused long lines and high prices, limited audiences for country and Tejano clubs on the outskirts of town. But new downtown club activity was on the rise, especially in the seedy Sixth Street district, where a trio of country bars—Alliance Wagon Yard (at the old 505 Neches location of Flight 505), River City Inn (304 E. Sixth), and the Cotton Exchange (formerly Toad Hall) at Sixth and Trinity—bonded to allow customers to barhop on only one cover charge. Meanwhile, the Lamplite Saloon, in the former 317 E. Sixth location of Wander Inn, hosted the Cobras, Storm, Fools, and other blues-rockers a year before Antone's opened two blocks west.

In October '74, Armadillo human mascot Jim Franklin and t-shirt printer Bill Livingood liberated the Ritz

Jim Franklin and Doug Sahm settling up at the Ritz, 1974. Photograph by Mack Royal.

Willie and Connie Nelson at a Steve Fromholz show at the Paramount, 1976. Photograph by Nancy E. Goldfarb LeNoir.

RIGHT: Margaret Moser jumped for joy when the Austin Opera House opened in 1977. Photograph by Ken Hoge. Courtesy of AusPop archives.

movie theater from its porn phase, and booked touring acts that might've otherwise played the Armadillo. Nobody ever thought Sixth Street was where you'd go to see J. J. Cale or Bo Diddley.

That the Texas Opry House came and went in the time it takes an onion to grow was bad news for Willie, who'd used it as his homebase after a run-in with those peaceniks at the Armadillo, who asked that Willie take Smith and Wesson off the guest list. His crew was packin' and that was fine with Shotgun Willie—he'd take his considerable draw elsewhere. Managed by Willie's pal Wallace Selman from River City Inn, Texas Opry House was looking good in its quest to take the Armadillo's crown, opening with Doug Sahm, Augie Meyers, and Freda and the Firedogs in April '74, then stealing the Eagles for the next weekend. Waylon Jennings recorded his great *Waylon Live* album, with the Willie jab, "Bob Wills Is Still the King," there in September '74.

The Opry House Annex, a small club in a room that would later be part of Arlyn Recording Studios, was home to Last Mile Ramblers, a Western swing band whose guitarist was a kid from New Mexico named Junior Brown. "It was a pickin' party every night," recalled Junior. "That was the spirit of the Austin music scene back then. Let's go see and be seen." Willie would come by and jam every night he was in town, which drew the other musicians. "There was so much sitting in," said Brown, "that there'd be a whole different band at the end of the set than the one that started."

Everybody loved the Texas Opry House except its Travis Heights neighbors, whose streets became the venue's parking lot, overrun by drunk concertgoers who couldn't find their cars. One neighbor even had to turn the hose on fornicators in his front yard. The party started before the concerts and went on long after.

The TOH rent was $5,000 a month, plus 10 percent of the gross, but first the owners had to pay sales tax to get their liquor license restored. This was an ongoing problem. Outbidding the Armadillo for acts made for cash flow problems.

The venue was dormant from '75 to mid-'77, and the Terrace Motel was way behind on upkeep and intake. To make matters worse, Dude McCandless was rumored to have had an unlucky run at the poker table. Willie, meanwhile, was on a massive winning streak, with 1975's #1 smash, "Blue Eyes Crying in the Rain," making him the international star he always knew he'd be. After the deal was struck, with Willie walking away with fourteen acres at South Congress and Academy, he partnered again with Tim O'Connor, who got to work in May 1977. The Austin Opry House was scheduled to open the next month with Willie and Waylon Jennings. Thirty days to turn a carcass into a concert hall with a dancefloor.

"There was a lot of amphetamine," recalled Roger "Oneknite" Collins, who was the venue manager. "We'd hand out those little white pills like candy." The unemployment rate of hippie carpenters and stagehands was zero in Austin the month of June 1977. O'Connor brought in a field kitchen to keep the workers from going out to dinner and maybe not coming back to their exhausting, low-paying jobs.

"We built the stage and risers, and Tim ordered seats," recalled Collins. "When the truck came, we thought, 'There's no way 1,800 seats could fit in there,' but the chairs were in three parts. Plus, there weren't any nuts and bolts!" Assembling and installing the seats was a two-day, around the clock job, finished just a couple hours before the doors opened on June 28, 1977. There's not a drug with more upside than speed.

The 200 Academy Drive complex included the ballroom, a banquet hall and other rooms—forty-two thousand square feet in all—so Willie's nephew (Sister Bobbie's son) Freddy Fletcher built Arlyn recording studios in 1984. Named after his father Arlyn "Bud" Fletcher, it's where Stevie Ray Vaughan and Junior Brown did much of their recording, and where Gary Clark Jr. still does.

Because of its maze of hallways and back doors, the Austin Opry House was notoriously easy to sneak into. Every musician in town knew about the unguarded loading dock door. Or they waltzed right in through the Arlyn hallway to the best seats in the house—the infamous "cocaine catwalk."

The month after Willie and Tim opened, they were hit with a trademark infringement lawsuit from Houston's Texas Opry House, opened in '75 by one of the old Austin partners. At the trial, attorneys for Willie and O'Connor showed the jury a Bugs Bunny cartoon set at an "Opry House" to show the common usage. They seemed to be winning the case, when Nashville's Grand Ole Opry also sent a cease and desist. Hands were thrown up and in September 1978, the name was officially changed to Austin Opera House, though ads still used the Opry House logo for another year or so. Everybody still called it "the Opry House."

Even with everybody's hero Willie involved, the neighborhood was not keen with all the hippies and druggies and roadies and musicians who had moved into the former Oak Terrace Apartments and bungalows. Stretching across Academy, all the way to the back of the Continental Club, this was "Willie World," a trailer park without wheels.

Opening day of the Austin Opry House, June 28, 1977. Photograph by Scott Newton.

Piedmont
Piedmont Cigarettes of Quality
For Cigarettes
Virginia Tobacco
is the Best
Town Crier
THE BEST
flour
Dirty's

O'Connor wanted a place on "the 14 Acres" where the Opry crowd could drink until 2 a.m. after shows, so he had his crew convert the motel's former front office at the corner of South Congress into the Backstage Bar, with a big beer garden. West Travis Heights had become Party Central against its will.

Nelson sold his majority share of the Opera House in 1988 to brothers Morris and Clark Lyda, who pulled out the seating and renamed it "The Terrace" like the old days. They put on some good shows, including the Pixies, Red Hot Chili Peppers, Neville Brothers, and SXSW showcases with Little Village, Morphine, and a True Believers reunion, before concentrating on the banquet business. The Lydas sold the building, which is still standing, to the YWCA in 1993. It's been various offices, but not a music business, for the past three decades.

Spellman's, 1974–81

Opened in 1974 by UT student David Spellman, who invested an inheritance on a place where he could hang out, drink beer, and play dominoes, this ramshackle restaurant/club on West Fifth was neighbors with a hobo camp, a pillow factory, and the city's shortbus barn. Not exactly a lovely setting, but to the groovers who lived in big party houses on Sixth Street west of Lamar, Spellman's was paradise!

Spellman stocked the jukebox with his favorite records (lotsa Willie), served good food and twenty-five-cent longnecks—who needed more? The joint didn't become known for live music 'til the namesake got his masters and moved away to teach college math.

Under new owner Charles Walthall and managers Tom Brown and Kerry Reid, Spellman's became "the home of the old hippie," so tagged by John Kelso in a 1980 *Statesman* column, which also called the Spellman Burger, on a wheat bun with sprouts, the best he'd ever had in Austin.

OPPOSITE: Blaze Foley plays outside of Spellman's. Songwriter Bobby Martinez to his right. Photograph by Dana Kolflat.

Texas Monthly also blurbed about the food until Walthall asked them not to anymore. He was tired of well-heeled TM-ers coming in, recoiling at the Spahn Ranch vibe, and then getting the hell out.

Lucinda Williams, Bill Neely, piano player Robert Shaw, John Clay and the Lost Austin Band, Mandy Mercier, and many others played here from '78–'81, when there was live music seven nights a week. Townes Van Zandt and Blaze Foley were regulars, often sleeping in the barfly bunkbed—one on the pool table and the other underneath it. The janitor also slept at Spellman's, and it was okay with Walthall because there was nothing worth pawning. And it meant he didn't have to come in early to let him in.

ABOVE: They got the billing right. 1980.

Townes Van Zandt peeks through longnecks at the Alamo Lounge. Photograph by Dana Kolflat.

XIII.

Townes's Time in Uncle Seymour's Clarksville

Born in Fort Worth, making his name in Houston's folk scene, and thriving in Nashville, the late, great Townes Van Zandt has been claimed as a native of all those cities, and also Austin, though his most prominent residency here was for less than a year. From September 1975 until about July 1976, the brilliant, troubled songwriter lived in a floppy trailer with a seventeen-year-old girlfriend in the West Austin neighborhood of Clarksville.

It was supposed to be just a couple months, but after the trailer owner died in a plane crash on a marijuana haul, the stay was extended.

When director James Szalapski came to Clarksville in December 1975 for an all-access look at Townes and friends for the acclaimed *Heartworn Highways* documentary, the most unforgettable scene was an old Black man with tears streaming down his face as Townes sang "Waitin' 'Round to Die." That was former blacksmith Seymour Washington—"Uncle Seymour" to the hippies.

"Unk" was seventy-nine with terminal cancer and would be dead within a year. But the tears could also have been for a Clarksville community, founded by freed men after the Civil War and taken back when all of West Austin meant Rich Austin.

In the one hundred years after 1871, when an emancipated Charles Clark bought two acres at W. 10th St. and sold lots to fellow former slaves, Clarksville was almost all African American from West Lynn to Exposition. It was a densely wooded "freedman's town" of dirt roads and shanties, where the people were self-sufficient—hunting and fishing and growing their own vegetables. To make money, they worked as domestics for the white folks of Old Enfield, just a few blocks away.

Clarksville was nearly invisible to the city of Austin, which withheld services to Black residents not living in the designated "Negro District" (via the 1928 masterplan) of East Austin. But that was fine by those who didn't mind using an outhouse if it kept them out of the white gaze. They were country folk who wanted to be left alone.

The construction of MoPac Expressway, which began in '69 and lasted several years, changed all that. As the bulldozers cleared a wide path through the tight-knit community, as many as sixty Black families were displaced. Some were given as little as $4,500—the appraised value—for their homes, many of which lacked running water or electricity. Clarksville, which used to oil its dirt roads to prevent dust, didn't get paved until 1975.

Bohos and musicians integrated Clarksville in the late 1960s/early 1970s, when rent was still dirt cheap. Longtime residents looked suspiciously at these long-haired freaks with their guitars and braless girlfriends, but they were welcomed by Washington, the unofficial mayor of Clarksville. The old man loved the Bible and his bourbon. His front porch, next to a rusted lawn ornament on four wheels, was the gathering place.

Washington "could've been a good preacher if he wasn't a blacksmith," Richard Dobson wrote in his *Gulf Coast Boys* memoir. "He got right into it when the spirit moved him." He sang in the choir of Sweet Home Baptist

Townes Van Zandt sings at the 1976 porch wedding of Little Suzy and Chito. Photograph by George Geier.

Church, the community bedrock on the next block, but they wouldn't let him preach because he drank.

But Unk used scripture to justify the daily imbibing. "People condemn whiskey, but they have no right to," he told Townes and the documentary camera in 1975. "When God created heaven and earth, he created all things. He also created barley, rye. If he didn't think those things were good for man, he wouldn't have let those things grow." "Amen!" was Van Zandt's reply.

God also created the poppy plant. "Clarksville was basically a place where we were all on heroin, all shooting up," Van Zandt's then girlfriend Cindy told R. E. Hardy in the *No Deeper Blue* biography. Nau's Pharmacy sold syringes, in addition to those great cheeseburgers.

"Tell you the truth, Townes was too bad of a drunk to be a good junkie," said Phyllis Peoples, just eighteen when she moved into a garage apartment (forty dollars a month) across the street from Uncle Seymour in 1969. Most of the heroin crowd were chippers. They did any drug available.

Van Zandt had released six albums up to that point, recording "Pancho and Lefty" on 1972's *The Late Great Townes Van Zandt*, but his songs were mainly heard only by other singer-songwriters. David Allan Coe ripped him off by copying "If I Needed You" for "Would You Lay with Me (In a Field of Stone)," which Tanya Tucker took to #1 in 1973, so Townes was bitter and broke. But Emmylou Harris put him on the map by covering "Pancho" on 1977's *Luxury Liner*, then did a hit duet with Don Williams on "If I Needed You" in 1981. After that success, Van Zandt moved to Nashville, then had a #1 hit when Willie Nelson and Merle Haggard covered "Pancho and Lefty." Friends worried about what Townes would do with all that money coming in, but he took a shot at sobriety, several shots.

But in 1976 he was too drunk to sing at the Uncle Seymour benefit at Soap Creek, so he told corny jokes instead. Many of us have thoroughly endured that Townes set. The show was to raise money to fix up Unk's house, which had running water only in the kitchen, so he could wait around to die at the domicile that was part of him. As Greezy Wheels were setting up, an announcement was made: an angel had stepped forward to pay for the complete renovation. Money raised that night would go towards a full-time nurse. It was a joyous occasion, but Seymour Washington never got back to Clarksville, passing away in the nursing home just ten days later on November 12, 1976. He's buried in Evergreen Cemetery, section E, lot 75.

Described as a "soft-spoken, highly intelligent man" in a 1953 *American-Statesman* profile by Billy Lee Brammer, Washington had retired by then from his role as "the Walking Blacksmith," shoeing horses at ranches from Buda to Blanco, and also for the circus when Barnum and Bailey came to town.

In semiretirement he kept horses of the well-heeled, well-shoed, working for the West Enfield Riding Club, as well as a woman from New York who trained show horses. In a short doc about Clarksville in 1970, Washington talks about "ginging" horses for an advantage in the show ring. "You chew up some root ginger in your mouth and then you raise the horse's tail and stick that hot ginger in his rear end," said Washington. The burn makes the horse arch its back, impressing judges.

He had the hardest time working with mules, he told Brammer. "God made the horse and the donkey, but man made the mule. That's why he's so mean." Brammer ended his article by declaring that Seymour Washington's "heart is bigger than a mule. He's a God-made man, you see."

Uncle Seymour's funeral packed Sweet Home Baptist Church with a mix of longhairs, Black neighbors, and relatives, who Unk's young friends had never seen before. "It took a long time for us white kids to be accepted in Clarksville," said Phyllis Peoples. "I would say it was more of a lifestyle thing than skin color. They were hard-working people, and we were drinking and partying and playing music every day."

Songwriters Richard Dobson and Townes Van Zandt on Seymour Washington's porch, circa 1976. Photograph by George Geier.

XIV.

Austin City Limits: This Brand Could Be Your Life

Terry Lickona has been the face and speaking voice of *Austin City Limits* for as long as anyone can remember, so it's hard to believe he was living in Poughkeepsie, NY, when the show launched. Lickona had a nightly radio program on WPDH-FM, where he could play whatever he wanted, which included a lot of the mainstream-bucking country music coming out of Austin.

"There were probably more blues and jazz musicians here than country musicians," *ACL* cofounder Bill Arhos described what was happening in '70s Austin. "But the only moneymaking gigs were in country. So they played jazz and blues inside the country music, and that developed a new art form." KRLU producers Paul Bosner and Bruce Scafe cocreated *ACL* with Arhos to activate Studio 6A in the brand-new rust-colored communications building at the University of Texas.

That was 1974, the year Lickona and his best friend Dan Del Santo, a bluegrass/country guitarist, trekked to College Station for the second Willie Nelson Fourth of July Picnic, then spent three days in Austin recovering. Though they came for the country music, it was hearing the pulsating conjunto sounds coming out of Las Palomitas nightclub on a drive up Sixth Street that convinced them to stop picking their toes in Poughkeepsie and to start living with the pickers of this musically diverse city. Flamingo Cantina is where Las Palomitas was.

"Dan thought his music would fit right in, but when he saw that everyone else was doing the same progressive country style, he decided to do something new," Lickona said. Del Santo became Austin's king of "world beat," as he tagged the mix of African, South American, Mexican and Caribbean music he'd play on KUT every Friday night. He also fronted an Afro-Cuban group, the Professors of Pleasure, who were the surprise Band of the Year winners at the 1983 Austin Music Awards. Since the Professors' Sunday night residency at Club Foot drew only about one hundred fans a week, the joke was that Del Santo made his marijuana customers fill out a ballot before he'd send them off with a green-filled mason jar. Del Santo's weed was reportedly better than Willie's, but he might've went too far by posing in a marijuana field for a promo photo. He was busted in Virginia in 1992 for conspiracy to distribute more than a ton of pot, and, facing serious time, fled to Mexico. Del Santo lived the last nine years of his life in Oaxaca where he died at age fifty from internal bleeding caused by painkillers he was addicted to after two car crashes.

Like his friend Dan, Lickona also got a show on KUT, spinning bluegrass, but in late '75 he moved to TV as public affairs reporter for KLRU's *Newsroom Nine* nightly broadcast. He also started volunteering at *ACL*, and when producer-director Charles Vaughn left after the third season, Lickona convinced station manager Larry White to hire him. There was no money to recruit someone with experience.

"By the fourth season (1978), the progressive country Armadillo spark had begun to fade along with the view of Austin as the anti-Nashville, and the show had already begun to recycle the acts," Lickona told Kevin Curtin of the *Austin Chronicle* in 2014. His vision of Austin City had no Limits, so taping eighty-five-year-old blues primitive Elizabeth Cotten and psychedelic Mexican accordion player Steve Jordan made sense. Tom Waits was also a first-year booking for Lickona, who had to wake up the singer from the hallway couch when it was time to go on.

"Without Terry, I don't think the TV show would still be around," Robert Earl Keen said in 2008 when the Americana Music Conference gave Lickona a lifetime achievement award at the Ryman Auditorium. "Artists love to play *ACL* because Terry pays attention to what they need." Sometimes the requests are simple, as when the great Leonard Cohen answered can-I-get-you-anything with "a bottle of tequila would be nice." The singer and his band did shots of Cuervo before the 1988 show, one of Cohen's first national TV appearances. Delighted by the response, Cohen asked, "Is this a real audience or were you brought in for occupational therapy?"

Executive producer Dick Peterson was an unsung hero of Studio 6A, the behind-the-scenes "honey do" man who stressed professionalism in every aspect of production. Austin native Peterson started working at KLRU just out of college in the '60s when it was still called KLRN and shared time with San Antonio. A move to Hollywood in the '70s saw him work on *The Bob Newhart Show* and *Maude* as an editor. But public TV was his passion, so he returned to KLRU in '84, and eventually became executive producer of *ACL* during its 2000–2009 rebirth decade.

In 2003, *Austin City Limits* became the first TV show honored with a National Medal of the Arts at the White House. That was also the first of five years that Capital Sports & Entertainment, which later became C3 Presents, coproduced the show with Lickona, who gave their Austin City Limits Music Festival credit with "breathing new life into the brand." But Terry and his staff were used to doing things their way and there was some butting of heads on that thirtieth-anniversary season. For example, minutes before Ben Harper's taping in 2004, CSE's top client (and Harper friend) Lance Armstrong called to ask that the starting time be held up because he was still at dinner. That shit didn't ride at 6A.

But Lickona was relieved to finally have some financial stability, as CSE guaranteed funding even if it had to come out of their own pockets.

The program didn't take much dough to get started. Arhos wrote a proposal to do a live music show from Austin and received $7,000 from PBS in 1974 to produce a one-hour pilot starring B. W. Stevenson, who'd just had a top ten hit with "My Maria," and Willie Nelson. Sound glitches deemed B. W.'s set unairable, so Willie got the whole hour. Three years later, Gary P. Nunn's "London Homesick Blues" was chosen as the *ACL* theme song. And then along came Terry.

It wasn't until 1982 that the show first used the Austin skyline backdrop, which has fooled many TV viewers into believing the show is taped outdoors.

Producer Jeff Peterson and Lickona in 1990, at the fifteenth anniversary of *ACL*. Photograph by Lisa Davis. Courtesy of Austin History Center.

The late '90s were the leanest years, with KLRU having to take a bank loan to cover production costs when main sponsor Agillion went under.

This all led up to the 2002 launch of the music festival that licensed the Austin City Limits name for a percentage of ticket sales—about $100,000 that first year. Promoters were praying to break even at thirty thousand fans each day that September weekend at Zilker Park, then were elated—and overwhelmed—when forty-two thousand bought twenty-five-dollar tickets on Saturday and thirty-five thousand on Sunday.

Terry Lickona was sky high when he saw the culmination of his previous twenty-five years fill the fields with music lovers. The *Austin City Limits* name had value! He was walking through the crowd when a young hipster couple spotted his "all access" badge and asked Lickona what was his connection to the festival. "I produce *Austin City Limits*, the TV show," he said, to which the kids responded, incredulously, "There's a TV show?"

Lickona tells that crashing-down-to-Earth story with a big laugh. There's no laurel-resting in public TV.

The challenge is always there for *ACL* to keep working hard to turn folks onto great music. And to give acts the stage many dreamed of playing when they hit their first G-chord.

When Lickona booked Uncle Walt's Band to play in front of a national PBS audience in 1980, the trio was unsigned, playing small clubs. "I was looking for something different than the cosmic cowboy electric sound that dominated the scene, and being a bluegrass fan, I loved their acoustic vibe," said Lickona. UWB had the songs that deserved to be heard by many, and that was always good enough for Terry.

Terry Lickona, Willie Nelson, and *ACL* director Gary Menotti get ready for a taping. Photograph by Scott Newton. Courtesy of Terry Lickona.

'alter Hyatt, David Ball, and Champ Hood at
'aterloo Ice House. Photograph by Kathy Hill

XV.

That's Right, They're Not from Austin: Uncle Walt's Band

"Of all the musical groups which have moved here since the Austin music scene began to develop about six years ago, I don't think any have intrigued, captivated, hypnotized or won the hearts of Austin fans like Uncle Walt's Band."

TOWNSEND MILLER of the *Statesman*, announcing the trio's reunion, after a three-year hiatus, at Liberty Lunch in July 1978.

Townsend hadn't seen nothin' yet. The rebirth was sensational, as Uncle Walt's Band—and their diehard fans—found a musical home at the original Waterloo Ice House at 906 Congress Avenue for the next five years. It was as strong a marriage of room and talent as Austin has ever seen.

UWB played completely acoustic at first, but the crowd's size and enthusiasm called for mics. "People went crazy over them," Waterloo Ice House owner Stephen Clark said of guitarists Walter Hyatt and Champ Hood and bassist David Ball, who all hailed from Spartanburg, SC. "Someone called them 'the Bluegrass Beatles,' but they played a bit of everything." Their trademark was harmonies so crisp they could remove wrinkles.

The trio was championed by fellow musicians, especially Lyle Lovett, whose sophisticated country/jazz style came right from Hyatt. "Uncle Walt's Band gave me my career," said Marcia Ball, who'd been singing country covers as Freda with the Firedogs. "When they brought that first album (the self-released *Blame It on the Bossa Nova*) to town, there was a cover song on it called 'In the Night.'...I asked Champ what that was and he said 'that's Professor Longhair' ... and there I went."

You can also hear the influence of David Ball's "Don't You Think I Feel It Too" on the songwriting of Lucinda Williams, another Waterloo Ice House regular.

Clark opened the burger/beer joint in March 1976 with Roger Swanson, but didn't have live music in the beginning. The first booking, Ain't Misbehavin', dictated that the Ice House would be a swing club, not a folk joint. Eaglebone Whistle, featuring future Lyle Lovett cellist John Hagen, was another regular act, as was David Ball, who'd recently moved back to Austin from Spartanburg to try to get a new band together.

Instead, the countertenor (dude sings like a lady) got the old band back. Hyatt and Hood were living in Nashville, where their five-piece roots rock band the Contenders were building a cult audience and working with R.E.M. producer Don Dixon. But Walter and his first wife Mary Lou, who managed Waylon Jennings, were in the process of breaking up, so Austin was looking good. To sweeten the relocation, Clark gave the trio free rehearsal space upstairs from the club, so Ball had to move his standup bass just down the stairs for gigs. The trio received 100 percent of the door which, at three dollars cover, put as much as $200 in the pocket of each musician, twice a week. That was livin' XXL in Austin in 1978.

Uncle Walt's Band had everything—the looks, the songs, the harmonies, the musicianship, the cool covers. It felt like history was being made on Congress Avenue. Soon, the trio would be a national act, so enjoy the up close and personal experience while you still could.

But stardom never came, and after five years back, UWB broke up again in 1983, with Ball, the best singer of the group, headed to mainstream country success in Nashville ("Thinkin' Problem," "Riding with Private Malone"). Hyatt and Hood continued as a duo for a few weeks, but two-thirds of the trio drew less than half of the former crowd. Walter and his second wife, the former Heidi Narum, moved to Nashville in the mid-'80s to be near his daughter Haley. His acclaimed 1990 solo LP *King Tears* (the name of an East Austin mortuary) was produced by Lovett, but Hyatt was one-and-done on MCA.

Champ stayed in Austin, where his guitar and fiddle (self-taught as an adult) backed many acts, most notably Toni Price for nine years of Tuesday "Hippie Hour" shows, and the Wednesday night sessions at Threadgill's. His violinist son Warren Hood and guitarist nephew Marshall Hood have kept the Uncle Walt repertoire alive every Wednesday for years at ABGB.

Tragedies felled Hyatt and Hood in their forties, with Walter perishing in the 1996 ValuJet crash in the Florida Everglades, and Champ succumbing to cancer in November 2001.

Their music, most of which they put out on their own, was gloriously reissued by LA's Omnivore Recordings from 2018–21. Listen to the first album, 1974's *Blame It on the Bossa Nova* (self-titled by Omnivore) and there's little doubt that Uncle Walt's Band was one of Austin's all-time greatest groups. The Lost Gonzo Band certainly thought so, covering such Walt Band origs as "Getaway," "High Hill," and "I'll Come Knockin'" on their MCA albums.

Walter, Champ, and David first touched down in Austin at the invitation of Willis Alan Ramsey, who saw them in Nashville at Our Place on March 5, 1972. Ramsey's sure of the date because it was his twenty-first birthday. He was also celebrating that day's completion of recording the album that would make him the Harper Lee of redneck rock.

Ramsey brought the trio to his Hound Sound studio in a shack on Baylor Street, but like the earlier sessions UWB recorded in Nashville with producer Buzz Cason, there was not much label interest. There was no proven market for what they were doing.

But the trio was smitten with Austin, where they drew crowds to the original Saxon Pub, and to Castle Creek. Big fan Gary P. Nunn gave the trio a place to stay at his "Public Domain Inc." complex on N. Lamar, where scruffy cottages rented for fifty dollars a month.

"The boys from Carolina" (as Lovett immortalized the band in "That's Right, You're Not from Texas") especially loved how quietly attentive the audiences were when they played, then erupted at the end of the song. "Uncle Walt's was not a bar band," Ball said in a 2019 interview. "We were a listening band." Not everyone in this guitar town got their fresh take on "folk swing," however. "We had some people ask us, 'Why do y'all sing at the same time?'"

The closest UWB—the Unpeggable White Band—got to a major label deal was when they were briefly courted by Warner Brothers in '75. The Walts were viewed as the next Dan Hicks and His Hot Licks, but when that well-promoted group failed to sell many records, WB eventually passed.

That heartbreaking process facilitated the trio's first breakup. Hyatt and Hood went to Nashville, while Ball went back to Spartanburg and opened a bar. Three years went by.

And nobody forgot them.

OPPOSITE: Champ Hood holds son Warren, with Walter Hyatt, 1985. Fiddler Warren Hood does much to sustain the musical legacy of his father's trio. Photograph by Niles J. Fuller. Courtesy of Dolph Briscoe Center for American History.

Crowd at the ZZ Top Barndance during Joe Cocker's opening set.
Photograph by Van Brooks. Courtesy of AusPop archives.

XVI.

Let's Take It Outside: A Bash, a Barndance, and Two Breaks

Willie and the Elevators at Hill on the Moon, 3/17/73

In the early '70s, everybody was trying to put on the next Woodstock. The Austin rock crowd's greatest attempt was 1973's "Last Bash on the Hill," a free all-day festival starring the 13th Floor Elevators just a couple months after Roky Erickson was released from Rusk State Hospital for the criminally insane. Also, on the bill at Hill on the Moon, off City Park Road, were Jimmie Vaughan's Storm, Conqueroo, Freda and the Firedogs, Becky Franke's Tanglefoot, and a surprise guest who turned out to be Willie Nelson.

"Willie showed up in a Winnebago with Sammi Smith," recalled Roger Collins, one of the organizers. Smith, who sang her big hit "Help Me Make It through the Night," was married to Willie's guitar player Jody Payne, and they had a baby named Waylon. "He drove right through the crowd down to the stage." Willie's first Fourth of July Picnic, four months later, was partially inspired by how the rock crowd approved of his country set with unbridled hoots and hollers.

About three thousand were expected at the Last Bash, but when local radio stations talked up this free concert with the 13th Floor Elevators back at it again, fifteen thousand showed up. RR 2222 was backed up for miles and folks were ditching their cars to hike up the hill.

Brothers Crady and Barry Bond, who inherited the scenic, sloping ten acre festival site, as well as the houses and sheds in the back, where bands lived and practiced as loud as they wanted, had put on a few outdoor concerts there previously. But the local police, assisted by Texas Rangers and DPS, had been regularly hassling and arresting attendees and staff. The Bonds' security crew wore American flag armbands for identification, and when one wore his upside down he was taken to jail for desecrating the American flag. Another fifty-eight were arrested at Austin's first-ever rock festival at the Hill in August 1970, with three cars and a truck seized

The surprise guest at the free 1973 festival was Willie Nelson. Poster by Gary Oliver.

for containing narcotics and sold at auction. The long-haired, pot-smoking subculture was the enemy of the authorities, whose greatest weapon was the law.

Barry Bond, twenty-two, was found dead five months later at the base of Mount Bonnell, though it was never determined if he jumped or fell. The Hill on the Moon concerts just weren't worth it anymore, so Crady's partners in police harassment, the One Knite, suggested a final blowout. They'd book the bands and bring the beer, and Bond would provide the site without charge. "We just wanted to have the biggest party Austin had ever seen," said Collins. All the businesses listed on the poster contributed to the beer expense—sixty-two kegs of Lone Star which would be given out free. "We didn't care about making money, just like at the One Knite."

Songwriter Harvey Thomas Young had moved to Austin from Lubbock a year earlier "and I was wondering what the big deal was," he said. "But then I went to that concert at Hill on the Moon. That show made me realize that rock and country and blues could all fit together." Was there another city in 1973 where Willie Nelson and Roky Erickson and Jimmie Vaughan and Marcia Ball could share a stage while fifteen thousand drank for free?

ZZ Top's "Barn Dance": September 1, 1974

In September 1970, UT sponsored an unnamed rock festival at their Clark Field baseball diamond (Red River at 26th) featuring the Allman Brothers (with Duane and Berry still alive), Leon Russell, and It's a Beautiful Day. The concert went off splendidly, but the next big outdoor festival at a UT sports facility would not be such a groovy affair. On Labor Day weekend 1974, ZZ Top headlined an all-day blowout at Memorial Stadium that would have Coach Darrell Royal screaming, "No more concerts!" What that crowd did to his precious football field! Just two weeks before the home opener.

To celebrate the breakout success of *Tres Hombres*, featuring that instant classic "La Grange," the rockin' trio from Houston hosted the "First Annual Texas Size Rompin' Stompin' Barn Dance and Bar B.Q.," featuring Santana, Joe Cocker, and Bad Company, with Jimmy Page on guitar.

The university was ready for a crowd of thirty thousand max, but nearly twice that showed up. Many without tickets crashed the gates, as the overwhelmed and underpaid security force could only watch and shake their heads. The stadium ran out of food and water even before a very drunk Joe Cocker was finished heaving onstage in the brutal afternoon heat. Anarchy reigned, as the plywood field-covering was pulled up in places and many in the crowd tattooed their initials or an outline of Texas in the brand new astroturf with lit cigarettes. Coach Royal was well-known as a music fan, but you can bet he never listened to ZZ Top after that.

Sunday Break Concerts, 1976

The big rock festivals moved to where there was not much to damage. On May 2, 1976, a twenty-eight-year-old first-time promoter from Dallas named Win Anderson and financial backer Jack Cooper, who owned Houston tire stores, drew a crowd of fifty-six thousand to a big field near the intersection of Hwy 290 and I-35 for a "Sunday Break" concert with America, Santana, Peter Frampton, Gary Wright, and Cecilio & Kapono. Booking Frampton for middle act money, then watching his *Frampton Comes Alive* album become a monster as the festival approached, was a grand slam for Anderson's Mayday Productions, which split a profit of $120,000 with Cooper.

That was easy, let's do it again!

Scheduled just four months later, on the Sunday before Labor Day '76, "Sunday Break II" hoped to attract one hundred thousand fans to the much-bigger Steiner Ranch near Lake Austin, with a bill of Chicago, Fleetwood Mac, The Band, Steve Miller Band, England Dan and John Ford Coley, and Firefall. Tickets were $10 in advance and $12.50 at the gate ($50 and $60 in today's money) for that lineup, but with only one two-lane road leading to the site, traffic backed up for over ten miles and only six thousand tickets were sold at the gate. Total paid attendance was just twenty-eight thousand, but many of those never made it. The only option was to ditch your car and walk several miles, but it's hard to fully appreciate "Landslide" and "The Joker" with a tow truck on your mind.

It was even harder for Anderson and Cooper to enjoy the festival when they paid the bands over $400,000 (Chicago got $210,000), against total ticket sales at around $350,000. The Band made $50,000, but they had to cancel the next week's shows because keyboardist Richard Manuel suffered a neck injury on Lake Austin when a speedboat he was riding in hit a wave.

Promoters lost nearly half a million dollars, and stiffed day workers on their three-dollars-an-hour wage.

For those who did get in and acquired some immunity from the ninety-five-degree heat by having attended that

Sunday Break II looked like a success until the numbers came in. Paid attendance of twenty-eight thousand meant losses of nearly half a million dollars. But it was a great day of music. Photograph by Scott Newton.

year's Willie Nelson Fourth of July Picnic in Gonzales, it was one helluva festival! Great performances from everyone, topflight production, plenty of room. Who cared that promoters were losing their asses?

Five lawsuits were eventually filed, including from the Houston bank that lent Mayday $415,000. Landowner Tommy Steiner received $10,000 upfront to rent his ranch, but was stiffed on the promised 10 percent of the gross.

As if it made a difference, Mayday blamed the financial fiasco on counterfeit tickets—seventy-thousand in all! But those upstarts didn't even keep ticket stubs. Going through the trash that hadn't been hauled away, Texas consumer affairs officials found about 3 percent of the tickets—not 70 percent—were fake.

DPS officials had put the crowd estimate at one hundred thousand, but they always pad those numbers to make themselves look more heroic in controlling the masses. An aerial photograph was examined by crowd-counting experts who estimated twenty-four thousand were in attendance.

Mayday Productions filed for Chapter 11 bankruptcy protection and was never heard from again. Their only concerts were the two that bookended the summer of '76.

Covering the messy aftermath for *Texas Monthly*, Richard West found a curious incident in Win Anderson's past. In 1973, he pleaded nolo contendere to the charge of setting fire to the Texas School Book Depository building in Dallas. He was a patsy, working for the building's owner Aubrey Mayhew, a record producer and songwriter who discovered Johnny Paycheck, and started Little Darlin' Records in 1966. Mayhew was also a Kennedy fanatic with dreams of turning the tragic building into a memorial. He was facing foreclosure when Anderson and accomplices poured gasoline and lit matches on five floors of the building in July 1972. The sprinkler system and nearby firemen put out the fire in twenty-four minutes, with damages of only $5,000. Mayhew was never charged in the arson, Anderson did only a few months in jail, and the building's ownership reverted to D. H. Byrd.

There was one more music festival at Steiner Ranch, two weeks after SB II. The Bicentennial Outlaw Concert, starring Willie Nelson, Waylon Jennings, Tracy Nelson, Asleep at the Wheel, David Allan Coe, and Marcia Ball, needed to sell twenty-five thousand tickets to break even, but after the Sunday Break fiasco only six thousand showed up. And that was it for concerts at Steiner.

'aughan on the verge: Stevie Ray and former Cobras bassist Alex Napier in 1979. He'd have a connected new manager the next year. Photograph by Nancy E. Goldfarb-LeNoir.

XVII.

SRV Finds Management at Deadhead Downs

Stevie Ray Vaughan was a mind-blowing '80s guitar hero, but he toiled in Austin clubs for ten years before he took off nationally. The manager who helped orchestrate his rise was Chesley Millikin, a former Epic Records exec and Grateful Dead associate who came to town in 1980 to take over management of Manor Downs horserace track from his best friend Sam Cutler (former Stones road manager of Altamont infamy).

Cutler's girlfriend and partner in Out of Town Tours was Frances Carr, an oil heiress from Corpus Christi. They lost their main client when the Grateful Dead took an extended break after playing five consecutive nights (three shows?) at Winterland in SF in 1974. So Carr came back to Texas and bought a dormant 1960's horse track twelve miles east of Austin called Manor Downs. She was "through with show biz," she told the *Statesman* in March 1975, which is what the regulatory boards and conservative Manor neighbors wanted to hear.

The Downs would be an equine-training facility, with quarter horse racing on weekends. It was also pitched as the new home for the Travis County Fair and Livestock Show, which Austin's City Coliseum proved inadequate to handle.

The renovated Manor Downs debuted in May 1977, and just five months later, the Dead played the infield of the racetrack for the first of five times in the next eight years. The track's new slogan was "Horse Racing and Rock and Roll." So much for Carr's retirement from the music business.

In 1979, Manor Downs hired Bobby Hedderman, the former Armadillo booker, as director of special events. He had a big first year with the Fish Outta Water Festival (a jab at the square Aqua Fest), featuring the Allman Brothers, Jerry Jeff Walker, and Johnny Winter. Then came Waylon Jennings, with the original Crickets opening, and Cheap Trick with Graham Parker, and the Kinks after that.

Another memorable show was in 1982 when the Fabulous Thunderbirds opened for Jerry Lee Lewis, who'd just had major surgery. A doctor in a white coat would occasionally come out to check Jerry Lee's heart, then try to lead him offstage, but the Killer would come storming back a la James Brown's cape routine.

Traffic was a downer, with only a two-lane road leading in, but parking was ample, beer was only one dollar a cup, and outdoors under the stars had a lot more ambiance than the Erwin Super Drum, which opened in late 1977. Manor Downs was the site of the big festival scenes from *Roadie*, the stranded Meatloaf vehicle filmed there in 1979.

Lotta happenings out there on the infield of the racetrack, or playing to the stands, but for its effect on Austin music, Manor Downs is more significant for what happened in its offices. Avid horseman Milikin, who first came to North America from Ireland in the late '50s for horse-jumping competitions, started Classic Management with Carr. She had the money, he had the charm and connections. "Carry on" was his infectious sign-off.

"There were a lot of musicians here, but not much music business," said writer Joe Nick Patoski of Millikin's arrival. "Chesley helped legitimize Austin as a music town to the rest of the world." The facilitator who had

Sam Cutler introduces the Grateful Dead at Manor Downs, 1977. Photograph by Watt Casey.

introduced his client David Lindley (in Kaleidoscope) to friend Jackson Browne in the '60s, let it be known he was looking for talent.

Manor Downs accountant Edi Johnson raved about a phenomenal guitarist working the blues mines downtown, and took Millikin and Carr to see Stevie Vaughan at Steamboat in late '80. His singer Lou Ann Barton had left him to join Roomful of Blues, so Stevie was a frontman for the first time. His incredible guitar playing had Millikin speaking Chinese.

Ho lee fuk!

After signing a management deal, Millikin got a copy of a VHS tape Steve Dean recorded of Stevie at the last night of the Rome Inn, and played it for Mick Jagger and Jerry Hall when they came down to look at horses in April '82. A mightily impressed Mick wondered when he and the rest of Stones, staying in New York, could see Stevie and Double Trouble live.

Millikin hastily arranged a private showcase at the Danceteria nightclub, attended by members of the Rolling Stones and a handful of others—maybe fifty people in all. Jann Wenner got wind and a photo and blurb appeared in the Random Notes section of *Rolling Stone*. It looked like SRV was going to join Peter Tosh on the roster of Rolling Stones Records, but Jagger passed, because the blues just didn't sell.

That's why Stevie languished in Texas clubs for so long. Yeah, he's amazing, but where does that go from here? Even Johnny Winter couldn't sell albums anymore. The punks certainly didn't like what Stevie and Double Trouble were playing, booing them heartily when they opened for the Clash on June 8, 1982, at City Coliseum. Not all of Chesley's moves worked.

Jerry Wexler had already lost a lot of Atlantic Records' money on Austin, so he didn't sign SRV either after having his eyebrows singed at the Continental Club one

Left to right: Doug Sahm, Randy Thornton, Gary P. Nunn, Sam Cutler, Jack Barber at Manor Downs. Oct. 12, 1977, the first of five Grateful Deadshows at the racetrack. Photograph by Ken Hoge. Courtesy of AusPop archives.

Wednesday night in '82. Instead, Wex put in a call to Claude Nobs, who owned the Montreux Jazz Festival in Switzerland. "I don't have any of his music to send you," said Wexler, "but trust me on this one." Stevie and Double Trouble were the first unsigned act to ever play the main stage of the vaunted jazz festival.

Stevie Ray Vaughan's life changed on July 17, 1982, in Montreux. Unlike bluesman John Hammond Jr., who played solo acoustic in the concert hall named after Stravinski, Stevie and Double Trouble came out blazing with their full-on blues-rock set. It was the Austin club version of Dylan at Newport in '65, with scattered boos from the purists. But SRV didn't flinch, and afterwards David Bowie stopped by his dressing room with praise, enticing the twenty-seven-year-old Texan to play guitar on the upcoming *Let's Dance* album. Jackson Browne offered the Vaughan gang his studio in Los Angeles free of charge. And Hammond called his father John Sr. with a new name for a discovery wall that included Billie Holiday, Bob Dylan, Aretha Franklin, and Bruce Springsteen. Signed to Epic, Stevie ripped under the radar no more.

Back home in Starfucker, TX, playing with David Bowie was considered the highlight of Stevie's career, but Millikin foresaw bigger things for "Junior," as he called his charge. Vaughan was set to go on the *Serious Moonlight* tour with Bowie in '83, but with the Texas Flood debut coming out around the same time, Chesley said it made more sense to promote that record instead of being Ziggy's hired gun. He made last-minute demands on Bowie's management and then pulled Junior while he was waiting for his ride to the airport. People in Austin thought Chesley Millikin was off his meds! You don't turn down David Bowie when you've been playing for the same fifty people back home.

But Chesley was right, and by the end of the year, SRV was his generation's new guitar hero, almost single-handedly resurrecting the blues while never forgetting the pioneers. He was Austin's "Pride and Joy."

Millikin also put sixteen-year-old Charlie Sexton, whom he didn't manage, in a New York City studio with Ron Wood. That's where Bob Dylan first met his future guitarist. "Chesley knew everyone," Carr told me in 2001, when I was working on Millikin's obituary. "He was incredible at putting people together."

The Irishman saw Austin as a land of unrealized potential, and lifted the scene wherever he could. Meanwhile, the Stevie Express he'd engineered had become a runaway train, fueled by drugs and alcohol. A silver platter piled with cocaine was as much a studio necessity as headphones, whether Stevie was recording his own album or producing one by his hero Lonnie Mack. Chesley, who was also ridin' that train, was a bit of an enabler.

The scene was shocked in 1986, when Stevie and Chesley parted company. Who fired who? The word from Classic was that Chesley dropped his drug-addled client, but SRV biographer Patoski wasn't buying that. Even with the substance abuse problems, Stevie was bringing in a lot of money.

"Chesley didn't want to be the manager that got the phone call that said Stevie was dead," said Widgeon Holland, the guitarist Millikin was grooming as the next Stevie when the manager was felled by emphysema in 2001 at age sixty-seven. When Millikin got the diagnosis eight years earlier, he moved for his lungs to Indian Wells, in the Palm Desert of California.

At Manor Downs, the breakup with Vaughan was set aside for the big news that Texas legalized pari-mutuel wagering, to take effect in '87. With the focus on getting the track in shape for thoroughbred racing, Carr really was done with show business this time. Millikin began managing an MS-stricken Ronnie Lane of the Faces, whom he convinced to move to Austin.

Farm Aid II, which doubled as Willie's Picnic, was the last big show at the Downs on July 4, 1986. Stevie kicked ass, but ten weeks later he was in an ambulance in Germany, after cocaine and Crown Royal had conspired to kill him. Back in the States, he checked into rehab, as did bassist Tommy Shannon, and remained happily sober the last four years of his life. Vaughan opened *In Step*, his final album with Double Trouble, with "The House Is Rockin'," blasting the crutchspeak that getting high is better for creativity. By example, he showed many others the Higher Power from within. And then he was called home in August 1990 after just thirty-five years on Earth.

The Grateful Dead played only two more concerts in Texas—Houston and Dallas in '88—after their last show at Deadhead Downs. Jerry Garcia died on August 9, 1995, the day of the only Lollapalooza festival in Austin. The news broke before Hole took the stage at Southpark Meadows. "I can see Jerry in the moon," said Courtney Love, whose estranged father was in the Dead's inner circle.

Manor Downs, beat out by the more-modernized Retama Park in Selma as the premier horse track in Central Texas, closed in 2010. The 146-acre property Frances Carr owned with brother Billy was sold in 2021 to a Dallas developer of industrial parks. For about five years, though, Manor Downs was Austin's connection to rock royalty, and the office that sent Stevie Ray Vaughan and Double Trouble out into the stratosphere.

Stevie Ray Vaughan and Double Trouble at Sam's BBQ in Austin. Photograph by Watt Casey.

Frances Carr, 1977. Photograph by Watt Casey.

The I. S. gang *L-R:* Nancy Weeks Stoner, Steve Goodwin, Ginger Sledge, Joani Crenshaw, Richard Dorsett, Neil Ruttenberg, Joe Bryson) unveils Guy Juke sign that signaled a new-wave direction for the store circa 1982.

XVIII.

The Record Stores

"A scene itself can be defined as an overproductive signifying community; that is, far more semiotic information is produced than can be rationally parsed. Such scenes remain a necessary condition for the production of exciting rock n' roll music capable of moving past the mere expression of locally significant cultural values."

BARRY SHANK, *Dissonant Identities; The Rock n' Roll Scene in Austin, Texas* (Wesleyan University Press, 1994).

Shank played guitar in '80s Austin band Black Spring before writing a master's thesis in the dense style of academia that worked because, last we checked, he was a professor of comparative studies at Ohio State.

Having attended public school in Hawaii, I'm barely educated, so I see a scene as where you can have fun every day without making plans, *semiotic* or otherwise. It's a cool club that anyone can be a part of for the price of a cover charge, or the ability to thumb through albums for two hours with fifty cents in your pocket. A scene requires at least two good bands, for the purpose of argument, and a dozen charming middling ones to get drunk to. An adventurous radio station is nice, but not required, as a cool record store is fully capable of turning kids onto new music.

Inner Sanctum

Inner Sanctum on 24th St. began as the place to buy the hippie country records heard on KOKE-FM in the early '70s. In the next decade it was new wave central, as Raul's was switching from Tejano to punk. Next door to the west was Mad Dog and Beans, which did creative things to char-grilled burgers, and featured an average of one recording artist in the kitchen at all times. (Stripped to their skivvies in the summer heat.) To the east was Les Amis of *Slacker* fame, which sold more beer than usual for a vegetarian restaurant.

Joe Bryson opened Inner Sanctum on August 28, 1970, three weeks after the Armadillo World Headquarters, in the former location of Phil's Records on W. 24th St. at Rio Grande. The twenty-two-year-old UT senior from Corpus was a rockstar-looking guy, the face of Inner Sanctum, but the employees made the place (which Bryson sold in 1982). Buyers James Cooper, Neil Ruttenberg, and Richard Dorsett knew more than what the people wanted. They knew what they should want.

Soon after Sanctum relocated to Bluebonnet Plaza at 504 W. 24th, "Cowboy" Cooper decided to move up, literally, from Les Amis waiter to manage the record store he watched through the restaurant window above.

That view was just too enticing for a fan who, as his nickname implies, knew country music inside-out. Former shoppers at CBS-owned Discount Records (2310 Guadalupe) started going to Inner Sanctum to see if the new B. W. Stevenson record was out yet, or to replace a record they ralphed on. (Never take the plastic wrap off *¡Viva Terlingua!*) As the name implies, Inner Sanctum was a hangout where all music lovers were welcome.

Until the labels found out and freaked, Bryson's vinyl emporium had a one-dollar rental policy for LPs, which were usually taped, returned, and reshelved at fifty cents off. Sanctum also started the record store keg party on Fridays, with bands playing in the parking lot. That's how you *move past the mere expression of locally significant cultural values*.

There was also Record Exchange on the south end of the Drag. Back and forth, back and forth we'd walk, between record stores, between Mad Dog's avocado cheeseburger and a full-pounder from G&M Steakhouse, which was nicknamed S&M because the owner was borderline sadistic.

The Drag was like paradise without tourists. You'd always run into people you knew, and learned which crazy-looking street people to give a wide berth to, and which sane-looking folks were Scientologists (wider berth). Walking the boulevard that separates UT from the real world has long been Austin's favorite waste of time.

Waterloo Records

You could never walk on South Lamar, where Austin's next great record store opened in 1982. Waterloo was in a building the width and length of an automated car wash, because that's what used to be at 221 S. Lamar. Partners Louis Karp and John Kunz ran their twelve-hundred-square-foot store on customer service and trust. Not only could you listen to a record on headphones before buying, Waterloo offered refunds on returns within ten days. No questions asked, even if the clerk knew you weren't returning *Purple Rain* because you didn't like the music. A surprisingly small percentage of customers abused this policy by making copies and getting their money back. If you loved music, you respected Waterloo (even if you took a handful of bumper stickers to slice into new words, which used to be a thing).

Waterloo was a unique indie record store because it was organized, like a chain store, but funky. It was Sam Goody with Mardi Gras beads, staffed by music nerd scenesters who kept their condescension to themselves. Working in various record stores, including Zebra Records on Lavaca St., Kunz spent years plotting what he'd do differently when he got his own place. He'd call it Eclipse Records.

Karp had the same dream while managing Sound Warehouse on Burnet Road, and opened Waterloo by himself on April 1, 1982, the day after Kunz quit his record store job in Highland Mall. Instead of competing, the pair became friends and, within a few months, partners. Kunz put away his hand-drawn Eclipse logo.

One of Waterloo's greatest innovations was shelving its albums alphabetically, without regard to genre. You can't calculate all the time that has saved customers who, for instance, just wanna buy that Talking Heads record they heard on KGSR, without having to wonder if it's in "new wave" or "rock" or "Stu's Picks."

By day he was running Austin's cool record store, but at night Kunz paid the bills by waiting tables at Jeffrey's, a job he held from '82–'91.

Karp sold his 50 percent share to Kunz in '87 to start a video rental business for hospitals, then went into store management for Whole Foods. In '89, Kunz moved Waterloo to a bigger space, five times the size, at Sixth and North Lamar. That was one of downtown's first retail centers—and look at that corner now!

Inner Sanctum made it twenty-seven years, closing in 1997. Waterloo passed the forty-year mark in 2022.

Considering record stores have been disappearing like phone booths, four decades in music retailing is a landmark achievement. The Stevie statue, Continental Club, Broken Spoke, and Waterloo Records remain the top four pilgrimage stops in town for music fans from abroad.

Waterloo doesn't organize in terms of genre, but we do. Let's explore significant Austin acts in their respective categories of gospel, rock, jazz, and punk.

Waterloo Records store.

Joe Gracey and James "Cowboy" Cooper (in hat) at a KOKE event at Inner Sanctum. Photograph by Watt Casey.

Sara Hickman performs from the counter at an instore from the just-opened Waterloo Records at Sixth and Lamar. Photograph by Bill Leissner.

Big Boys play a Record Exchange instore for *Lullabies Help the Brain Grow*, 1983. Photograph by David C. Fox.

OPPOSITE: Anchoring the south end of the Drag. Photograph by Cristobal Bouroncle, UT Student Publications. Courtesy of Dolph Briscoe Center for American History.

RECORD EXCHANGE
OPEN
Open

Brothers-in-law Junior Franklin and Bill “The Mailman” Martin

XIX.

Franklin: First Family of Gospel

This Mailman Delivered the Good News

Bill "the Mailman" Martin was an actual letter carrier in East Austin when he took over for his mentor Elmer Akins (1911–98) as Austin's face and voice of Black gospel music. Martin was a religious music DJ on KIXL (which became KGLO) for over three decades, and also promoted gospel concerts.

Martin came to Austin in 1953 as an airman at Bergstrom Air Force Base, with the goal of attending Julliard on the G. I. Bill. Martin was a sax player influenced by fellow North Carolinian John Coltrane, but his musical course was rerouted when he met a Huston-Tillotson student named Evelyn Franklin at her grocery store checkout job in East Austin. He asked her out and she said, "You gotta talk to my daddy first."

Can't imagine there are too many things in life more intimidating than facing E. M. Franklin, the stern pastor of St. James Missionary Baptist Church, and asking him to entrust his daughter to your care for an evening. Rev. Franklin asked the airman what church he belonged to and when Martin said he wasn't a member of any church, the audition was over. But Bill was in the front pew at St. James the next Sunday, and served the church with enthusiastic dedication for almost sixty years. The Mailman and Evelyn, who everyone called "Tutter," were married for fifty years until she passed away in 2005.

Paramount Singers

Born in 1910 in the Pilot Knob community nine miles southeast of Austin, Ermant M. Franklin was one of seventeen children born to Ananias, a porter, and housewife Callie Franklin. Brought up in the church, E. M. cofounded Austin's first recorded gospel group, the Paramount Singers, with his younger brother A. C. in 1936.

"We loved to look up at that Paramount Theatre marquee," A. C. Franklin told music historian Clay Shorkey in 1987. "But after a few minutes a policeman would come by with a billy club and tell us to move along to the Ritz."

Named after a theater they couldn't attend during segregation, the Paramount Singers had a radio show on KTBC for five years and were recorded by John Henry Faulk for the Library of Congress in 1941.

World War II broke up the a cappella group when the other cofounding brothers, Kermit and Geno Terrell, were drafted. Upon returning from the war, the Terrells settled in Oakland and restarted the Paramount Singers, without the Franklin brothers or fifth original member James Haywood Medlock, who had joined the Soul Stirrers in Chicago. The Franklins decided to remain pastors of their churches—A. C. in Los Angeles and E. M. in Austin. Everybody in Austin knew A . C., who preached alongside the Rev. Martin Luther King Jr. at Victory Baptist Church in Los Angeles in 1968, as "Uncle Koot."

The Chariettes

Evelyn Franklin and her sister Dorothy were members of gospel girl group, the Chariettes, who released a 45 in 1954 on Houston's Duke/Peacock label with "Step by Step." That tune and its flip side "Prop Me Jesus" were written by Lavada Durst, the KVET DJ who also managed the group. Rosalie "Miss Kitty" Alexander, the hottest gospel piano player in town, was brought on board, but church commitments kept her from touring. Since some of the Chariettes were still in high school, they couldn't hit the gospel highway either, so Duke's Don Robey dropped the group after the single didn't sizzle.

Another Franklin sister Barbara was almost disowned when she left the choir to go on the road with Ray Charles in the '60s as a frugging Raelette. After a couple years, though, she came back to town and married a preacher.

Junior Franklin

Oldest Franklin sibling Ermant Jr. had the most success in music, moving to LA in the late '50s with brother Elmo and starting a new version of their Austin group Sensational Wonders. They played the same circuit as a teenage Holy Ghost shouter from Alabama named Willie Joe Ligon, who approached the intensity of June Cheeks and Archie Brownlee, the two greatest hard gospel voices of the era. What set the Wonders apart was a full band backing, with electric bass, drums, guitar, and organ, almost unheard of in gospel at the time. With Ligon as lead singer, they became the Mighty Clouds of Joy, a group that revolutionized religious music after signing with Peacock Records in 1960. They were later called "The Temptations of Gospel" for their soul and choreography. But even more significant was the funk bass lines they brought to spirituals.

Though the Clouds, who had a disco hit in 1975 with "Mighty High," were frowned upon by religious purists, they brought church to the charts while never losing the sanctifying conviction.

Junior Franklin moved back to Austin in '79 to see after his ailing mother and organized a female group—the Golden Echoes. Featuring the Bonner sisters of McCallum High, the Echoes were the first Black gospel group many of the white rock crowd had ever heard, playing Soap Creek and before the SXSW keynote. Franklin fathered a child by the oldest sister, who still sings gospel as Jacqueline Bonner-Calhoun.

Junior Franklin encouraged his brother-in-law Martin to stick with radio after a disastrous first show on KIXL in 1980. "I didn't know I was supposed to turn off the mike when the records played, so they heard me talking on the phone over the music," Martin said, shaking his head. "I was so embarrassed; I tried to hide from everybody. But Junior kept telling me I could make a difference in gospel music if I stayed on the radio." The Mailman delivered that joyful noise every Sunday for thirty-four years.

Elmer Akins

His mentor was Elmer Akins, a man he met on his mail route. Also originally from Pilot Knob, Akins had the *Gospel Train* radio show on KVET from 1947 until his passing in '98, and also promoted concerts by national gospel acts, usually at Doris Miller Auditorium. They'd attach a loudspeaker to the top of Akins's car and Martin would drive while Akins promoted.

The father of educator Charles Akins, the first African American principal in the Austin Independent School District, Elmer Akins had friendly competition from Junior Franklin, who promoted gospel shows by acts he was personally connected with through the Mighty Clouds. Junior wanted to do his own posters, so he went into the printing business, guided by an instructional book he checked out of the library. The Franklin–Stewart Printing company was raided by federal agents in 1981, who charged Franklin with conspiracy to counterfeit. The charges were dropped the next month, but Junior's reputation was sullied. But one local artist had fun with the situation, producing a hundred dollar bill in Franklin-Stewart's trademark dayglow colors.

Junior Franklin became a minister in 1991 and died of a stroke in 1996 at age sixty-four. Carrying out the Franklin family legacy at St. James is Claudia Williams, who has been choir director at St. James since she was sixteen. Claudia was handpicked by E. M. Franklin after she led a bicentennial choir at the church in 1976. In the ensuing decades, Williams, whose frantic motions and facial contortions resemble Mick Jagger as much as anyone in gospel, has become nationally known in mass choir circles.

Also, she'd been a mail carrier for over three decades before a recent retirement. The mailbag was also passed, along with the torch!

Clarksville's Bells of Joy had the biggest gospel hit of 1951 with "Let's Talk about Jesus" on Houston's Peacock Records. Label owner Don Robey put a drumbeat to quartet singing to create a religious crossover unsurpassed until the Edwin Hawkins Singers recorded "Oh Happy Day" in 1969. Peacock publicity photo. Courtesy of Andrew Brown Collection, University of Houston.

Singer Bruce Bowland leads Krackerjack at the Armadillo, 1973. *Left to right*: Uncle John Turner, Jesse Taylor, Tommy Shannon. Keyboardist Mike Kindred is obscured. Photograph by Van Brooks. Courtesy of AusPop archives.

XX.

Austin Rocks! (In a Hard Place)

In the thirty-plus years since *Billboard* started using Soundscan to more accurately measure album sales, rap and hard rock have been dominant genres on the charts. But as of 2023, the live music capital of the world has not produced a single hit rapper, not even close. And aside from Dangerous Toys, whose self-titled 1989 LP on Columbia took five years to go gold, no rock/metal band from the scene has broken out.

In the '90s, the weekend didn't start until KLBJ's Johnny Walker played "Bonecrusher" by Soulhat on Friday afternoon. But that's another major label Austin rock band (Epic Records) that never made it too far out of Travis County.

Austin's Greatest Unsigned Band

Austin's repute as a hard rock/hard-luck town starts with Krackerjack, a huge local band that never released a record. Though they were together only from 1970–74, Krackerjack is revered this many years later by those who experienced live their hard-rockin' blues, draped in glam. Groupies became aware that taking a member of the 'jack home for the night was not just an invitation to bed, but to their closet.

Drummer Uncle John Turner and bassist Tommy Shannon played Woodstock with Johnny Winter in 1969, and came back to Texas dressing like Jimi Hendrix and the Who. They were the rhythm section on the three albums that announced the albino guitar hero's arrival. But their departure came when Winter's manager Steve Paul convinced the guitarist to shed the blues and play rock 'n' roll, backed by the McCoys ("Hang On Sloopy") of Rick Derringer.

Winter sent Turner and Shannon away with a righteous severance, which they used to put together their new band Krackerjack.

While Johnny was recording "Rock and Roll, Hoochie Koo," Unc and Tommy were in Dallas convincing Oak Cliff rockers Bruce Bowland (vocals) and Mike Kindred (piano) to leave the Mystics for their new band. In San Francisco, where they went to teach those flower children how to rock, they found guitarist Jesse Taylor, who played like the freight train from Lubbock he rode in on.

Their first big show was at the Matrix, where "everybody said they were too loud," said Jillian Bailey, Uncle John's girlfriend during the Krackerjack years, and also the band's road manager. "They couldn't get booked after that."

Texas couldn't come quick enough, though the band was often denied service on the drive through West Texas for their long hair and freakish garb. "We even got turned away at a gas station," said Bailey, a Chicago native who hoped the rest of Texas wasn't like that. The open arms of Austin let her finally exhale.

"When we first got here we lived at the Armadillo," Bailey recalled. "They had all these little rooms and Eddie Wilson let us crash in one of them." Free isn't always without cost. "We hated Shiva's Head Band because they were always practicing. It was hard to get any sleep."

Krackerjack eventually settled in a house on 16th Street between Trinity and Red River, just six blocks from the New Orleans Club, where they were the biggest band since the 13th Floor Elevators. Were Krackerjack shows as crazy as the Elevators? "Times three," answered New Orleans Club manager Ron Coleman. The sellout crowds would spill out to the sidewalks. Inside was drunken delirium.

"We became, almost overnight, the biggest, most popular band in Austin," Jesse Taylor said in a 2005 interview. "And that lasted for a couple of years."

"I didn't miss too many Krackerjack shows at the New Orleans," said Vickie O'Bannon, who started going to rock clubs as a sophomore at Reagan High in 1967. "They were the best band in town. And probably the most nationally underrated band ever." Ms. O'Bannon, married for a time to Leonard Arnold of Lavender Hill Express, is in possession of studio tracks the band recorded in its heyday that prove Tommy Shannon drove that bus. He and Uncle John were a tremendous rhythm section. And Bowland was a forceful, wiry-voiced, rock 'n' roll singer. Krackerjack was Aerosmith before Aerosmith, plus they had a secret weapon in Kindred, the best piano player on the scene, who gave them a Faces feel. Jesse Taylor led the murderer's row of guitarists, followed by John Staehely, Robin Syler, Stevie Vaughan, and Gary Myrick.

"Playing guitar for Krackerjack was kind of a rite of passage," said Jimmie Randall, bassist of Jo Jo Gunne. "But I think one of the reasons they didn't get a record deal was because they were changing guitarists all the time."

Randall was a member of Smiley, who played the New Orleans Club, and also shared a stage with Krackerjack in 1970 at King's Village Rock Grounds. That was a short-lived, but fondly remembered outdoor venue in a predominantly Black neighborhood at I-35 and Howard Lane, owned by Krackerjack's booking agent Charlie Hatchett and Coleman from the New Orleans Club.

"One of our best concerts had ZZ Top, with Krackerjack opening," recalled Coleman. Krackerjack went over bigtime, which drew a good-natured reprimand from ZZ Top manager Bill Ham. "He said 'don't you ever make my band follow Krackerjack again.'"

Tragedy struck Kings Village in September '71 when popular sausage vendor Francisco "Paco" Carrasco, a UT grad student, was shot and killed outside the venue's entrance. Trying to prevent someone from the neighborhood stealing a sausage sandwich cost him his life. (He received his master's degree posthumously.) HACO Productions packed it in at Kings Village soon after, though a new owner kept the concerts going another year.

Krackerjack seemed on the verge of taking it to the next level, but Clive Davis, who had signed fellow Golden Trianglers Johnny Winter and Janis Joplin to Columbia, passed on them. "We went to New York with tapes of the band and met with him, but he thought they needed more development," said Bailey. The raw, energetic music that drove the kids crazy at the New Orleans was kept down on closer inspection by sometimes-banal lyrics.

The K-Jack repertoire included "Medicine Man," "Til Tuesday," "It's Another Thing," "Gimme the Gun," and "Chicken Slacks." That latter song came from a lyrical misunderstanding. "We were listening to Sam Cooke's 'Twistin' the Night Away' and I said 'What are chicken slacks?'," laughed Bailey. Cooke's "chick in slacks" gave birth to a Krackerjack favorite about buying new pants because your ass is hanging out of your ripped jeans.

After the New Orleans Club closed, Coleman moved operations to Waterloo Social Club at 705 Red River, with an E. Seventh St. entrance. Krackerjack rotated with Jimmie Vaughan's Storm and Stevie Vaughan's Blackbird at the club until it was renamed Waterloo Country in '73 to chase that prog Western market.

Krackerjack played every rock club in Austin over the next two years, and they were also big in Wichita Falls, Odessa, and Waco. But the grind was brutal. Jesse Taylor was the first to leave, replaced by John Staehely. When the Austin native left to join bassist brother Al Staehely in Spirit, Uncle John, who always called the shots, hired two guitarists—Syler from Dallas and Stevie Vaughan.

"Unc was pushing for Robin to be the featured guitarist, and me and Tommy (Shannon) would be going, 'Stevie's the one!'" said Bailey. Turner stuck with Syler and let Vaughan go.

"Unc was very particular about how the band looked onstage," said Bailey, "and one night Stevie was up there with a big fat wallet in his front pocket. I guess that was the last straw." Ironically, Krackerjack is best known today for the three months its membership included Stevie Ray Vaughan.

By the band's second year, Bowland's alcohol and drug use was becoming a problem, though he was usually able to get it together onstage. Shannon was in and out of jail/rehab. Then there was friction over material, since the band wrote its own. "Mike (Kindred) was the best songwriter and he wanted to sing more," said O'Bannon, who lives in Williamson County near the reclusive Kindred. "But Unc wanted Bruce to sing everything." Kindred left the band in '73 and cut off contact, though Shannon had to play Kindred's "Cold Shot," a cowrite with W. C. Clark, every night with SRV.

Krackerjack's last guitarist was Gary Myrick of Dallas, whose 1974 exit to LA, where he formed Gary Myrick and the Figures, marked the end of Austin's greatest band to never release a record. Myrick achieved what everyone on the Austin rock scene predicted of Krackerjack, having a big hit with "She Talks in Stereo" in 1980.

ABOVE: Jesse Taylor, Tommy Shannon, Mike Kindred, Bruce Bowland, and Uncle John Turner were Krackerjack. Photograph by Burton Wilson.

RIGHT: Fire closed Mother Earth on North Lamar in November 1976. Courtesy of *Austin American-Statesman* Photographic Morgue at the Austin History Center.

Too Smooth

Too Smooth was another local sensation that never caught on nationally. The quartet signed with Woodstock promoter Michael Lang's Just Sunshine label in '74 and recorded an album at the fabled Record Plant in Sausalito, California, but it never came out. "Gulf & Western decided to get out of the music business, so they sold Just Sunshine to ABC Dunhill," said Clark. The new folks didn't know who Too Smooth was, and they didn't care.

During its 1974–79 heyday, Too Smooth played the Armadillo 76 times, more than any band besides Greezy Wheels (123) and Balcones Fault (84). And they packed Mother Earth every time, too. But because they weren't part of the romanticized outlaw country, psychedelic rock, or electric blues scenes, they've become almost forgotten.

They were Austin's Grand Funk Railroad, but Too Smooth never released an album (just a 45 on Buddah Records) until two decades after their 1981 breakup. *The Still* (2011) compilation was a keepsake for a small, yet devoted cult called the Smoothies.

Interlocking guitarists Brian Wooten and Jeff Clark, bassist Danny Swinney, and drummer Tom Holden were each distinctive players who brought something special to the group. Two sang, three wrote songs, and all four worked out arrangements, making for a sound that was all over the place but rooted in riff-wailing guitar rock.

The members regarded their unclassifiable repertoire to be their strength, but labels saw a lack of focus. Not grandiose enough to be lumped with King Crimson or Yes, but higher reaching than "Smokin' in the Boys' Room," Too Smooth was stuck in the unmarketable middle ground.

The band formed in 1973 when Wooten replaced Stevie Ray Vaughan in Stump, which also featured Clark and Holden. "Stump was always a compromise because Stevie and (bassist) David Frame wanted to play blues, and Tom and I were more into rock," said Clark. Former West Coast radio exec Jon Fox flipped over the new Stump at the Black Queen and signed them to a management/publishing deal. Their new name came from an associate everyone called "Too Smooth." He had a handshake that ended with a finger snap, so the band had artist Ken Featherston incorporate that image into their logo.

When touring acts Golden Earring, Ted Nugent, and Lynyrd Skynyrd made their initial forays into Austin, the Armadillo booked Too Smooth as the opening act to ensure a full house. Greezy Wheels and Alvin Crow served the same function for country acts—and Bruce Springsteen's first Austin shows at the Armadillo in 1974.

Why didn't Too Smooth make it? Was it the soft name that made them sound like Seals & Crofts devotees? Was it bad luck with labels? Those things were a big part of Too Smooth's regional-locked popularity. But you can also point to the law of averages. A lot of great bands never break out nationally. Rock 'n' roll is a vicious game, as the Ray Wylie Hubbard song says.

Clubland Paradise: Hard Rock Havens

MOTHER EARTH, 1972–81

After the Jade Room and New Orleans Club closed, the rock box circuit of the '70s was Mother Earth at 10th and Lamar, the Black Queen on West Sixth, South Door off Riverside, Flight 505 on Neches near Sixth, and Eli's Club on North Lamar, which burned to the ground in 1974, but was rebuilt three blocks north (current Yellow Rose location).

Late in their eight-year run, Too Smooth had competition in hard rock supremacy from Fools, led by powerhouse blues-rock guitarist Van Wilks. Managed by Bill Ham's Lone Wolf Productions (ZZ Top, Eric Johnson), Fools opened the wildly successful Sunday Break I concert in May '76 and seemed on their way to national prominence when they signed to Mercury a couple years later. That deal yielded only the Van Wilks solo album *Bombay Tears*, allegedly released by the label in 1980.

Also packing Mother Earth with regularity were Dallas bands Lynx, Werewolves, and Bugs Henderson.

"The thing that really set Too Smooth apart from the other bands was their dual lead guitar sound," says Lowell Fowler, who ran the light show at Mother Earth (the original home of Whole Foods) and went on to cofound concert lighting giant High End Systems/Barco. During the day, Mother Earth was his showroom.

At night, M. E. was an eleven-thousand-square-foot rock emporium, selling more Budweiser than any bar in the state—and #3 in the country. On weekly "Drink and Drown Nights," you bought a personal pitcher for three dollars and could fill it up as many times as you wanted.

Mother Earth had been a struggling nine-month-old club when Mark and Steve Weinstein, just twenty-one and twenty at the time, came down from Dallas to buy it from another pair of brothers in '72. The Weinsteins had club owner DNA, their father being notorious Dallas impressario Abe Weinstein, whose Colony Club

(1939–73) made Juanita Slusher famous as Candy Barr. But the only stripping the Weinstein brothers promoted was hard rock that could peel the paint off the walls. And they made sure the party kept going for two hours longer. The Weinsteins were key in getting the alcohol curfew extended to 2 a.m. in May 1975, spearheading the "Don't Throw the Lock Before 2 O'clock" campaign. It passed by 101 votes.

Fire closed Mother Earth on North Lamar in November 1976, but rockers followed the club to the former 1907 Riverside Dr. address of Caesar's lounge act haven the next year. Mother Earth had five years on E. Riverside until the rock got stale and the Weinsteins, seeing an underserved audience, converted it to upscale urban dance club Tootsy's. That place was an instant success, but lasted only a couple years before the Weinsteins went Tejano with Club Festival.

BACK ROOM, 1973–2006

Originally located at the current Rivertowne Mall home of Thundercloud Subs, the Back Room grew out of the pinball craze in 1973. That was also the year the legal drinking age dropped from twenty-one to eighteen in Texas, putting a serious crimp in the fake ID business, but filling the Back Room with UT students living in nearby apartments.

Even in that small room, owner Ronnie Roark booked music—Angela Strehli and Southern Feeling, Blind George, Ace in the Hole (not George Strait's band, Louis Jay Meyers's). He had the foresight to buy his own pinball machines, bypassing the vending companies and eventually growing into one of the biggest quarter-gulpers in town. If you ever played pinball or pool at the Hole in the Wall, Continental Club, Mother Earth, or Raul's, you gave some of your money to Mr. Roark.

Roark bought the building at 2015 E. Riverside that we all knew as the Back Room around 1977. With it came the adjoining Copper Dollar, formerly a bikers' bar that Roark filled with pool tables. This version of the BR, booked by Wayne Nagel from '81 until he left to tour-manage Charlie Sexton in '85, had a few booths and tables, with a small dancefloor, and a capacity of about a hundred for live music. There was never a cover.

During the '80s there was not much reason to go to East Riverside besides the Back Room, whose first big regular draw was the Friday evening residency of Dan and Dave, which went back to '75 in the original location. Moonlighting executives Dan Burke and Dave Henry, with Dr. Hans Langsjoen coming down from Scott & White in Temple to play bass, were like the Smothers Brothers, with a lot of witty repartee, but they played country music, not folk. *Legends in Our Spare Time* was the album sold at gigs.

The Back Room doubled in size in April '85 by knocking down some walls and combining the Copper Dollar. All the games went to that room, which opened up the live music venue. Jim Ramsey was hired to book the BR from 1985–93, during which time it became a hair band club for men. The Back Room was as close as Austin nightlife got to New Jersey.

The business model was described by former club employee Ray Seggern in six words: The door. The bar. The games. If the last two were making money, the first one didn't matter, so the club with a six hundred capacity could overpay bands, with a relatively low ticket price, and still turn a profit. We got to see Public Enemy and the Ramones and Motorhead and Jane's Addiction and Marilyn Manson and Warren Zevon and Rage Against the Machine and Pearl Jam and Pantera (who blew out the PA on their first note) and many more music hall acts in a rock 'n' roll club.

Bubble Puppy was one band to make the transition from Vulcan Gas Company to Mother Earth, 1978. Photograph by Ken Hoge. Courtesy of AusPop Archives.

XXI.

Austin Jazz

Kenny Dorham and Gene Ramey

This town is a country and blues burg, a rock-without-borders haven, a place that embraces songwriters who can make poetry from their past. You don't hear much about Austin's legacy as a jazz town, but a pair of Austinites—trumpeter Kenny Dorham and bassist Gene Ramey—not only backed the likes of Charlie Parker and Lester Young, but played on many of the late-'40s and early-'50s Thelonious Monk sessions one critic called "among the most significant and original in modern jazz." To go from L.C. Anderson High School in East Austin to 52nd Street in Manhattan is a trek only talent can guide. But Dorham and Ramey, who both picked up a lot of session work by knowing how to best shade the outline of the spotlight, are not widely known. Dorham was in the shadow of the top trumpet players of the bop era: Miles Davis and Dizzy Gillespie. But he'd settle for the "thinking man's trumpet player" tag.

Ramey (1913–84) went to Anderson High before B. L. Joyce started the venerated band there in 1933. He played tuba with George Corley's Royal Aces at the Cotton Club on E. 11th, and got further education following Eddie and Sugar Lou's Band. Those transplants from Tyler featured Oran "Hot Lips" Page on trumpet for a time. When Ramey went to Kansas City for college he met Hot Lips' half-brother Walter Page of the Blue Devils, who helped him transition from tuba to string bass. Ramey got his big break in 1937, joining the Jay McShann Orchestra, then convincing the bandleader to hire his brilliant, yet irresponsible friend Charlie Parker on sax. McShann approved the hire under one condition—Ramey was in charge of Bird's sax after gigs so it wouldn't be pawned.

Ramey didn't drink or do drugs and was naive to the demon ways of an addict. "We were coming from Port Arthur to Austin for a date," Ramey told John Bustin in 1964, "and Bird and Walter Brown, the blues singer, got sick. They were sweating and moaning and looking real bad, so I called my mother and told her I was bringing home a couple of sick boys from the band and for her to get a doctor." After Parker and Brown were treated, the doctor took Ramey aside and scolded him for bringing junkies to his mother's home. "I was shocked because I hadn't even realized that was what was wrong with them." Parker died of a heroin overdose in 1955 at age thirty-five.

Eleven years younger than Ramey, fellow Parker collaborator Dorham came up in the Anderson High Yellow Jackets, who won several statewide marching band contests between Black high schools. "If we came in second it was a big disappointment," said Ernie Mae Miller, tenor sax player with the band from 1940–43. After college at Prairie View A&M, where she toured with the Co-eds swing band, Miller was a beloved mainstay on the local club circuit, with a six-nights-a-week residency (1951–67) at the downstairs Creole Room of the New Orleans Club.

Jazz singers like Miller and Damita Jo (DeBlanc) received early training at Dinty Moore's, a café/bar on West Sixth and Colorado that was so popular you couldn't get in on weekends if owners Flo and Dave Robbins didn't recognize you through the sliding peep-slot at the front door. After Dinty's was torn down in 1950 to make way for the American National Bank building, Flo and Dave, transplanted New Yorkers, opened the Manhattan deli at 911 Congress Avenue, whose backroom saloon was, unofficially, Austin's first gay bar circa 1957.

Damita Jo, who had a couple of R&B hits in '60 and '61 with answer songs "I'll Save the Last Dance for You" and "I'll Be There" ("Stand by Me"), grew up in East Austin, the cousin of future Supremes musical director Gilbert Askey. But after her father, a Creole chef from New Iberia, LA, enlisted in the Navy during WWII and was stationed in Santa Barbara, Damita Jo attended high school there, and didn't have the Yellow Jacket experience so vital to aspiring Eastside musicians. The Anderson High School Band represented the entire community.

For most of the '40s, '50s, and '60s, the predominantly Black neighborhood on the other side of the freeway might as well have been in another county. But when the Yellow Jacket Band marched down Congress Avenue to the state capitol during inauguration parades, East Austin's presence was full and pronounced. Wow! Other marching bands would almost rather follow horse manure.

A master tailor who worked out of his house on E. 14th St. and taught the trade at Samuel Huston College, Benjamin Leo Joyce was also a musician who played tuba in the army band during World War I. With a desire to give Black students the same kind of musical training available in the white schools, Joyce canvassed East Austin looking for kids who wanted to play. He also solicited neglected instruments.

"Mr. Joyce didn't put up with an ounce of foolishness," said Ernie Mae, whose grandfather Laurine Cecil Anderson was the school's namesake. "You couldn't play no jazz either." Horn players would jam after school in the backyard of the Patterson brothers, Alvin and Roy, with Dorham, Askey, and trombonist Buford Banks regulars. Dorham would have a profound influence on Buford's trumpet-playing son Martin Banks, who toured with Ray Charles and played in the Apollo Theater house band for a decade.

Joyce bent his strict "no jazz" rule only one time that trumpet player Alvin Patterson could remember. "We were playing football against our rival, Wheatley in San Antonio, and they were beatin' us," he recalled. "But even worse, their band was showing us up, playing all these hot big band swing numbers. So, Mr. Joyce called me over and said, 'What was that swing thing you guys were playing the other day when you thought I was out of range?' I said that was 'Tuxedo Junction' and he said, 'OK, let's hear it.'" As Dorham played the Erskine Hawkins part perfectly, even Joyce had a smile on his face. The crowd went nuts, rallying the Anderson football team to victory.

Joyce was forced to resign in 1953 when a new statewide rule required high school band leaders to have music degrees. His replacement was protege Alvin Patterson, who held the job until school desegregation forced Anderson to close in 1971.

In a 2004 interview, Patterson told me Dorham was "very thoughtful and perceptive" and would often defer to the older players, especially Hermie Edwards, "who everyone knew as the baddest horn player on the Eastside."

After high school, Dorham attended Wiley College in Marshall, where he studied chemistry. But after only a year in college, Dorham was drafted into the army. He was discharged in 1943.

Just two years later, Dorham replaced Fats Navarro in Billy Eckstine's orchestra, the first bop big band, from whose ranks flowed the likes of Parker, Davis, Gillespie, Dexter Gordon, and Sarah Vaughan.

On Christmas Eve 1948, Miles Davis couldn't make a gig with the Charlie Parker Quintet, so he recommended Dorham as a replacement. The gig lasted two years, including a sensational stint in 1949 in Paris, at that city's first international jazz festival.

Although Dorham played with Parker on the sax great's final public performance in 1955, he spent most of the early '50s freelancing for Monk, Bud Powell, Sonny Stitt, and others. In 1954, he cofounded the highly influential Jazz Messengers with Art Blakey and Horace Silver. Ramey was also a Messenger for a time. The L.C. Anderson alums crossed paths often.

Later, Dorham led several of his own groups, recording such highly regarded albums as *Afro Cuban* in 1955, *Jazz Contrasts* in '57, and his most highly regarded LP, *Una Mas*, in '63.

"In Miles' autobiography, he writes about what an underrated player Kenny Dorham was," said Thomas Heflin, whose New Six Jazz Project played a birthday tribute to Dorham at the Elephant Room in 2008. "He wasn't flashy like Dizzy or quite as stylish as Miles, but there was so much lyricism in the way Dorham articulated notes."

With such tenderness and vulnerability in his dark tones, Dorham has been called the most poetic of trumpet players.

Dorham and Ramey, along with Nat King Cole's guitarist Oscar Moore, are the greatest representatives of Austin-raised talent to the jazz world because their playing was in service to the song. Counting Austin-born

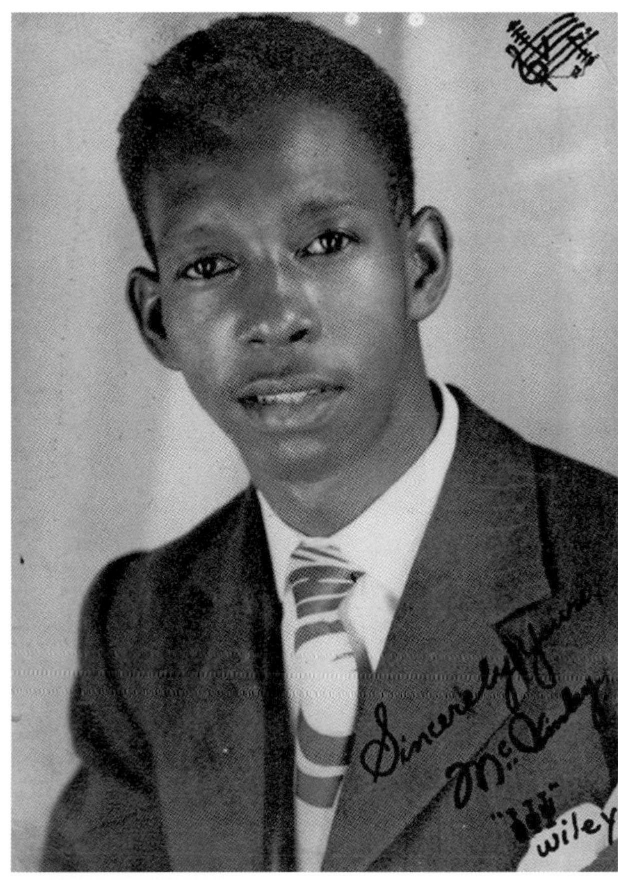

ABOVE: Ernie Mae Miller at the New Orleans Club, 1950. Photograph by Neal Douglass. Courtesy of Austin History Center.

RIGHT (TOP): Kenny Dorham was known for his introspective trumpet tone. Courtesy of Texas Music Museum.

RIGHT: Trio of Austin jazz greats Teddy Wilson, Alvin Patterson, and Kenny Dorham reunited at the 1966 Longhorn Jazz Fest. Courtesy of Austin History Center.

pianist Teddy Wilson, who moved to Alabama at age six, there's not a musical genre in which Austin has produced more icons than jazz.

Dorham died of kidney disease in 1972 at forty-eight. Ramey retired to a farm in Williamson County, where he lived out the last eight years of a fruitful life. Moore died in 1981 at age sixty-four.

James Polk: Passenger's Driver

The most influential leader on the local jazz scene was James Polk, a multi-instrumentalist who came up from Corpus Christi in 1959 to attend Huston-Tillotson College. Polk left town from '77–'87 to play organ with Ray Charles, eventually expanding into an arranger/conductor role, but he had a rich musical life in Austin before and after. Unlike Dorham and Ramey who left Austin right after high school, Polk made his mark right here in the clubs.

Austin's jazz scene was happening in the mid-to-late-'70s, with the Casablanca and Blue Parrot clubs at 15th and Lavaca, Mackedrick's Treehouse on Dawson at Barton Springs, Piggy's on Congress, Buffalo Grille on W. Sixth, and the preroof Liberty Lunch. The most highly regarded musician in the bunch, Polk led a mid-'70's quintet which would become Passenger—Leonard Cohen's band for awhile.

Bassist Charles "Roscoe" Beck, guitarist Mitch Watkins, sax player Paul Ostermayer, keyboardist Bill Ginn, and drummer Steve Meador first backed the Canadian songwriting legend on 1979's *Recent Songs* and subsequent tours. The band grew out of UT's Jazz Ensemble, though they could play anything, backing Joe Ely on 1984's *Hi-Res* project.

A child of musical parents, Polk was taught violin in grade school, and played trombone in the Coles High School band. He also played bass, well enough for Lionel Hampton to take him on a world tour. The gig started at San Antonio's HemisFair in 1968, when Hamp's bassist didn't show up, and the vibe great plucked Polk from the house band. He could also play sax, but keyboards were his kingdom.

Polk was also a member of the popular Blue Crew, with drummer Gerry Storm and Brazilian bassist Luis Natalicio (a UT professor), and led an octet, featuring Pat Murphy, Fred Smith, and Melvin Scott on saxes, Bob Bruno on bass, and either John Whitehurst or Leotis Duffy on drums. Polk and experimental accordionist Bob Sardo were the two most prolific bandleaders in the Austin jazz scene.

His '60s soul band James Polk and the Brothers, featuring trumpeter Martin Banks and W. C. Clark on bass, would play weekends at the Hideaway Club on E. 19th, but they had trouble getting booked west of the freeway because of their name and their Afros. "Club owners thought we were gonna burn their club down," Polk said. He integrated the Brothers in the early '70s, with Lubbock natives Angela Strehli on vocals and John X. Reed on guitar, and got booked downtown at Muther's, before it became Castle Creek. "I used to go and see him perform before I was a professional," Strehli said of Polk to *Blues Blast* magazine. "To be in a band of his was just an instant education about the tools you need to run one yourself." Which she and W. C. did next with Southern Feeling in 1972.

That the audience was nonexistent at Casablanca in the beginning made James Polk's group of young Caucasians better. "He'd stop right in the middle of a song and come over and play the beat that he wanted," drummer Steve Meador recalled. It was taken in the spirit of instruction and used for improvement. These jazz kids in their twenties were looking for mentorship, and they got a great one. Within months, the Casablanca was packed. A live recording of "Polk Chops" from that era is high-energy jazz at its funkiest. "Nobody could ever accuse us of laying back," Beck said with a laugh.

Polk's legacy is in leading. A teacher and music director at Booker T. Washington High in Elgin after graduating from Huston-Tillotson in '62, Polk has always been a natural instructor. When he returned to his hometown in 1964 to play the Corpus Christi Jazz Festival, his sixteen-piece band was made up almost entirely of his high school students. He then went on to teach a whole generation of notable jazz players.

Album cover photo from James Polk's 1984 LP *You Know the Feeling?*

ABOVE: Trumpet great Freddy Hubbard joins James Polk and the future Passenger at Casablanca. Courtesy of Roscoe Beck.

Eric Johnson and the Boys from Abilene

We all know about how the influx of musicians from Lubbock—Jesse Taylor, Joe Ely, Angela Strehli, Junior Medlow, all the Hancocks, Jimmie Gilmore, John X. Reed, Bob Livingston, Kimmie Rhodes, and so on—have enriched our musical way of life in the River City.

But let's not forget the Great Abilene Migration of 1971, when two groups of musicians, who'd known each other since childhood, took that four-hour drive to Austin and never looked back. Those bands—Sundance and Cadillac—didn't get record deals or headline at the Armadillo, but its members, including the Neece brothers—Tim and Murray—Stephen Grisham Barber, Bill Maddox, Keith Landers, David Baldry, Lee Pence, and Noel Kelton, plus soundman Richard Vannoy, went on to have a great impact on the Austin music scene.

Sundance drummer Tim Neece opened the Rockola record store on W. 24th St. and managed a cover band called Good Question, which would find greater success as Christopher Cross, necessitating a move to LA Managing Charlie Sexton, who signed with MCA as a seventeen-year-old in '85, eventually brought Neece back to Austin, where he switched from managing artists to running concert venues. In '96, Neece was hired by Tim O'Connor's Direct Events (Backyard, Austin Music Hall, La Zona Rosa), then he helmed the Bass Concert Hall for seven years, and was the first general manager of ACL Live at Moody Theater.

His Sundance bandmate David Baldry worked at Strait Music for fifteen years before opening Musicmakers on South Lamar in 1989.

The 1972 wreckage of Cadillac resulted in two quite different followups. The more vocally gifted Landers and Kelton came up with Johnny Dee and the Rocket 88's, a popular oldies band on the lucrative private party circuit for four decades. Maddox and Barber went all the way in the other direction.

Fifteen-year-old Eric Johnson recorded an album with Mariani in a forest near McDade, 1970. Photo by Mariani singer Jay Aaron Podolnick.

After dabbling with a piano/drums prog duo called AUSSENHOROWITZ, drummer Maddox and keyboardist Barber, joined by another Abilenian, bassist Kyle Brock, cofounded the Electromagnets, the first great jazz-rock fusion band in town, in 1973. "Billy Maddox was the gorilla glue that kept it all together since the Abilene days," said Barber. The drummer's father, a dentist by day, played big band dance music on weekends with his Ray Maddox Orchestra. "Billy would sit in. He could play just about every instrument and was always pushing us to be our best." Maddox could play drums with one hand and a keyboard with the other.

One day they went to a rehearsal space on Crady Bond's Hill on the Moon compound, and jammed with a recent Holy Cross High School graduate named Eric Johnson. "We loved Frank Zappa and wanted to have a guitar in the band," recalled Barber, "but to say Eric blew us away is an understatement."

The son of a Hyde Park anesthesiologist with a diverse record collection, Eric Johnson's first instrument was the piano, which he mastered as a child. He got his first guitar at eleven and had his first band Sounds of Life at thirteen. At fifteen, he was recruited to join Mariani, whose adventurous drummer Vince Mariani had put out a couple drum instrumentals á la Sandy Nelson on Bill Josey's Sonobeat label in 1969. In his Eric Clapton/Peter Green phase, Johnson played his Gibson 335 all over the Mariani album *Perpetuum Mobile* the next year. But after Josey shopped it to every major label and had no takers, Sonobeat put out only a 45.

Mariani opened a memorable Deep Purple concert in San Antonio in 1970, when they were asked to play an additional set by the promoter because guitarist Ritchie Blackmore was too ill to go on. A kid who said he knew all the songs on guitar was plucked from the audience to stand in for Deep Purple's guitar legend. His name was Chris Geppert, aka Christopher Cross.

The likes of Emerson Lake & Palmer and Yes were replaced as models in the exploratory rock scene by Chick Corea's Return to Forever, Weather Report, and Mahavishu Orchestra. There was a new, mind-blowing "jazz fusion" scene in Austin, including Tomas Ramirez and Jazzmanian Devils and 47 Times Its Own Weight, but when E. J. joined the Abilene gang in late '73, the Electromagnets went to the top of the class. They sounded like Jeff Beck's *Blow by Blow*, but that groundbreaking jazz-fusion LP wouldn't come out for another year.

"We were wondering what's with these Abilene guys," said Podolnick, who went to Holy Cross two years ahead of Johnson. "They were intense. Eric had found these really, really strong players." Zappa was a fan, calling Electromagnets, "the Mahavishnu Orchestra if they had a sense of humor." The Magnets often played the *Bonanza* theme song and cartoon music from the '30s to go with their full-on jazz-rock liftoff.

The band went into Odyssey Sound on W. Sixth in the summer of '74 and made an LP of originals with their manager Park Street producing. With the album getting raves, the Magnets went from smaller clubs like Castle Creek and Soap Creek to larger venues like Mother Earth and the Armadillo.

On the road they were sometimes too far out for the crowd. One night in Huntsville the manager timidly approached the stage after the first song with the band's pay in an envelope. "Thanks for coming, but we're gonna go with the jukebox from here on."

Johnson's star power was so obvious that no one was surprised when the Electromagnets changed their name to "Eric Johnson" in 1976. Maddox and Brock continued as the rhythm section, while Barber moved to New York to study under a Julliard master. He rejoined Johnson's touring band in the '90s but is best known today as a classical composer and arranger.

Maddox was also a gearhead and studied at the Southwest School of Electronics. In January 1984, he got a job on the three-man manufacturing staff of PC's Limited, which became Dell Computer later that year. One of the first "Dellionaires," Maddox eventually cashed out,

Electromagnets. *Left to right:* Eric Johnson, Billy Maddox, Kyle Brock, Stephen Barber. Photograph by Park Street.

got sober, and helped other alcoholics recover. He kept his hand in music, rejoining Johnson on the Alien Love Child side-project in 1994, and playing with the Fabulous Chevelles, a party band led by former Cadillac booking agent Charlie Hatchett.

Maddox played the Abilene Country Club with the Chevelles on December 21, 2010 and noted during dinner that this was also the site of his first paying gig, playing drums for his dad's group at age thirteen. It ended up being the last place he played.

After visiting Landers regularly in the Scenic Brook neighborhood in West Austin, Maddox bought a house whose backyard abutted the Landers property. The pair had been best friends since elementary school and now they would grow old together.

But random, unspeakable tragedy struck the Abilene brotherhood on December 27, 2010, when Maddox was murdered by a deranged neighbor, a jogger off his meds who threw a rock through the glass front door and entered the house. He fought with Maddox, whose wife called 9-1-1 and got the pistol, shooting the intruder. But the sixty-three-year-old neighbor was able to get the gun away and shot Bill Maddox. The killer died three days later of a head injury suffered when a wounded Maddox threw him through a wall to protect his wife. Maddox was fifty-seven, and twenty-four years sober.

More grief came ten months later when Landers passed away from kidney failure. He was sixty.

"There's not a day goes by I don't think of Billy and Keith," said Barber, speaking for the entire Abilene gang, who lived and breathed music in their boring hometown, then took their talent to an Austin scene that had not yet seen their likes.

The Raul's scene gathers for an *Austin Chronicle* portrait which never ran: *Standing left to right:* JJ Jacobson, Cindy Marabito, Mikey Donaldson, Pat Doyle, Karla Eppler, Pat Deason, Tony Johnson, Tomas Levy, Gary Floyd, Brad Troxel, Craig Legg. *Front row left to right:* Tommy Pipes, John Slate, Chris Wing, Mellissa Cobb, Robbie Jacks. Half of them died young. Photograph by Ken Hoge.

XXII.

Clubland Paradise: Punk /Alternative Clubs

Raul's, 1978–81

On December 31, 1977, Roy "Raul" Gomez, Joseph Gonzales and Bobby Morales opened a bar at 2610 Guadalupe Street where they wanted to feature Chicano music. But the Sex Pistols made for other plans. Nine days after Raul's opened, the British punk rock sensation played San Antonio, and every cutting-edge music fan from Austin was in the crowd thinking, "I could do that, if I only had the guts."

Three who did were Kathy Valentine, her classmate at Greenbriar "hippie high" Marilyn Dean, and Carla Olson, who started a band called the Violators. Future Go-Go Valentine wanted it to be an all-girl group, but they couldn't find a bass player, so she enlisted her friend Jesse Sublett, from Jellyroll, who was also working with Olson's boyfriend, guitarist Eddie Munoz, on a band called the Skunks.

The 2610 Guadalupe address had been the site of many failed bars: Buffalo Gap, Hungry Horse #2, Sunshine's Party, and Gemini's all opened and closed in the six years before Raul's, which was also headed to an early grave, as the target audience of construction workers just wanted to get the hell out of West Campus when the whistle blew. Opening a Tejano bar near UT was like a coffeehouse at BYU.

Raul's booked a few of the holdovers from Gemini's, including prog rock band Project Terror, featuring former Electromagnets drummer Bill Maddox on guitar and Glenn Fukunaga on bass for a time. Terror's drummer Stevie Wilson was dating/teaching Marilyn Dean, so the Violators got the opening slot about two weeks after the Pistols ravaged the punk rock Alamo that was Randy's Rodeo. Gonzales liked their desire so he booked the Violators and the Skunks as the first all-punk show of local bands two weeks later. Both Raul's bands played mainly covers—"Pretty Vacant," "Mystery Dance," Stooges, Mott, Damned.

Punk dives were sprouting all over the country, and Austin had its very own CBGB, though instead of real Bowery rats, Raul's had a huge mural of them on the wall, painted by Sarita Crocker, while her Dykes with Dicks bandmate Claire LaVaye read aloud Edgar Allan Poe.

Because this was already a live music city with a standard of aptitude, the groups were generally good, not just drunks stumbling around onstage and taunting the audience, though there was some of that, too.

The Big Boys and the Dicks, led by chubby, gay singers Biscuit and Gary Floyd, respectively, were like no other bands in the country—as ferocious as they were outlandish. Then you had the art rock of Terminal Mind, F-Systems and Reversable Chords, the melodic thrust of Standing Waves, D-Day, and The Norvells, and the wild front man-focused bands like The Next with Ty Gavin and Boy Problems of Billy Problem (Pringle).

"Raul's was Austin proving, yet again, that its local players can hold their own with the best music from elsewhere," summated Margaret Moser. *Live at Raul's*, a 1982 album with Big Boys on one side and the Dicks on the other, has been called one of the top ten skate punk albums (*Phoenix New Times*). And noted SST helmsman Glen "Spot" Lockett, who moved to Austin in the mid-'80s, named The Dicks' *Kill from the Heart* above classic LPs by the Minutemen, Black Flag, the Descendents, and Husker Du as his all-time favorite production.

Bands plant their flag on the wall of Raul's.
Courtesy of Tony Pitts.

Raul's sign. Courtesy of Tony Pitts.

Austin's first punk band, the Violators,
sit on the rubble from the former Mother Earth
rock palace. Courtesy of Jesse Sublet.

ABOVE: Terminal Mind was Steve Marsh *(center)* and the Murray brothers Greg and Doug. Photograph by David C. Fox.

F-Systems, led by singer Lorenda Ash, at Club Foot, February 1981. Photograph by Ken Hoge.

BELOW: The Next, with singer Ty Gavin, at Raul's. Photograph by Ken Hoge.

Led by Gary Floyd, the first openly gay punk frontman, the fearless and ferocious Dicks also featured Buxf Parrot on bass, Pat Deason on drums, and Glen Taylor on guitar. Their "Dicks Hate the Police" remains the most enduring Austin punk song.

"Absolutely nothing phony about the band or the recording" he told *Punktastic* magazine in 2015.

While Sublett was concentrating on the Skunks, the female Violators moved to LA, and did what you do when you leave the comforts of Austin. "We were so homesick," Valentine said, "we'd go out to see every Texas band that played L.A." Valentine and Olson called their next band the Textones.

On a visit home, Valentine had a fling with Billy Pringle, as all our girlfriends seemingly did before they met us. And on the plane back to LA she wrote "Vacation" about how she couldn't seem to get him offa her mind.

Hun's Bust

The Raul's scene started gaining a national rep with "The Huns Bust" of September 19, 1978, when overzealous cops mistook staged chaos onstage for real, and started busting heads. Six clubgoers, including future *Austin Chronicle* publisher Nick Barbaro and Richard Dorsett from Inner Sanctum Records, were taken to jail for defending themselves.

Punk rock in Texas?! That night put Austin on the map as a place where other types of music besides cosmic country and white blues were played. It also established Austin as a town that doesn't take itself too seriously. "I saw a cop walk onstage and I couldn't believe it," Huns drummer Tom Huckabee told the *Daily Texan*. "We said on posters, 'No Police.'" A noted filmmaker, who passed away in 2022, Huckabee described the Huns as sounding like they had Sid Vicious on every instrument. But they were good enough to win the July '79 battle of the bands at Raul's, along with Standing Waves.

With *Rolling Stone* writing about the Huns bust, touring acts like Patti Smith, Elvis Costello, and Blondie popped in to jam at Raul's, and up-and-coming bands like Psychedelic Furs, the Cramps, and Black Flag started getting booked there.

Riots at punk shows were big news, as America wondered what the hell was happening to its young people. One of those who read the *Rolling Stone* story was a high schooler in Del Valle named David Yow, who joined the growing number of Raul's regulars. "It changed the way I thought about music," said Yow, the future Jesus Lizard front man whose first band Toxic Shock put up posters all over town before they had any gigs.

"If you cut your hair short, wore black and hung out at Raul's you became a target for frat boys and hippie rednecks alike," said Roland Swenson, the SXSW director whose entree into show biz was managing Standing Waves. "That bonded the kids in the scene in a way I've not seen since."

Many stepped over to the Raul's side four-plus decades ago and never came back. Or, like Phil Tolstead, they went the other way. The Huns' lead instigator

Big Boys 1980 publicity shot for first single "Frat Cars." Steve Collier, later of Doctors' Mob, was the drummer. Big Boys are recognized as skate punk pioneers. Photograph by David C. Fox.

Standing Waves play Duke's, co-owned by manager Roland Swenson. Photograph by Ben Tecumseh Desoto.

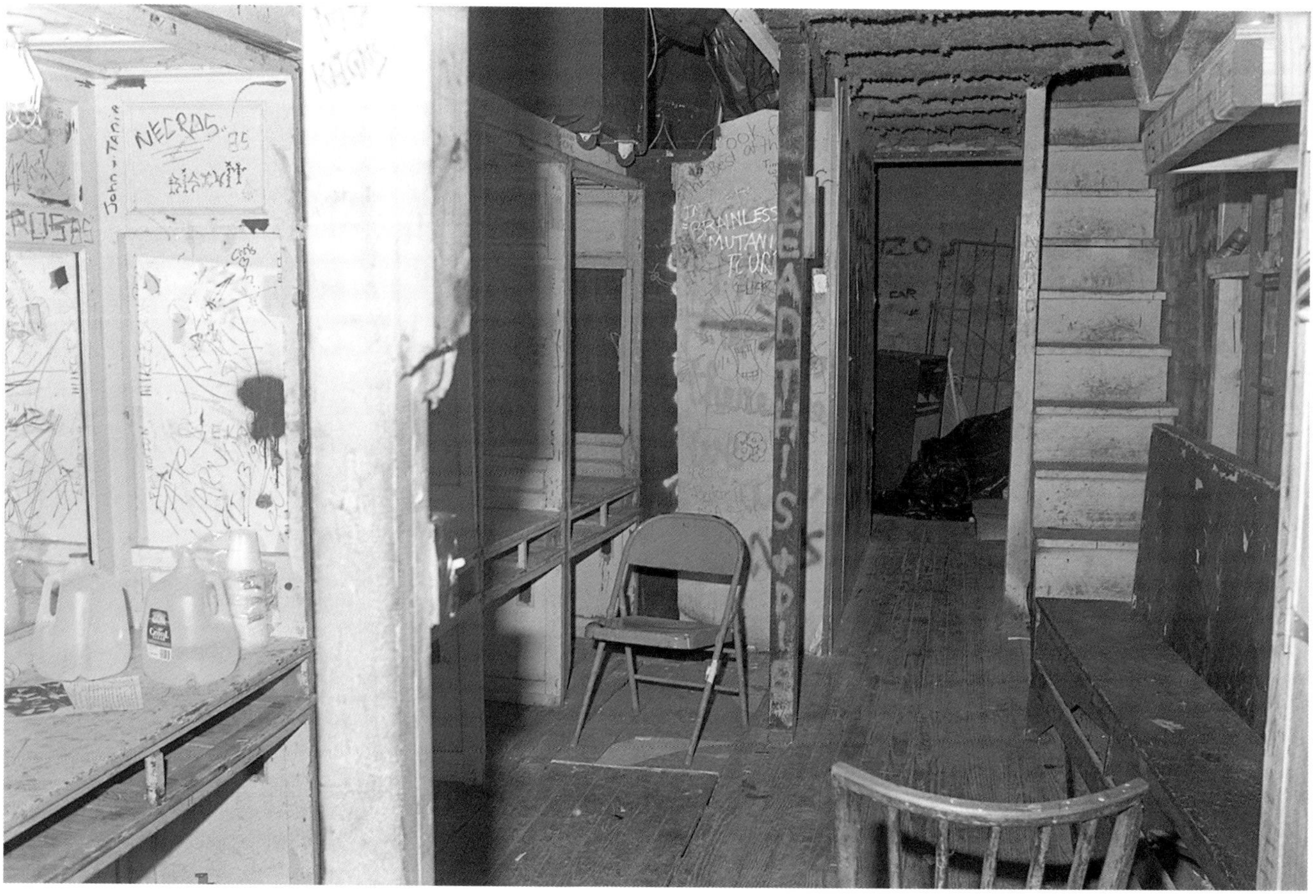
NECROS

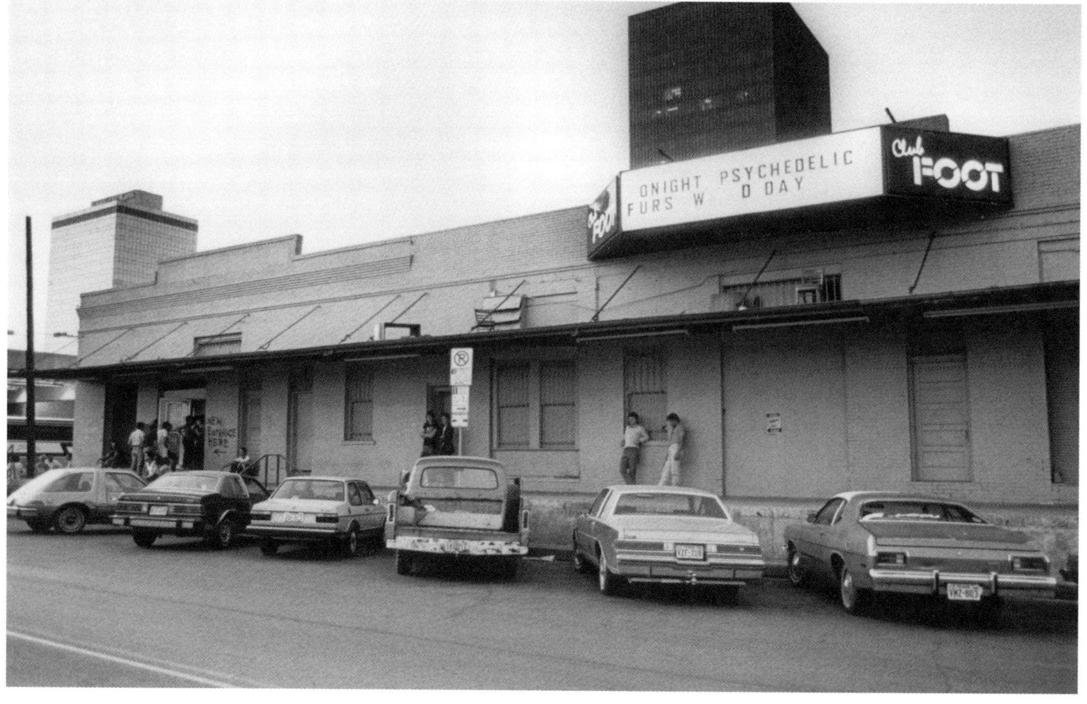

Club FOOT
ONIGHT PSYCHEDELIC
FURS W D DAY

became a soldier in Jerry Falwell's religious right crusade in the '80s. His new stage was *The 700 Club*.

LA's Rank & File was one of the last touring bands to play Raul's in the Spring of '81. Buoyed by the first audience to get their "cowpunk" meld, Chip and Tony Kinman ended up staying in Austin for about a year, before moving on without rhythm guitarist Alejandro Escovedo.

There would be other punk clubs—Duke's Royal Coach Inn, Studio 29, the Ritz Theater, the Beach, and that deathtrap Voltaire's in the basement of a bookstore at 4th and Lavaca. Even the Skyline and the former Charlie's Playhouse (as Club 1206) hosted punk shows, but Raul's was the first, and remains the most legendary.

The club closed the first time in February '80. Steve Hayden resurrected it two months later for one more year of anarchy in the ATX, with a new rule: no cover songs, because he didn't want to pay BMI's music licensing fee. Raul's closed for good on April 1, 1981.

The punk scene wasn't the first grasp of notoriety at 2610 Guadalupe St. In 1965 it was Roy's Lounge, owned by Roy Eazor, who resisted being forced to let Black folks into the club, defying the Civil Rights Act. Roy's was picketed for two months by the Student Interracial Committee, led by Jeff Shero (later "Nightbyrd"), who were often outnumbered by counter-protesters holding signs that said "Support S.P.O.N.G.E." (Society for the Prevention of Negroes Getting Everything). An ex-Marine named Charles Whitman is believed to have been one of the barking segregationists.

The Austin City Council, which called SIC "rabble rousers" and refused to meet with them, and the *Statesman*, which bemoaned that "the main result of the demonstration so far has been the expenditure of thousands of dollars of public funds," seemed to side with Eazor, a popular local figure who would later work on Lt. Gov. Ben Barnes's staff. After going private as Waterloo Club, a last-ditch attempt to legally segregate, Eazor went out of business in late '67, replaced at 2610 by Tex Vanzura's Pink Lizard Lounge. Texas A&M grad Vanzura included the "Aggie War Hymn" (under a different title) on the jukebox, which rankled more UT students than the building's racist past.

OPPOSITE (TOP): The Ritz dressing room during the 1980s punk era. Joe Rogan's fixed the place up as Comedy Mothership. Photograph by Bill Leissner.

OPPOSITE: Club Foot was a former General Electric Supply Center. Photograph by David C. Fox.

Club Foot, 1980–83

This 950-capacity, split-level club, built up vertically for better sightlines, booked several acts that were about to blow up: U2, New Order, Metallica, R.E.M., the Go-Gos, Bangles, X, Stray Cats, OMD, and on and on. But the club's most notorious bookings were a fifteen-piece Nigerian band and a hip-hop group from DC playing the "go-go" strain.

Brad First got fired in 1983 for booking King Sunny Ade, which ended up being one of the most celebrated concerts in Austin music history. The $7,500 fee was high for the three-year-old club, and First also had to charter a bus to bring the group to and from Houston. No touring African band had ever played an Austin club, so it was more risk than Club Foot owner John Bird was willing to take.

The venue at 110 E. 4th Street, behind the Greyhound station, would have to sell eight hundred tickets just to break even. "A $10 ticket was almost unheard of back then," said First, who couldn't risk not booking a band he knew would turn Club Foot into a den of delirium.

Promoted in conjunction with UT's African Student Union, and trumpeted by Dan Del Santo's *World Music* radio show on KUT, the King Sunny Ade show sold out, and those who were there describe it more in religious than musical terms. The Talking Heads 1980 show at the Armadillo on the *Remain in Light* tour primed the local audience in African polyrhythms, but this was the real thing! The crowd gasped in ecstasy after three solid hours of the original groove music.

Even though hurt by his dismissal, the booker was there at the show. "I wanted to see King Sunny, first of all, but I also wanted to see John Bird," First said. Looks like this show worked out, he told the owner, and asked for his job back. "No" was the quick answer. Bird had fired the staff, with plans to rebrand the bi-level club as Nightlife, and it would take more than one sensational concert to turn him around (though later he did rehire First as a freelance booker).

A budding entrepreneur whose dabbles included brokering horse semen to thoroughbred breeders, Bird reportedly "won" a failing gay disco called 110 Club in a card game. With its two-tiered sightlines, Bird returned the former location of Boondocks (whose Lorraine Dillard and her sons had the second level built in 1976), and Bob Porter's short-lived Crazy Bob's Saloon, to a live music format. Jim Ramsey's Spotlight Productions booked the club's first two roadshows—the Stranglers on October 28, 1980, and Gang of Four, with F-Systems

ABOVE: Gang of Four played Club Foot on the night Ronald Reagan was elected president. Photograph for the *Daily Texan*. Courtesy of Dolph Briscoe Center for American History.

BELOW: Pair of Kings: Sunny Ade and Joe Carrasco both had big impacts on Club Foot. Photograph by David C. Fox.

Duke's Royal Coach Inn used to be the Vulcan Gas Company. Photograph by Ben Tecumseh Desoto.

Brad First and some of the musicians he's booked through the years.
Photograph by David. C. Fox.

opening, a week later, on the night Ronald Reagan was elected president.

After berating the crowd of Americans for choosing "a B-list actor" to lead them, the politically radical Gang firehosed the room with danceable punk rock that left everyone dripping. "It was one of those great rock shows that crosses the line into pandemonium," said photographer David C. Fox, who attended with First. "You know that saying about how 'rock and roll saved my life'? That's how that night felt."

First walked back to Duke's Royal Coach Inn, the punk/new wave club he ran with Fox, Roland Swenson, and Sam Staples, and sat there in the dark with head in hands. Our days are numbered, he thought. There was no way bare bones Duke's, in the former Congress Avenue location of the Vulcan Gas Company, could compete with that new live music palace just two blocks away. He'd have to keep selling shoes at the mall to pay the bills.

Duke's had been a down-on-its-luck Mexican bar, taken over and rejuvenated by the punk/new wave scene, just like Raul's before it. When Austin's first punk club closed in February 1980, it created a void that Duke's rushed to fill. But Raul's was back just two months later, booking aggressive punk bands, while Duke's catered to the new-wavers: F-Systems, Terminal Mind, 5-Spot, Gator Family, Standing Waves, Skunks, the Shades, the Next.

With Swenson moving to NYC, temporarily it turned out, with Standing Waves, First met with Bird (the brother of author Sarah Bird) as soon as he could about working at Club Foot. "Duke's had Joe King Carrasco booked, a big draw," said First. "So he said, 'if you can bring Joe King Carrasco to Club Foot instead, you've got a job.'"

Carrasco and the Crowns, who called their bouncy Tex-Mex sound "nuevo wavo," were Austin's big breakout act of 1980, signing to hip British punk label Stiff

Records and taping a crazy, high-energy segment of *Austin City Limits*. They easily sold out Club Foot on their return from a three-month tour of Europe. X was another act First diverted from Duke's.

Ramsey was a freelance promoter, who booked most of the new wave shows at the Austin Opera House, and various other rooms, but Bird wanted someone fully committed to Club Foot. Someone who could fill the calendar seven nights a week, which, First said, caused some of the club's financial shortcomings. Local bands on weeknights rarely broke even.

Brad started booking Club Foot the week the Armadillo closed for good. This is called timing. Antone's was also soon between locations, with an eighteen-month gap between Great Northern Boulevard (#2) and 2915 Guadalupe St., so Club Foot got B. B. King, James Brown, Sam & Dave, Willie Dixon, Albert Collins, SRV, Fabulous Thunderbirds, John Lee Hooker, and other acts that would've went with Austin's "Home of the Blues."

But the club was better known for the acts that exploded on MTV. First convinced Bird to upgrade the club's video screens and sound system. "The perfect club, to me, was one where the people stay after the show and hang out and dance," he said.

Everybody loved Club Foot, but the live music business, with all its overhead and speculation, is not for entrepreneurs. It's for diehard music fans who are delighted to break even on a great show. Thinking all the press and big names meant Club Foot was raking it in, the owner of the building—a former General Electric Supply Center—notified Bird that the rent would increase from $3,300 a month to $11,000 at the end of the lease, and that was it! Bird moved on with new investments, including the Golden Chick franchise.

Brad's final sensational booking at 110 E. 4th, by then called Nightlife, was August '83, when Trouble Funk headlined with the Big Boys opening. Go-go and punk had never shared a stage before, but the Big Boys had added a horn section and were mixing punk and funk a year before Red Hot Chili Peppers. They campaigned for the unusual double bill.

Using "call and response" from the church, Trouble Funk roamed the soundscape in search of the deepest groove and once they found it, they didn't let go. Repetition became hypnotic, with no breaks between songs. The most self-conscious people during the Trouble Funk set at Nightlife were the handful not dancing. Nobody on hand has ever forgotten that night.

The club's final official show was Standing Waves December 17, 1983, though Big Boys rented it for a BYOB punk blowout on New Year's Eve.

The Afro-party moved to Liberty Lunch, where King Sunny and Ebenezer Obey packed the place, plus their mentor, the great Fela Kuti, played there twice. "Direct from Africa" on a club ad guaranteed at least six hundred paying customers, though when Fela played at the soul-less City Coliseum in '86, the show lost money. "There were no dressing rooms at the Coliseum, so we had to put the band in a big bathroom behind the stage," recalled Louis Meyers, who copromoted the show with First. The headliner barked at Meyers: "You do not put FELA in a shithouse!"

First went on to his greatest financial success in 1984, teaming with Jennifer Jaqua and Richard Luckett on Club Iguana—a genius concept that kept all the door, with minimal overhead. A hip dance club without an address, Iguana was straight night at the gay disco, rotating between Hall's in the Warehouse District, Backstreets Basics (later Red 7) on E. 7th, and Oz on Red River each week. But after two years it made like a fad and fizzled.

Cave Club, 1986–88

First missed booking live music venues, so when Oz closed at 705 Red River (current home to Elysium), Brad became his alter ego Feet First, jumping back into the band biz without hesitation.

He painted the walls black, removed the groin-high mirror at the urine trough and rush-opened the Cave Club on Halloween Night 1986.

How long was Cave Club open? Ask a scenester from the '80s and they'd guess four or five years, because it's become so vaunted. But First's club was open only fifteen months. In that short time, the Cave gave the Red River club scene its swagger back and introduced live aggro to this country/blues/folk stronghold. Just a block and a half from Sixth Street, the Cave was christened by Skinny Puppy, Ministry, and DJ Phil Owen, who would go on to form Skatenigs.

Things just seemed to get crazy inside that industrial sweat lodge, which didn't have air-conditioning at first and then only two small window units after a "Cool-Aid" benefit in the summer of '87. You'd get a blast of cold air at the entrance, then step inside the swelter of jampacked shows by Screaming Trees, Scratch Acid, Tackhead, Pussy Galore, Sonic Youth, and a hastily relocated Woodshock 1987.

In a building that served as a mule barn for the army

Artist Frank Kozik *(left)* made his name with posters for the Cave Club, then Emo's. That's Charles "Doug the Slug" Gunning III to his left, and Jason Angola of Nice Strong Arm behind him. Unknown female. Photograph by Bill Leissner.

during WWI, the Cave was just too uncomfortable during the five-month Austin summer. But all that oppressive heat seemed to work for the Butthole Surfers, who did some of their most gloriously warped Austin shows at the Cave during their *Locust Abortion Technician* era. This was when they had the freaky topless dancer who sported a braided goatee (attached with pasty glue). Gibby and the gang could do whatever they wanted, including selling out the joint for their Jack Officers side project, then partying backstage while the programmed experimental dance music played on an empty stage.

The Cave's aura of giddy danger was stroked by the whimsically demented posters of Frank Kozik, the former Atomic City toy boy, who went from nobody to somebody in record time. A lot went on at the Cave, which closed between the first SXSW and the second. First then worked for SXSW, handling the downtown clubs, which led to him being asked to take over Club Coyote, a Wylie's spinoff (get it?) across Sixth Street from the Black Cat in late '88.

Cannibal Club, 1989–91

First renamed it Club Cairo, then Cannibal Club—Sixth Street's first live music venue devoted to alternative rock. Sixth Street had the best live original music scene in town for the first time ever in 1989.

Musicians got in free, and several worked there, with Wammo as DJ, and bartenders Max Crawford and John Nelson (Poi Dog Pondering), Kathy McCarty (Glass Eye), and Kay Klier (Bad Mutha Goose). It felt like the musicians ran the place, which was fine by Brad and bar manager Amanda Bowman, who came over from Wylie's.

During a sweaty show by Afghan Whigs on June 15, 1991, singer Greg Dulli attempted to cool down the crowd with water from a plastic pitcher, but it slipped from his hand and struck a young woman on the forehead, which required stitches. The woman sued the club and won a judgement, and since First didn't have insurance, constables or sheriffs could come by at any time and clean out the cash registers. Unprepared for the first such visit, the Cannibal lost hundreds of dollars in bar sales, which could've gone towards back taxes. After that, First started hiding the money at regular intervals, but the constable kept showing up and taking what he could. The Cannibal was finished, but we'd hear from Mr. Dulli again.

Jesus Christ, What a Hoot?!

The "hootenanny" cover-song-swap tradition in Austin goes back to Threadgill's Tavern on North Lamar, which was packed every Wednesday night during the late '50s/early '60s folk boom.

The concept was an old one, but Wild Seeds leader Mike Hall started the modern "Hoot Night" era Tuesdays at the Continental Club circa 1986. They were pretty loose, like an open mic, except the participants were established musicians doing acoustic covers, as well as new originals.

When Hoot Night moved to Club Cairo in '88, that's when folks started getting creative with the concepts. There was "Exile on Sixth Street," where Jesus Lizard debuted with "I Just Wanna See His Face." Not the one with David Yow in Chicago. This Lizard was a one-off group with Larry Seaman, Randy Franklin, John Ratliff, Sherry Baby, and Darcie Fromholz. That Stones Hoot Night was pretty much stolen by Pariah, recent arrivals from San Antonio, who blasted hair all over the walls on "Rip This Joint."

The Cannibal Club Hoot Nights had a lot of energy because a different person hosted each week, and they'd round up some of their favorite musicians. Band From Hell led a night of songs from *Kiss Alive*, Brenda Hutchison put together a salute to her hero Elton John, and visiting artist Vic Chesnutt took over the Replacements vs. R.E.M. Hoot, berating Austin musicians for doing safe 'Mats covers from *Let It Be* and *Tim* and ignoring *Sorry Ma*. There was even a disco Hoot Night.

You got a lot of fun and recognizable music for two dollars. Especially on July 25, 1989, a night that will live in infamy in local music lore. "Jesus Christ Superhoot" set a standard that nobody could top. A cast of dozens, backed by members of Glass Eye, the Reivers, Stick People, and Poi Dog Pondering, performed the Andrew Lloyd Webber rock opera in its entirety, with the jam-packed audience chanting "Crucify him!" at the right time.

I was living in San Francisco when I heard about this Hootzilla, and suffered serious POMO. I mean, the pain of missing Kris McKay as Mary Magdalene singing "I Don't Know How to Love Him" was too much. Glenn Benavides as Peter? C'mon! Steve Chaney, Robbie Jacks, Malford Milligan, Gretchen Phillips, and Alejandro Escovedo all singing Tim Rice's lyrics!

Paul Swift as Jesus Chris was a revelation. Casting director Kathy McCarty picked the Wild Seeds bassist because he had long hair like J, but no one knew he was

The mother of all hoots revived Jesus Christ Superstar, in track order, with dialogue. Photograph by Bill Leissner.

a musical theater star in college.

The project began when McCarty of Glass Eye started going to Colorado Street Cafe to listen to the Irish music jams and became friends with guitarist Rich Brotherton. Both fans of Richard and Linda Thompson, they started performing the former married couple's breakup songs in public, and also realized a deep affinity for *Jesus Christ Superstar*. "I remember Kathy and Rich sitting in the back of Big Mamou singing and playing the entire album (from memory)," said Mike Hall. Soon, they attracted a singalong throng.

The Superhoot was a natural. McCarty was in charge, with Brotherton the music director, and also playing Judas Iscariot. In the normal hoot process, musicians would pick the song they wanted to do, and sing them in random order. But McCarty pushed for a beginning-to-end presentation including the sing-song dialogue! And they pulled it off with only one rehearsal.

"It was just a transcendent night," said McCarty. "People had tears in their eyes. It was so beautiful."

There was virtually no costuming—one of the apostles was wearing cut-offs—but the music was right on. "It was a turning point for me," said McCarty, "because it showed that I was good at making things happen. I didn't know I could do it."

Copied by the Indigo Girls and other Atlanta acts three or four years later, "Jesus Christ Superhoot" was never redone in Austin because it was next to impossible for everyone to be available again on the same night.

After the Cannibal turned to Jelly in '92, the quirky cover action moved briefly to the Hole in the Wall, where one memorable theme was songs about cross-dressing. (Bands seem to be always looking for excuses to wear women's clothing.) And then Hoot Night kinda ran its course. It was a lotta fun while it lasted. Plus, the bar always did well, with no bands to pay. Like Chicken Shit Bingo at Ginny's Little Longhorn, Hoot Night originated elsewhere, but was perfected in Austin.

The Neville Brothers became part of the Austin music scene whenever they played Liberty Lunch. Photograph by Bill Leissner.

XXIII.

Liberty Lunch Was the Armadillo in the Trousers of '80s Austin

A Dillo Connection

To those of us who moved to Austin in the '80s and had to hear about how we missed all those amazing '70s clubs, think of how much worse that would have been if we didn't have our own AWHQ in Liberty Lunch. But this sacred venue also had a date with the 'dozer, wiped away in 1999 to make room for Computer Sciences Corporation headquarters. The bare-boned venue's demise was determined by two words: city owned. The rent in this prime downtown location was only $600 a month, so the Lunch's days were numbered. For twenty-four years!

Shows were general admission, and we all had our favorite Lunch spot: mine was stage right, six paces back, where the pot smoke from the patio hit the jet stream of sound. The best doorman for the bands and the worst for the pest list was the guy named David who used to perform weird folk as Blanche. He was stone-faced as a Palace guard but couldn't quite mask delight when he made someone from the *Austin Chronicle* pay cover.

Physically, there wasn't much to the room that used to store lumber (and still did in its first few months). No place to sit. No place to shit, at least in private. When preshow adrenaline loosened the bowels, acts had to use the gross prison bathrooms because there wasn't running water backstage. "Are you going to play 'Stinkpot?'" a fan asked a stall-less, squatting member of Soul hat one night. "I'm playing it now."

What made this Lunch so fulfilling was the ever-smiling staff, who got their reward when audience members mouthed "thank you" with a hand on their heart on the way out.

You felt safe at Liberty Lunch, which was all-ages, so many parents just dropped their kids off so they could go out for a quiet dinner—or home for loud sex.

Besides great roadshows, like the February 1992 triplet of Dinosaur Jr., My Bloody Valentine, and Babes in Toyland (Christmas for audiologists!), the Lunch nurtured several local scenes, including funk-rap with Bad Mutha Goose, Do Dat, Bouffant Jellyfish, and Retarted Elf. Any kind of live dance music worked there. Any kind of music really.

"I always thought of it as the Willie Nelson of Austin venues, that one infallible place," said David Garza, who sold out the Lunch with Twang Twang Shock-a-Boom in 1990. When he left the group, prematurely it seemed, only a hundred showed up for his first solo gig at 405 W. 2nd Street. "Lunch don't lie," he laughed.

On a dead night—and there were more of them than Nevilles—the room was so big it was kind of embarrassing for everyone. But a great night, like when Bonnie Raitt jammed with the Meters, or when Ween played for four hours, with never a dull moment, or when Replacement fans burned *Austin Chronicles* in a trash can for heat, was hitting the nightlife jackpot.

Mark Pratz and Jeanette Ward, now married, ran things from '83–'99, but let's not forget the Austin couple that founded Liberty Lunch. Before Esther's Follies, former UT drama students Shannon Sedwick and Michael Shelton took over the site of a former Calcasieu

This is the face of "killed it." Joe Ely at Liberty Lunch, circa 1987. Photograph by Bill Leissner.

Liberty Lunch as it opened in 1975. It was formerly a diner owned by a blind man. Courtesy of Shannon Sedwick and Michael Shelton.

OPPOSITE: Mark Pratz and J'Net Ward arrive at Liberty Lunch, which they rented from the city. Photograph by Bill Leissner.

lumberyard on December 9, 1975. They planned to call this food/performance space Progressive Grocery, but while scraping the paint off the front of the building they saw the name Liberty Lunch from when the smaller, enclosed room was a café in the '50s owned by a blind man, Harold Carlson. During the bicentennial patriotism of 1976, Liberty Lunch was the perfect name.

With chef Emil Vogley, the club's Cajun-flavored restaurant got a rave in *Texas Monthly* soon after opening, but the staff was overwhelmed by the demand. The first Liberty Lunch reputation was for excruciatingly slow service. But the music and the beer in the big, open-air space next door gradually took over, with exotic local bands Beto y Los Fairlanes (salsa), the Lotions (reggae), and Steam Heat (funk), inspiring dancing on the pea gravel floor that created dust storms. This was around when Doug Jacques painted the tropical mural that seemed especially out of place years later when GWAR played and sprayed it with "blood.".

The city wanted to shut down Liberty Lunch and all those half-naked stoned hippies almost from the very beginning. "Liberty Lunch has always been a point of contention with the city," said Sedwick. But something cool was happening. And pro bono lawyers like to dance, too.

After Sedwick and Shelton left to reopen former Lege hangout The Tavern, plus Buffalo Grille on W. Sixth, Charlie Tesar took over the Lunch in 1980. After constant rain canceled shows in the summer of '81, Tesar built a roof over the Lunch with girders, trusses, and beams from the razed Armadillo. A spiritual connection had been forged with these bones of the Dillo, but the old Lunch crowd hated it not being alfresco. Austin was so much cooler before roofs.

The doorman since '78, Pratz started booking the club in '81, then joined with Louis Meyers, manager of Killer Bees, in '83 to form Lunch Money Productions. Reggae, African juju music, and, of course, the Neville Brothers from New Orleans, did especially well. Burning Spear would sell out every time.

The eleven-hundred-capacity Lunch was also the perfect launching pad for breakout bands like Red Hot Chili Peppers, Nirvana, Oasis, Replacements, Foo Fighters, Beck, Pavement, and Alanis Morrissette, too big for the Continental Club, which Lunch Money also booked. You'd see k.d. lang, when she was a rockabilly singer, and then the next night would be Black Flag and then the Count Basie Orchestra.

Stage-diving was a constant distraction at punk shows, but Fugazi had a brilliant solution when they made their Austin debut, opening for Bad Mutha Goose, at the Lunch in May 1989. Ian MacKaye announced that anyone from the audience that jumped on the stage would get a kiss on the mouth. The set started, some young punk still thinking Minor Threat, got on stage and started his leap into the crowd. But MacKaye tackled him, somebody held him down while, for all the audience to see, MacKaye planted a big kiss on the kid's mouth. Homophobia killed stage-diving at Fugazi. For at least half an hour.

In 1998, the city council voted to end the Lunch lease and rent the land to a high-tech company. Mayor Kirk Watson pushed for it, based on an expanded tax base. In December of that year, the Greg Dulli incident happened.

After an Afghan Whigs show, the singer got into a fight

Peter Zaremba and the Fleshtones were always wild at Liberty Lunch. The party continued at the Imperial 400 Motel on S. Congress. Photograph by Bill Leissner.

with a stagehand, was knocked out, and hit the back of his head on the concrete floor, which sent him to Brackenridge with a fractured skull. His lawsuit against the Lunch was eventually dropped, but the club got a black eye in the national music press, with bands vowing to never play there again. It didn't matter that witnesses said Dulli was the instigator; a dark PR cloud was overhead and Liberty Lunch was leveled eight months later. You can't even tell where it used to be.

It was only a building, and a homely one at that, but for over two decades Liberty Lunch was a structure where musicians and fans were at their best, because on a good night it couldn't get any better.

G-L-O-R-I-A-thon

The venue's perfect swan song came in July 1999, when Michael Hall of the Wild Seeds (and *Texas Monthly*) had the ridiculous idea of enlisting Austin musicians to keep playing "Gloria" by Them for 24 hours continuously. Who's going to play at 5 a.m? Or two in the afternoon?

One of Hall's short-lived bands the Brooders started the one-song marathon at 9 p.m. Friday July 23, kicking it off in a trance of vibrato guitars for 15 minutes. And then Hall started singing those lines that launched ten thousand bands; "She comes 'round here..." It was another forty-five minutes until the chorus was reached like a climax. "G-L-O-R-I-A, Gloria!" Twenty-three more hours to go.

The Austin music scene showed up like they do. All night, all day. Jam bands, blues players, shuffle drummers, and sax players. (One thing you'll never see on eBay is a "Gloriathon" bootleg.) One musician came offstage at 4 a.m. to find his car missing, so he went down to the station, filed a report and went back to the club in the morning light, played another hour—and then found his car exactly where he'd parked it. Fresh beers were distributed at 7 a.m., like coffee. The Gloriathon was a twenty-four-hour orgy with bodies coming in and out all day and night. It was just craziness, but everybody came together to put their hands on their hearts. Customers became musicians—playing on the stage where Trouble Funk, Wilco, Ebenezer Obey, Tragically Hip. and many

Davy Jones, Debbie Rombach, J-Net Ward, and Griff Luneburg sing G-L-O-R-I-A! Photograph by Kevin Virobik-Adams.

more kept them enthralled. The Toadies were the last touring band to play that stage, Rick Nelson the first.

At about three in the afternoon, Van Morrison's road manager held up a phone as Van the Man sang "Gloria" at a festival in Scotland, and it was piped over the sound system at the Lunch. He didn't normally perform the 1965 song anymore, Morrison said, but there were a crazy bunch of folks in Austin, Texas playing "Gloria" for twenty-four hours straight, so he dedicated it to them.

A great moment, for sure, but the superstar cameo was a deviation of what was really happening. We were not just toasting a beloved venue and the people who made it shine. We were saying goodbye to a paradise of our youth, a time and place that made us feel as if we finally belonged. The summer of '99 marked the end of the '70s and '80s in Austin. It was time to start families, to get on with the work that would define us, to see what we were really made of now that the fantasy was being torn down.

The last hour of the Gloriathon, with the finish line in sight, was the best. At 8 p.m., the crowd waiting outside to see Saturday's headliner Joe Ely let in, just as the stage was wailing, with about twenty people up there. Joe King Carrasco's dog yelped into the same microphone as his owner—an insane harmony that felt right. The newcomers urged on the hodgepodge orchestra, and for awhile there was no song, just players. It was challenging, abrasive, yet full of purpose, and the audience pumped their fists at the ugly and beautiful dissonance. But here she comes. When they hit the final familiar chorus, something beautiful burst. The whole place, now jam-packed, was singing along and stomping. There is no sadness in the climax.

Historic Night: Run-DMC Ushers in Rap Age on Juneteenth

The first rap concert in Austin was the last one at Municipal Auditorium before it became Palmer. A package show featuring Sugarhill Gang, Grandmaster Flash, Funky Four Plus One, and the bands Kano and Skyy drew three thousand fans on April 1, 1981. "We're not a band," Flash announced during his set with the Furious Five. "We're seven guys and two turntables." Since this show was just eighteen months after the first hip-hop record "Rapper's Delight," Austin was in on the underground sensation relatively early on. But four years later, Madonna's crowd hated her opening act at the Erwin Center, lustily booing the Beastie Boys on May 5, 1985. But the whiny, bratty Beasties were pretty terrible back then.

The golden era of hip-hop introduced itself to Austin audiences six weeks later when Run-DMC played a delirious Juneteenth show at Liberty Lunch. This was a year before *Raising Hell* and its Aerosmith collab on "Walk This Way" drew down the bridge between rock and rap, but Run-DMC had already become the first hip-hop act to record a million-selling LP with *King of Rock*. Joseph "Run" Simmons, Darryl McDaniel, and Jam Master Jay played Austin on a day off from the Fresh Festival package tour, which they headlined. They were hotter'n hell!

So it must've seemed strange when Harold McMillan of the sponsoring Black Arts Alliance picked up the trio at Robert Mueller Airport in his beat-up Datsun B-210 and took them to the seedy Stars Inn Motel on I-35 near 32nd Street. "They were saying 'Hey, man, this ain't in our rider,' but I had to tell them we were just a broke black arts organization," McMillan recalled. The BAA paid Run-DMC $5,000 and ended up making a profit of $6,000 on the $10 show.

McMillan's Datsun with the holes in the floorboard wasn't the only low ride the rap icons took during their twenty-four hours in Austin. When they showed up at Liberty Lunch before the show, they realized that they'd left their records on their Fresh Fest tour bus and enlisted copromoter Louis Meyers to take them to the record store, pronto. Meyers drove them to Sound Warehouse on Burnet Road so they could buy vinyl to rap over. "They

LUNCH

just climbed in the back of the pickup and we were off," said Meyers.

The sold-out crowd was about fifty-fifty Black and white—unheard of in Austin at the time—and they were united in ecstasy when Run-DMC charged out onto the stage. Only problem was that the plywood Liberty Lunch stage had some play in it and every time one of the rappers jumped or even stepped hard, the record would skip. Jay was doing his best to keep the beat going, but it soon became apparent that the only way to save the show was for Run and DMC to be as stationary as possible. They did a lot of that folding arm pose.

It was a thrown-together benefit, but the Run-DMC show is significant for validating hip-hop as a live music event to the rock crowd. This wasn't held at some dance club on Sixth Street, but the proving grounds of Liberty Lunch. Back in 1985, people still didn't know if rap was more than a fad. But when you felt the power of Run-DMC live, you knew it had legs like a Kenyan.

Run-DMC play a Juneteenth concert to remember, 1985.
Photograph by Bill Leissner.

Zeitgeist at the Beach in 1985. *Left to right:*
John Croslin, Garrett Williams, Kim Longacre, Cindy Toth.
Photograph by Bill Leissner.

XXIV.

True Believers in the Zeitgeist of '85

Zeitgeist/Reivers

The way a scene starts is that all of a sudden there are all these bands. Most of them have been around for a while, but it takes a new club or a new musical emphasis for them to find out they are not alone. In Austin in 1983, it was a room upstairs from a mechanic's garage on Justin Lane called Sparky's, though there wasn't a sign. Open only a few months, with sporatic bookings, Lyle Zurik's club hosted such tuneful guitar bands as Zeitgeist, Wild Seeds, and True Believers. "You brought in your own PA and set up in the corner and played," Alejandro Escovedo told the *Statesman*. "They didn't really give out the address because there was something illegal about it. But it was a lot of fun and it generated great spirit amongst the bands."

You could say that BYOB club "sparked" a musical clique that became full-blown at the Continental in South Austin, Liberty Lunch downtown, and the Beach near campus the next year. "I love this new sincerity," Jesse Sublett of the Skunks sniffed when watching a bill of these new *Murmur*-inspired bands at Steamboat. After the subtle diss made Margaret Moser's In One Ear column, the new scene wore insult as insignia, even though New Sincerity sounded like a feminine hygiene spray.

In 1985, Austin was in the throes of a real-estate bust (cheap rent!), but the music scene was booming. In August '85, MTV devoted an hourlong *Cutting Edge* episode to an Austin that the world was finding out was more than Willie Nelson and Stevie Ray Vaughan. "This Ain't the Summer of Love," the Dharma Bums sang in the midst of sweaty, delirious faces that said otherwise.

Austin-based music critic Ed Ward had a lot to do with *The Cutting Edge* coming here. He was in LA when I.R.S. publicist Cary Baker invited him to a screening of an earlier episode, which spotlighted North Carolina bands like Let's Active, The dB's, Dexter Romweber, and the Connells. After the screening, an unimpressed Ward said, "That's no scene! You wanna see a scene? Come to Austin!" Show producer Carlos Grasso took note and started planning a Texas sojourn.

"Everybody was real excited about MTV coming to town," said Pat MacDonald of Timbuk3, the married couple who had moved to Austin just nine months earlier. "We didn't think we had a shot, but you never know." Timbuk3 (no space, insists MacDonald) had a gig on Sixth Street at a place called Mid-City Roadhouse, and Pat made a poster that expressed wishful thinking when he tagged, "As seen on MTV" at the bottom. It just so happened that the producers, in town scouting talent before the shoots, saw the poster and admired the gumption. When Pat and Barbara K played at the Roadhouse the next night, Grasso was one of the only ones in the audience, and the show became an audition. At the end of their second set, I.R.S. president Jay Boberg, summoned by Grasso, was helping the MacDonalds load out.

"Timbuk who?" That's what everyone was saying when the unknown duo made the lineup for the MTV tapings over more popular bands. But by the time their debut LP became a big hit for I.R.S., which produced *The Cutting*

Alejandro Escovedo, Denny DeGorio, Javier Escovedo, and drummer French Acers—the True Believers—play a house party, 1984. Photograph by Bill Leissner.

Edge for MTV with some of that R.E.M. money, the talk turned to "I knew them when."

Timbuk3's "Future's So Bright, I Gotta Wear Shades" hit #19 on the *Billboard* singles chart, but *Greetings from Timbuk3* was just one of many defining recordings of that era: *Mud, Lies and Shame* by Wild Seeds, *Headache Machine* by Doctors' Mob, *Huge* from Glass Eye, the *Scratch Acid* EP, *Sun Tunnels* by the Texas Instruments, *Poison 13* on Wrestler.

The Lost Generation of Jangly Guitars was officially ushered in, however, with the 1985 release of *Translate Slowly*. That Zeitgeist album was proudly Texan (covers of Willie's "Blue Eyes Crying in the Rain" and the instrumental "Hill Country Theme"), yet exotically powerful and artfully accessible.

Talk about chemistry; the interplay between John Croslin's deadpan growl and Kim Longacre's angelic harmonies sounded like Lou Reed joined the Mamas and the Papas. This was a dynamic band of four individuals, including bassist Cindy Toth and drummer Garrett Williams, who swirled in song.

If the major labels drafted unsigned acts like their pro sports counterparts do players, Zeitgeist would've been a lottery pick. The band signed with Capitol, home of the Beatles. They were on their way. Everybody knew it.

They had the songs—"Freight Train Rain," "Things Don't Change," "Sound and the Fury," "Araby," "Secretariat," and so on—that charmed college radio, but Zeitgeist was even better live. Their shows at Liberty Lunch were events, with the front row diehards led by Rob Thomas, who would go on to create *Veronica Mars*. After the show there was always a big, jubilant party 'til the kegs ran out and the speed wore off. Those were nights forgotten by next weekend yet remembered years later.

"Things don't change, they never do," sang Zeitgeist in 1985. Then they had to change their name.

In the summer of '87, the band lost nearly all its momentum when a Minnesota choral group claimed "Zeitgeist" (which means "spirit of the times") in a cease and desist letter. To avoid a lawsuit, Capitol wouldn't put out the next record, the Don Dixon-produced *Saturday*, until Austin's Zeitgeist found a new handle. I suggested Whitegeist, but they went with the Reivers, after the William Faulkner novel. Zeitgeist was such a perfect name.

1985 lasted only two years. A punishing bodyshot came in September '86, when the drinking age rose from 19 to 21, hurting the clubs at the register and the bands in the amount of energy they got back. The Beach closed the next day. But the uppercut knockout was in August '87, when the Mark/J'Net Continental Club shuttered its doors. That was also the year the True Believers broke up, which to the Austin music scene was like an American bald eagle committing suicide.

True Believers

During my four years writing for the *Austin Chronicle*, I was ringside for Joe Ely, Lou Ann Barton, the LeRoi Brothers, the Fabulous Thunderbirds, the Tycoons (Austin's greatest unknown band), Stevie Ray Vaughan, Charlie Sexton, Omar and the Howlers, Evan Johns and the H-Bombs, and on and on. These bands could all raise the roof at a bomb shelter, but each was expendable in our roots-rock-heavy scene. If, say, Joe Ely moved to Montana, Bill Carter could throw on some turquoise gabardine, and hire Bobby Keys, and though it still wouldn't be Joe Ely, it wouldn't be so far off as to make you think about a roadtrip to Butte.

There was no one, however, who could replace the True Believers, the roots band who worshipped T-Rex and the Stooges, creating *glamericana*. They were the only "New Sincerity" band that dressed like rock stars.

If *Slacker* was more realistic there would've been a scene where two people walk down the street and argue True Believers vs. Zeitgeist as Austin's best band, with Teresa ("Madonna Pap Smear") Taylor, popping out of the alley to say that the only correct answer was Butthole Surfers.

Though both bands were influenced by the Velvet Underground, Zeitgeist was harmony-driven, while the Troobs of Alejando and Javier Escovedo, plus Jon Dee Graham, just wanted to fry your nosehairs. On a great night you'd forget your name.

"Who else can make it feel like 5 a.m. in a town that shuts down at 2?," I wrote in 1985. "True Believers can almost make you shoot up the rent money while some skinny skirt trash in troll doll hair leans over the side of the bed, throwing up loud enough to be almost heard over a cranked-up *Fun House*."

But a 1986 self-titled debut album, produced for under $10,000 by Jim Dickinson (Big Star, Replacements), didn't exactly capture the explosion, focusing too much on vocals and lyrics we ignored live. (I had thought their first single was about a lazy party guest ducking cleanup: "Lorraine Won't Help You When It's Over.")

EMI saw potential in *True Believers*, and, having seen them live at the Lone Star Café in NYC (on a night bassist Denny DeGorio was caught in a drug sweep of Union Square Park and replaced by Doctors' Mob bassist Tim Swingle), bought out their contract from Rounder. Our boys were on their way, with a big budget earmarked for the follow-up, produced by Jeff Glixman whose "Keep Your Hands to Yourself" by Georgia Satellites was a huge hit.

Everybody was thinking "She's Got" would be the lead single off TBII. But while finishing touches were being applied, EMI was folded into Manhattan Records, on its way to becoming absorbed by Capitol. The band wasn't lost in the shuffle—they were firehosed.

True Believers died soon after Benedict Escovedo joined MCA recording artists Will and the Kill, who had a tour bus. After five years on the Troobs' hard road, Javier was ready for his own bunk. That "career-making" True Believers album didn't come out until 1994, seven years after the breakup, when Rykodisc combined both the band's albums into *Hard Road*.

After all the media attention on Austin and the emergence of Timbuk3, it was '73 all over again, with bands moving to town in droves. South by Southwest launched in '87 and everyone was looking for a record deal. The amp was blown on a scene that was hyped up to eleven. By the early '90s, even the Butthole Surfers weren't cool anymore.

Austin was tagged the next Athens, GA. But we never produced an R.E.M. or a B-52s, just a whole lotta Pylons and Love Tractors and Guadalcanal Diaries.

In 1985, that was more than enough.

Clubland Paradise: The Two Continentals and the Beach

The Continental Club closed its doors for good on August 29, 1987. It was replaced on New Year's Eve, four months later, by the Continental Club, no relation. Ski Shores owner Steve Wertheimer bought the club from the Shuler family and recast it as a fifties-style hamburg er joint with red-and-black-tiles, and live music at night, like Hut's. He actually put in windows, which made you wonder, was it a diner or a nightclub? It didn't matter,

Junior Brown and guitarist/wife Tanya Rae became a local sensation with songs like "My Baby Don't Dance to Nuthin' but Ernest Tubb." Photograph by John Carrico.

The Beach on San Jacinto was formerly a UtoteM store. The college kid hangout closed the morning the drinking age rose from nineteen to twenty-one. It's been the Crown & Anchor Pub since 1987.

people stayed away those soulless first couple years until Junior Brown's Sunday night residency christened it in roots/country/blues. The guit-steel maestro didn't draw in the beginning, and Wertheimer pulled money from the bar register to keep him coming back. But after word got out that the room was perfect for a guy who sang like Ernest Tubb and played guitar like Jimi Hendrix, the line outside the Continental on Sundays would go all the way up to St. Vincent DePaul. Then, Alejandro Escovedo provided an indelible link when he rocked delirious fans as he'd done with True Believers. Today, the Continental of Steve Wertheimer and his veteran staff has grown into an internationally known roots-rock haven.

BEACH CABARET, 1984-86

During the Pratz/Ward era, the Continental's rival for rock dive supremacy was the Beach Cabaret in a former UtoteM store at 2911 San Jacinto St. In the late '70s/early '80s, it was folkie hangout You Scream Ice Cream (later Folkville Ice Cream), where Michelle Shocked got her start as Michelle Johnston. If you lived north of the river, the Beach was your favorite club.

The Continental was a much better live room, but the Beach was more of a scene. What Chris Mossler's club had was a great big patio that made the Beach feel like the Dog N' Duck outside and Raul's inside. You'd nurse pints and talk about music, then you'd go inside and get blasted, like a cold shower after the sauna.

When MTV came to town in '85 to film cutting-edge Austin bands, they didn't use the Beach, shooting most of the live stuff at Liberty Lunch and the South Bank (Mossler's new club). The Beach may have looked too much like a hangout than a viable venue, but bands like Scratch Acid, Criminal Crew, Cargo Cult, Vertibeads, and the Crybabies, who mixed it up on the calendar with all the bands inspired by R.E.M., loved playing the 150-capacity club because it was like rocking out in a living room jammed with friends.

A musician himself, Mossler had a simple booking policy: if you had a demo tape you could play the Beach. The patio would be packed most nights.

The adopted son of infamous Houston socialite Candy Mossler, Chris died in a one-car accident in 1990, at age thirty-seven. He was a passenger in a 1985 BMW he'd just sold to the driver, who was going 70–80 MPH on the 2400 block of Rollingwood Drive.

CONTINENTAL CLUB, 1955-PRESENT

For a room that was basically a black box, the Continental was a special place because of what happened onstage. From '84–'87, I'd see so many great shows in the cozy confines: Minutemen, accordeonista Steve Jordan, Billy Bragg, the Replacements, Johnny Thunders, the Skeletons, Mojo Nixon & Skid Roper, Del Fuegos, Meat Puppets, Green on Red, Bad Brains, and on and on. On a good night—well, they were all good nights—but on a great one, our own True Believers were the best of all. The no-frills Continental was where you went to make the music part of your face.

That started in September 1979, when the owners of the shuttered One Knite (at current Stubb's location) took over the lease at 1315 S. Congress. "It was a neighborhood bar with a pool table and pinball machine," recalled Roger "Oneknite" Collins, of the dive that opened at 7 a.m. and closed at 8 p.m. "Martin (Shuler), the owner, wasn't thrilled when he heard we wanted to put in live music. He was concerned about his vending machine money, so we had to guarantee in the lease he'd make a minimum amount from the pool table and pinball." Summerdog was hired as bar manager and Wayne Nagel booked the talent.

Stevie Ray Vaughan played every Wednesday, once sustaining a note that made a chunk fall from the ceiling. It seems the Continental stage just makes bands want to play loud, but nobody ravaged eardrums like the guit-slinger some called "Stevie Ray Volume."

Pratz, Ward, and soundman Terry Pearson took over the bare bones club in 1983, kicking up the national bookings with Louis Meyers on the phone, while keeping the focus on local acts that could draw. The club struggled each month to make rent, on top of all the other expenses in running a live music venue. Thank God they had Liberty Lunch.

We have celebrated significant Austin clubowners: Eddie Wilson of the Armadillo, Clifford of Antone's, the Majewskis of Soap Creek, and so on. But they had only one club at a time. Like Charles Gildon (Charlie's Playhouse, Ernie's Chicken Shack), Pratz and Ward ran two of the all-time greatest live music venues in Austin history, simultaneously. It was an insane amount of work.

When Liberty Lunch started getting touring shows in the '80s, it made more sense for the Pratz pack to concentrate there and close the Continental, which had three times the rent and a third the capacity. Still, it was crushing news.

Will Sexton celebrates his seventeenth birthday with a blowout at the Continental Club on August 10, 1987. Brother Charlie *(far left)* turned nineteen the next day. Photograph by Casey Monahan. Courtesy of *Austin American-Statesman* Photographic Morgue at the Austin History Center.

On the last night there were three times more people outside the club than were able to fit inside, where it was brutally hot and gloriously sweaty. Sitting in little clumps on the sidewalk and standing in the street behind the stage, the throng drank 7-11 beer, smoked joints, and reminisced about nights spent inside that windowless room, shut off from the world.

That final lineup was advertised as Glass Eye, Wild Seeds, and Zeitgeist (a month before the name-change to the Reivers). True Believers had another gig in town that night, but, thanks to the generosity of Zeitgeist, who were more of a Liberty Lunch band, they would play the very last set. The buzz went through the crowd as the Troobs turned up at the back door at 1 a.m. like gunslingers. With Brent Grulke (dressed in drag) at the sound board, the Escovedo Gang was so loud folks in the street needed earplugs. It was great, but True Believers blew out Zeitgeist's amps after about four songs. Lasting memory from loadout: John Croslin talking to TB bassist J. D. Foster about paying to repair the amps and Foster shrugging, "Hey, man, that's rock and roll."

The joint has been around since February 1955, when local businessmen Morin Scott and Dorsey Wier (Rusty's father) opened the Continental Club as a "private" lounge so they could serve mixed drinks. The opening week featured the Four Guys vocal quartet from Houston, with future *Hogan's Hero* actor Larry Hovis just out of high school.

OPPOSITE: Charlie Sexton and Eggbo Smith of Water the Dog play the first night of the Wertheimer Continental, December 31, 1987. Photograph by Bill Leissner.

OPPOSITE (BOTTOM): The VIP entrance at the Continental Club 1987. Photograph by Bill Leissner.

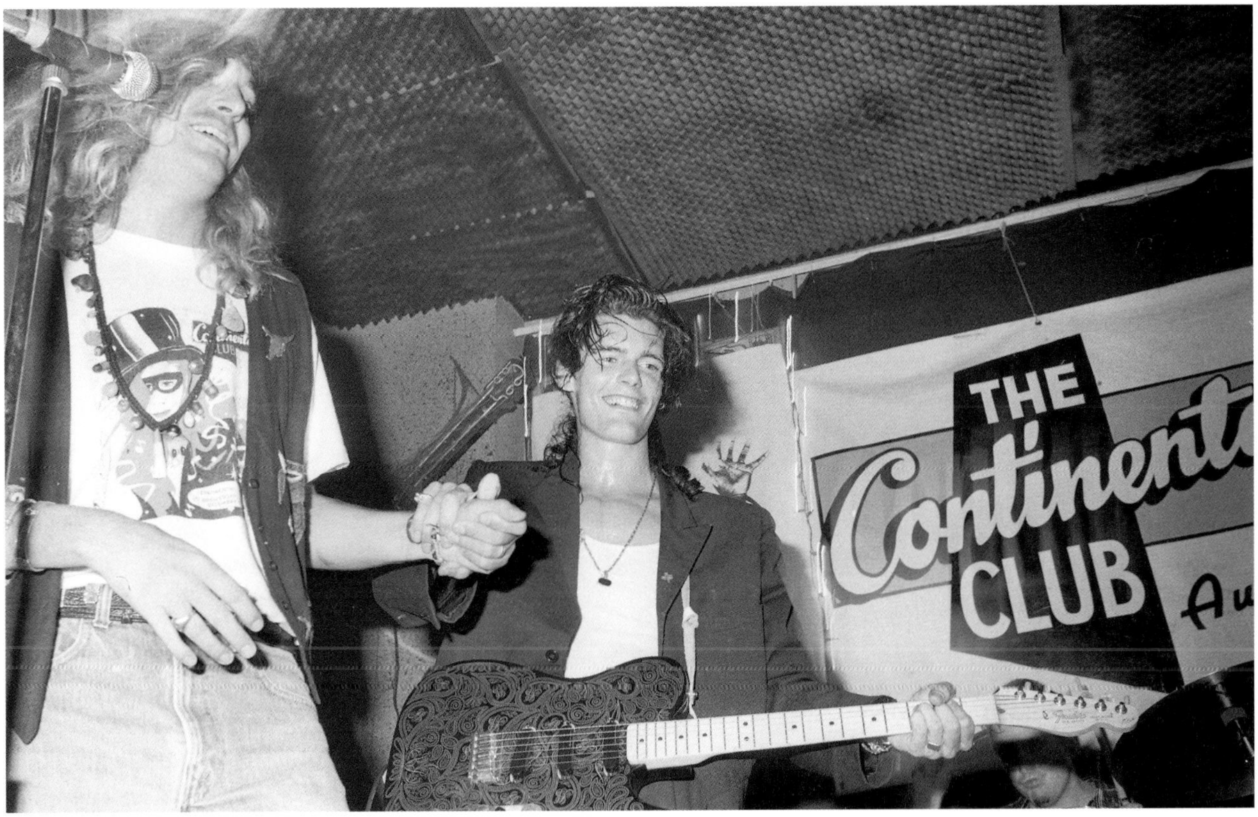
THE
Continental
CLUB

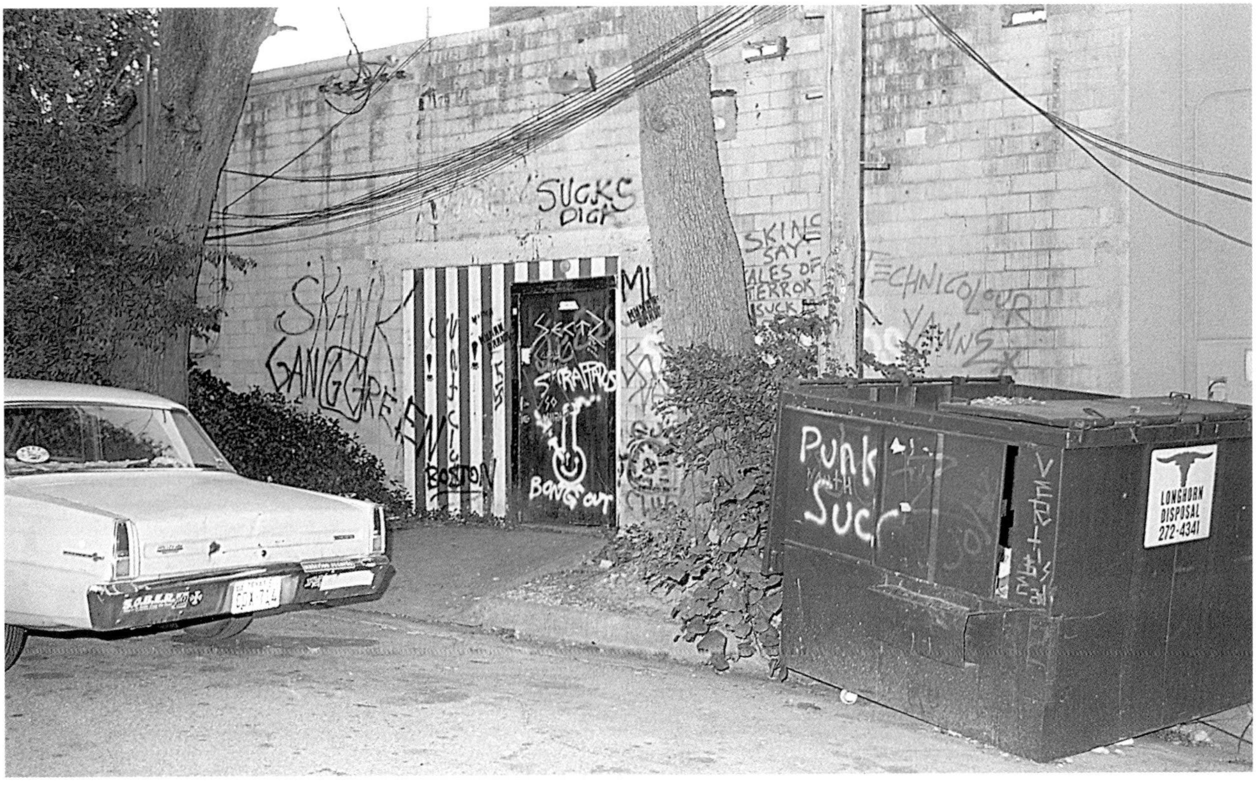
SUCKS
SKANK
GANGGREEN
BOSTON
TECHNICOLOUR
Punk
LONGHORN
DISPOSAL
272-4341

After nine months of operation, the Continental and another private saloon, Jesters Club at 3010 Guadalupe St., were challenged by the Texas Liquor Control Board on their loophole to sell mixed drinks (which wouldn't be legal in Texas until 1971). The clubs reportedly sold liquor to nonmembers. The result of that injunction was the Continental opening to the public in 1956, serving only beer and wine and setups to go with the jazz and Geezinslaws, who made the club their homebase.

In the mid-'60s, the Continental was a topless bar—the second in Austin after Frank Hoffman's Mardi Gras Club. Hoffman took over the Continental in '66 and was shut down a couple times for lewd behavior. The entertainment changed to go-go dancers in bikinis, often dancing to cover bands, the next few years.

It remained that way until Dorothy Armstrong bought the joint and got a permit to sell liquor by the drink in 1972. Thus began the club's barfly years.

The building at 1315 S. Congress Avenue, which opened in the '30s as Spears BBQ Kitchen, then became a washers-only Half Hour Laundry in 1947, has become a special, special place. This is still Austin as long as the Continental Club is rocking.

Unforgettable Night: Buck Owens Is in the House!

Austin is a Buckaroo town, more Bakersfield than Nashville, so it was natural that local musicians did a tribute night to the '60s honky-tonk hero whose twangin' #1s include "Act Naturally," "Sam's Place," and "Waiting in Your Welfare Line." Guitarist Casper Rawls of the Leroi Brothers, and drummer Tom Lewis of the Wagoneers, put the first Buck Owens Birthday Bash together in 1992 and the show was such a blast that it became an annual Continental Club event. Every Travis and Hays County country musician of note put it on their calendar and, as a courtesy, Rawls invited Owens, a native of Sherman, Texas, every year.

And in the fourth year, the country legend showed up! Only four people from the club—Rawls, Lewis, Wertheimer, and singer Kelly Willis—knew ahead of time that it was going to happen and even they weren't 100 percent until Owens came in the front door about an hour into the marathon show. Wertheimer whisked the ultraspecial guest to a roped-off spot at the corner of the bar, but he'd been spotted and it shot through the crowd: "Buck Owens is in the house!"

The seed was planted a year earlier when Owens, deeply touched by the annual birthday tribute, sent Rawls one of his red, white, and blue guitars. On the pick guard Owens had engraved, "To Casper, I might see you August 12, 1995!"

Indeed, Buck's private plane was en route to Austin that day, with singer-songwriter Jim Lauderdale and Buckaroos pianist Jim Shaw along for the jam.

After checking things out for a bit, Owens took the stage to sing a duet with Kelly Willis on "Loose Talk" and the crowd lost it. Later, Owens joined Rawls and the house band for three numbers: "Love's Gonna Live Here," "I Don't Hear You," and "I've Got a Tiger by the Tail." A birthday cake and a raucous singalong of "Happy Birthday" followed. It was a party no one present will ever forget.

Lewis said that the moment that's stayed with him came late in the show, when Buck came from his stool in the back corner to the side of the stage to watch the Derailers, who wore matching suits like the Buckaroos and modeled their sound after the Telecaster-driven band from Bakersfield. As Tony Villanueva and Brian Hofeldt tapped into the chemistry of Owens and his long-gone musical soul mate Don Rich, Buck had tears in his eyes.

ABOVE (TOP): Surprise guest Buck Owens is joined by Kelly Willis at the Continental. Photograph by Martha Grenon.

ABOVE: Continental Club ad, 1961.

RIGHT: Steve Wertheimer, circa 1988. Photograph by Bill Leissner.

When she first moved to Austin in the ’70s, Lucinda Williams was billed by first name only. Publicity photo. Courtesy of Briscoe Center.

XXV.

Folk Survives, Thrives in the '80s

Cactus Café, Alamo Lounge, emmajoe's, Chicago House

When the Texas Union reopened in 1977 after a two-year, $5.7 million renovation, it featured a new coffeehouse called the Cactus Café. But long before that, going back to 1933, the space was known as the Chuck Wagon. It was a campus restaurant that became more of a beatnik hangout in the early '60s—Janis Joplin sang there. During the Vietnam era of campus unrest, it drew radical hippies and runaways and was the site of a November 1969 riot, when police were called to remove longhaired townies. "Pigs Keep Out" was spray-painted on the wall to no avail. Twenty-one protestors were arrested and many heads were cracked. Days earlier, the Texas Union board voted to restrict the Chuck Wagon to students, staff, and faculty.

Defending the police, the *American Statesman* referred to "pot smoking nonstudent scum" and bemoaned the loss of the catch-all vagrancy charge "that covered every subject from street corner loafing to murder."

Cactus Café, 1977–Present

In its first two years as the Cactus, the 120-capacity venue was used mainly for plays, dance recitals, meetings, and symposiums, like the November 1978 "Is Rock Dead?" panel of famed music critic Lester Bangs, Sterling Morrison (ex-Velvet Underground), writer John Morthland, and Alex Chilton, who played Raul's the night before. The occasional music bookings in 1977 included jazz singer Natalie Zoe, folkies the Shucker Brothers, and the Cabaret Revue of show tunes.

Perhaps 1981 should be considered the true birth year of the Cactus because that's when student Griff Luneburg started working there, first as a bartender who taught himself to run the PA on Thursday night's open mic.

The next year, Griff was promoted to talent booker. He started charging cover—two dollars—with Nanci Griffith in October 1982. Lyle Lovett played for free his first year at the Cactus and eventually got three dollars at the door.

There had been a previous folk club in the Union from '68–'73 when Le Potpourri hosted singer-songwriters like Michael (Martin) Murphey and Keith Sykes from Memphis for a week at a time. But there was no scene there, no vibe. There almost never is on a college campus, but Griff's Cactus was different. It was stamped by Townes, who played there almost a hundred times in fifteen years, in all stages of readiness to perform. "He always had the songs," Luneburg said of Van Zandt's shaky final appearance at the Cactus, "and that's what people came out to hear." Van Zandt passed away on New Year's Day in 1997 at age fifty-two.

Guadalupe St. folk club emmajoe's closed during Luneburg's second year at the helm, leaving Austin's best singer-songwriters looking for a new place to play. They found it on campus seven blocks away. As an emmajoe's regular, Luneburg knew who he wanted playing the club he modeled in his mind after NYC's Gerde's Folk City.

Police clashed with protestors outside the Chuck Wagon, November 1969.
Courtesy of Dolph Briscoe Center for American History.

In high school in Houston, Griff bought an 8-track of Bob Dylan's *Blood on the Tracks* for something to listen to on the way to the beach, and has been a song freak ever since. That he was able to run a club at twenty-two that booked the best songsmiths out on tour was like being called up to the majors.

Not taking that opportunity lightly, Griff was why the Cactus was universally regarded as one of the top listening rooms in the country. He had great taste and knowledge, but that's not rare. He would go extra, like how he'd configure the seating according to advance ticket sales, so the room always looked full. The Cactus made you want to excel as an audience member. A "no talking" sign was not needed.

Distance and volume keep performers safe from revealing too much, but there was no place to hide at the Cactus. Bruce Robison, Darden Smith, Carrie Rodriguez, and Slaid Cleaves are just four of many popular Austin acts today who didn't know for sure that they could do this intimate thing until they bowled 'em over at Griff's Folk City.

Think of any acoustic act that's recorded a song in the past thirty years that gave you goosebumps—most of them played the Cactus. Among the best I saw were Bill Morrissey, Ralph Stanley, Kasey Chambers, Todd Snider, Maura O'Connell, Gillian Welch, and Ruthie Foster. But just as memorable are the shows I missed, but have replicated best I could in my mind, like Jesse Winchester and Townes Van Zandt so soon before their passings, and Butch Hancock on four of the six nights he played for two hours without repeating a song all week.

There's one Cactus night in particular I'll never forget.

I was one of only fourteen people or so to see John Hiatt in the Spring of '87. This was right before *Bring the Family* would revive a career almost destroyed by drink and drugs. Across town that night, the Back Room drew a sellout crowd of six hundred for Richard Thompson's solo debut in Austin. I just wanted to hear Hiatt sing "She Loves the Jerk," and head on over to the Back Room lovefest.

But Hiatt, wearing suspenders over a white dress shirt with rolled up sleeves, played as perfect a solo acoustic set as I'd ever witnessed. He opened with "Memphis in the Meantime," followed by other brilliant songs we'd never heard before: "Thing Called Love," "Tip of My Tongue," "Stood Up," all sung with the feeling of new sobriety that becomes addictive. He was in a zone and so were we, "the Cactus 14." At the end he went to the piano and played another brand-new song, "Have a Little Faith in Me." Think of how great that must've been and multiply by five. The Cactus math.

I stopped by the Back Room afterward, but my brain had no more room for music and drama that night. I lasted three songs, though everyone there will tell you Richard Thompson was fantastic.

Griff Luneburg made the Cactus Café a world class listening room. Photograph by Todd V. Wolfson.

THE CACTUS DEBACLE

In 2009, right before Christmas break, came unfathomable news: the richest state university was closing its world-famous Cactus Café listening room in a cost-cutting move. The outrage from the music community was swift and intense, and the protest became a national story. Chip "Wild Thing" Taylor quickly penned "Don't Let the Cactus Fail" with the opening line: "Will we not walk with heads bowed down/On the UT side of town."

The negative press for UT was unrelenting, and eventually the university caved, thanks to KUT stepping in to manage the Cactus and absorb any losses, which had been about $150,000 a year. But Griff's job was sacrificed. Over his twenty-eight-year tenure, he'd made the Cactus special, but Griff was getting sloppy with the bureaucratic details that come with a university-funded venture. His demotion to the union's underground bowling alley had some folks vow to never come back to the listening room.

The Cactus reopened, but it just wasn't the same—until someone with a guitar and words jumped the turnstile to your heart. When there's magic onstage, what's happening behind the scenes doesn't matter.

Remember the Alamo Lounge and emmajoe's!

Before the Cactus, one-name folkies Lucinda, Townes, Blaze, Butch, and Nanci played the Alamo Lounge and emmajoe's, which tag-teamed the folk scene from '79–'83.

"The night we closed the Alamo Lounge on November 13, 1981, we had Butch Hancock, Jimmie Gilmore and Joe Ely," recalled owner Bobby Nelson (not Willie's sister). "And the very next night we opened emmajoe's with Butch, Jimmie and Joe. It was a continuation in spirit of the Alamo, but emmajoe's was even more like home for the musicians."

Butch Hancock built the bar with wood from old doors the Alamo Hotel was going to scrap, and all the Alamo regulars had some input in the room's design and sound.

ABOVE: Butch Hancock built the bar and owned the stage at emmajoe's. Photograph by Dana Kolflat.

LEFT: Mandy Mercier and Tommy Hancock get ready for a fiddle jam at emmajoe's, circa '82. Photograph by Dana Kolflat.

In framed mugshots above the bar were those who inspired the name: early-twentieth-century radical socialists Emma Goldman and Joe Hill. The ladies room said "Emmas" and the men's room said "Joes."

The club's only recognized holidays were Labor Day and International Women's Day, which was a big mindset departure from the decade of topless joints, like Mr. Lucky's and Fox's Den, which preceded it at 3023 Guadalupe.

The Alamo Lounge and emmajoe's, both managed by Nelson's boyfriend Martin Wiginton, followed a turbulent baptism to the club business.

The Split Rail 16

In 1977, Nelson bought the Split Rail Inn, the redneck/hippie hang on S. Lamar, and reopened it as a workers' co-op. The plan was to keep it no cover, with conjunto music on Thursday and country music the rest of the time. But the young staff wanted changes, like a healthier menu and male servers in addition to females. "That turned off some of the good ol' boys, who were interested in pinching the waitresses," Rick Piltz of the co-op told the *Statesman*. The kids also wanted to book more rock and blues bands and less country music, which they found sexist and racist.

The Split Rail had been the first beer joint in town where longhaired liberals and good ol' boys coexisted without incident. But that changed fast when the commies took over. "The rednecks didn't like us and they let it be known," said Gary Floyd, the future frontman of the Dicks, who got a job at the Rail soon after moving to Austin from Palestine, TX. "Everybody did everything, so I cooked, served beer, bused tables, whatever was needed." He said the rift started when Wiginton began acting like the boss and not a member of the collective. He didn't want to alienate the regulars, who paid the bills.

A month after reopening, the co-op voted to remove from the menu all fried food, including the prized chicken fried steak and onion rings, and Wiginton barked, "No fucking way!" He lost his shit when a fifty-pound bag of brown rice was delivered, and started firing people. Thwarting this "capitalist takeover," the co-op voted to fire Wiginton instead. They also barred Nelson from the premises, but she had the lease, so she told them all to leave. When they didn't, she had them arrested for criminal trespass. Even after Nelson quickly dropped the charges, "the Split Rail 16" picketed the club for about a month.

The night of July 9, 1977, several Rail regulars, some jumping out of the back of a pickup, attacked the hippie protestors and sent one to the hospital. It was big news.

"We were putting on a play that night, spoofing Martin, and you could see him and Bobby looking at us through the window," said Floyd, who left before the violence the collective said Nelson, Wiginton, and Rail bartender David Apke participated in.

Nelson admitted slapping Lori Hansel in the face, but it was in response to the workers' rep calling her the c-word. The attackers claimed the prankster protesters were the instigators, and maybe they were. No charges were filed.

Eventually, the contentiousness died down and Nelson and Wiginton ran the Split Rail as they wanted. Some of the acts booked regularly were Alvin Crow, Jon Emery, Dixie Diesels with Shawn Colvin, and Partners in Crime with Buddy and Julie Miller.

But the club was torched in December 1978, by arsonist/s never found, who set the fire by burning balled up newspapers in scattered locations. The Split Rail of Freda and the Firedogs was a model of divergent cultures behaving themselves together, but a club by a collective didn't work. There was never any talk of running the Alamo Lounge or emmajoe's that way. Nelson and Wiginton learned their lesson.

Chicago House, 1987–95

There used to be an upstairs coffee shop with singer-songwriters on Trinity at Sixth Street called Chameleon's, but it opted out of the jungle after two years and moved to Brodie Oaks in '86. The relocation couldn't save it, however, and Chameleon's closed after less than a year on South Lamar.

That left Jimmy LaFave without a place to play. Nobody else in town would book the Stillwater, Oklahoma, singer-songwriter who tucked his jeans into his boots like an Okie would, so two of the four Chameleon's partners—Glynda Cox and Peg Miller—got the lease back at 607 Trinity. They took the name of the railroad workers hotel built in 1842 at that location.

"LaFave literally was the impetus for Chicago House to open," Miller told the *Statesman* in '89. Comparing his songwriting to Bob Dylan, with "the best voice you have ever heard," Miller said she and Cox "couldn't believe (LaFave) wasn't getting gigs. We thought, 'this is insane.'"

Chicago House opened in June 1987, with seats salvaged from the Varsity Theater, and somehow made it

Jimmy LaFave and Christine Albert were Chicago House regulars. Photograph by Randy Dees.

eight years, with Cox and Miller clawing for survival every step of the way, even bagging up aluminum cans to pay the electric bill. After six months they were able to renegotiate their $3,000 a month lease, but the duo never cut back on their commitment to provide a space that nurtured talent, not just in music, but experimental theater, poetry, and dance. They had two floors in the building and often hosted simultaneous performances.

Just ten months after they opened, the lesbian couple was attacked one night walking to their car, with Cox stabbed fourteen times with a screwdriver. But they were back on Trinity as soon as they were able, with Miller at the soundboard and Cox at the door.

If the Broken Spoke seems incongruous amongst the condos of South Lamar, consider a folk music club in the middle of a bass-thumping Sixth that was just starting to get Dirty. But on a magical night, Chicago House made you feel like you were in Greenwich Village in the '60s. Besides LaFave, regulars included Beaver Nelson, soon to be signed to Columbia by the A&R rep who found Destiny's Child; Tish Hinojosa, whose *Estrella Noche* (1991) was Watermelon's best-selling album; a nineteen-year-old kid from San Angelo named Will T. Massey, who would soon be signed to MCA and coproduced by Roy Bittan of the E Street Band; former attorney David Rodriguez, returning to his songwriting roots with *Man*

Against *Beast*, a fifteen-song cassette recorded live at Chicago House in 1990; and Jo Carol Pierce, a crisis hotline operator whose musical monologue *Bad Girls Upset by the Truth* brought her national recognition—and a tribute album—as a songwriter of rare depth and humor.

Austin is not a special music town for what happens in the big venues or weekend festivals. It's the small places on weeknights, like when Alejandro Escovedo, still smarting from the breakup of the True Believers, found out his songs didn't need to hide behind electric guitars. The Grackles of Kevin Russell and Jimmy Smith became the Gourds after a few run-throughs at the Chicago.

Not solely for nervous first-stagers, the Chi House open mic, which added Monday to Wednesday in year two, was also where veteran songwriters would unveil new songs, much like name-standups working out material in comedy cellars. Bluesman Chris Thomas King was signed to Warner Brothers based, in part, on a performance at the Chicago, but he kept coming back to open mics to keep his songs sharp and to soak up what he could from others.

"It was like a competition among songwriters," Barb Donovan said in Kathleen Hudson's 2013 book *Women in Texas Music*. "There was nothing in your world but writing the next song... I don't think a club has matched that energy since."

LaFave ran the Wednesday open mic until his career took off with an album he recorded live at Chicago House in 1991. The breakout track on *Austin Skyline* was a beautifully heartbreaking cover of "Walk Away Renee," a '60s pop hit by the Left Banke. Every songwriter's nightmare was having to follow that at a guitar pull.

The album's timing was good for LaFave because a year earlier, 107.1 FM changed formats from smooth jazz to an Adult Album Alternative playlist (AAA) with KGSR. As Joe Gracey had done before him at KOKE-FM, KGSR's program director Jody Denberg put an emphasis on local artists, so Joe Ely and Eliza Gilkyson held their own with Bob Dylan and Emmylou Harris. We love to hear our neighbors on the radio.

As the format, later called Americana, gained stations across the country, programmers checked KGSR's song rotation for tips on what to add, giving national airplay to not only LaFave, whose original "Only One Angel" lit up request lines, but other local acts like Ruthie Foster, Slaid Cleaves, Michael Fracasso, Jimmie Dale Gilmore, and Kelly Willis.

"It's amazing how you can slowly build your following for ten years, then you get a little airplay and 'Boom!' the next thing you know, your shows are packed and people are buying your record," LaFave said in '92.

But he never forgot Sweet Home Chicago House, returning to play benefits, or just dropping in unannounced to unveil a couple newbies. The rent and the Sixth Street hassles got too high, and the House was forced to close in 1995. Eight years is a miracle when you're not booking for bar sales.

The three heroes most responsible for "the atmosphere that produced a mountain of songs" (Donovan), all passed away in their sixties. But what a lasting impact was made by Glynda Cox, Peg Miller, and the singer-songwriter with the soulful whisper that inspired them to build their House of perpetual expression.

Jo Carol Pierce debuted "Bad Girls Upset by the Truth" at Chicago House. Photograph by Martha Grenon.

Big Joe Turner ("Shake, Rattle and Roll") has Clifford Antone

XXVI.

Clubland Paradise: Guadalupe Street

Antone's #3, 1982–97

Being a music critic in Austin in the '80s was the nerd version of *Goodfellas*. We just went where we wanted and if anyone complained, we hit them back so hard in the pages of the *Austin Chronicle* they'd never do it again.

The closest Austin got to Henry Hill's serpentine stealth entrance to the Copacabana was the kitchen back door at Antone's on Guadalupe. Waiting in line was for suckers.

The kitchen, built for Shakey's Pizza in the '60s, was no longer operational, so there was no banter with cooks. Instead, there were blues greats like Hubert Sumlin, Willie "Big Eyes" Smith, and Lazy Lester, just hanging out, shooting the breeze with Sugar Bear, the gentle giant who usually ran the back door. These guys would tell stories, like how the drummers in Chicago blues joints would hit the cowbell whenever someone's wife or girlfriend came in. They'd crack each other up, and you'd laugh too, even though you could usually make out only every fourth word.

Scene old-timers will tell you that the greatest location of Antone's was the first one, which opened in 1975 across from the Driskill Hotel. All the living legends of the blues played there, except Howlin' Wolf, number one on Clifford's wish list, who passed away after a long illness in 1976.

Everyone gets the Antone's they deserve, and I felt blessed with the one on Guadalupe. After Shakey's, that six-hundred-capacity place at 2915 Guadalupe was the Still dance club, then Hondo's Saloon, then A.J.'s Midtown, for a couple months before Antone's. It's where U2 famously jammed with the Vaughan brothers and T Bone Burnett after their sold-out show at the Erwin Center in November '87. This club helped resurrect the career of Buddy Guy, who had retired from touring until Clifford booked him for two delirious, sold-out nights. "You need a place like Antone's in order for people to know we're still around and alive and playing this music," Guy said in a 1988 interview, when he toured the West Coast in an Antone's Blues Revue with Kim Wilson, Albert Collins, James Cotton, Luther Tucker, and other Antonians.

Because of the platinum success of Stevie Ray and the Fabulous Thunderbirds, plus that killer house band of Derek O'Brien, Denny Freeman, Sarah Brown, George Rains, and Mel Brown, Antone's was fast becoming internationally known. Every celebrity passing through had to pop in, and if they thought they could play a little they jumped onstage. My favorite night was when Bruce Willis moonlighted as a blues harp player with the house band. Not that part, the next, when Snooky Pryor of Chicago followed and showed "Bruno" how it was done. Antone's was home of the blues snob, where that Hollywood shit doesn't count for much.

Blues education was big with owner Antone, who gave long "Cliffipedia" intros to little known sidemen like Wayne Bennett (Bobby Bland), Grady Gaines (Little Richard) and Matt "Guitar" Murphy (James Cotton). And nobody, heckled his resume-rattling because that was part of the deal. Clifford wanted everyone to love the blues like he did, though that wasn't possible.

Antone's second location, opening in September 1979 and closing fifteen months later, was on Great Northern Blvd., near MoPac and Anderson Lane. It

The third location of Antone's was formerly a Shakey's Pizza.
Photograph by Todd V. Wolfson.

Stevie Ray Vaughan in the studio with the Cobras.
Photograph by Van Brooks. Courtesy of AusPop archives.

Clifford Antone receives visitors Diana Ray and Connie Vaughan at Big Spring correctional facility on a day the Cobras played for inmates. Courtesy of Diana Ray.

was a big room, too big for the blues, and it was way north. Clifford booked some great shows—James Brown, B. B. King, Jerry Lee Lewis, and the night Iggy Pop sang "St. James Infirmary" with Bobby "Blue" Bland. But the club had to expand to country—George Jones, Johnny Paycheck, Gary Stewart, Tanya Tucker—and Mexican *orquestra*—Little Joe Hernandez and Ruben Ramos—to keep the lights on. In a September 1980 interview with Ed Ward, Antone said he'd rather just book blues, but those shows were break-even at best. Antone's #2 closed in early 1981.

Clifford looked for a place closer to downtown, with less overhead, and thanks to his Lebanese connections (relatives still own Centennial Liquors, El Patio, and the building where Antone's Records stands) found 2915 Guadalupe. With the perfect size and location, Antone's #3 opened in the summer of '82.

That was the year Antone was arrested for felony marijuana possession in a restaurant parking lot on Oltorf St. He pleaded guilty in '84 and spent fourteen months in the Big Spring federal prison, where the blues came to him. The Cobras were one of the Antone's bands to play for prisoners when Clifford was locked up. Club managers Diana Ray and Connie Vaughan made that three-hundred-mile drive when they could.

Antone's had a great run in the '80s, but business slacked off in the '90s, when Sixth Street dominated the nightlife. Maceo Parker's previous three-night stands, filled with wildly-dancing UT students, were cut to one. Even Antone was rarely seen at his namesake club, which hired SXSW cofounder Louis Meyers to book it in 1995.

Moving in '97 to Jellyroll piano bar on West Fifth was the new look Antone's needed, especially when Bob Schneider's filthy funk band the Scabs packed the place every Tuesday (with Bob's gf Sandra Bullock beaming side-stage.) One night a band called Summerteeth blew everyone away. That was Wilco playing under the name of the album they were in town recording.

After a short-lived move to East Riverside, where it was part of the Emo's complex, Antone's was back on East Fifth Street in 2015, moving into the former Maxey Glass Company. Just a few blocks from the original Antone's, they've started selling the family's po'boys again, which was one of the conditions of the loan that put Clifford in the club business in the first place.

Hole in the Wall, 1974–Present

When Antone's was cranking at #3, Guadalupe Street had three significant live music venues. The other two were the Hole in the Wall at 2538 Guad and Austin Outhouse ten blocks north of that.

From '84–'88 I worked or lived at 2712 B Guadalupe: China Sea Tattoo in the front and Mr. Lucky T-Shirts in the back. After Rollo Banks moved his shop to South Lamar, where El Meson is now, I took over the lease ($275 a month) and slept in a loft bed in the Mr. Lucky's portion. I rented the front to photographer Bill Leissner for his studio. My flop was two short blocks north of the Hole and two long blocks south of Antone's, plus the *Austin Chronicle*, which allowed me to get into those clubs free, was just a block away down the alley. The Lazy Daisy twenty-four-hour restaurant was at 2815 Guadalupe. I was making just $350 a month from the *Chronicle*, but living like a rockin' fella.

I also had Suzee's Chevron card as a parting gift/guilt offering so I could live off microwaved burritos across the street if I had to. But because they also sold beer, she took her card back after the first bill came. "How could you possibly spend $300 a month on 99-cent burritos?!" In my defense, she was the reason I had to get drunk every night.

The Hole and the Outhouse were similar dives, slutty sister clubs, where bands came to embrace the in-your-face audiences as part of the show. But there was one big difference. At the Hole, bands played in the picture window like some Bowery Esther's Follies.

Hole booker Steve Hiltz used to scout the Outhouse, and one night in early '85 he excitedly returned to tell owner Doug Cugini about his latest discovery. It was a married couple new to town, who played a kind of bluesy folk with a jambox for a rhythm section. "I thought he'd lost his mind," said Cugini. "He booked someone who played to a recording? At the Hole?!" A year later, Timbuk3 was all over the radio with "The Future's So Bright, I Gotta Wear Shades," and in telling their story, in print and on TV and radio, they made the Hole famous.

But not rich. Austin's *Cheers*, where everybody slurs your name, turns fifty in 2024, but it looked dead in the water in June 2002, when bartender/owner Debbie Rombach shuttered the club after ten days of blowout benefits. Some bands thought they were playing to save the club, and grumbled when the money raised went towards erasing debt.

The closing was front page news and covered by all the local TV news teams. But the Hole came back a year later, after Austin's Pizza's owners bought the building,

ABOVE: Pat MacDonald and Barbara K became a local sensation at the Hole in 1985 and returned as "Fred and Wilma" after stardom. Photograph by Karen Messerman.

Emmylou Harris jammed with Rosie Flores at the Hole in the Wall following her *ACL* taping on August 13, 1988. Terry McBride on bass, Steve Fishell on steel. Photograph by Casey Monahan.

BELOW: Commandos were *(left to right)* J. J. Barrera, Suzy Elkins, Phareaux Felton, Ram Garza. Photograph by Scott Van Osdal. Courtesy of Suzy Elkins.

cleaned it up, and recast the club to appeal to a broader audience than the daytime stool-flatteners and music fans who had to order over them. Added was a beer garden with a separate bar, so grad students could discuss Eastern philosophy and Vince Young over pints of ale without having to shout over the Rockland Eagles.

Previously, the Hole really wasn't much of a hangout for UT students. Rather than be part of the Charles Bukowski story unraveling inside the door with the baseball bat handle, students would pass by in droves on their way to the Texas Showdown in one direction or Abel's in the other.

Music was an afterthought at 2538 Guadalupe St., which had been Longhorn Cleaners for three decades, before the Cuginis—Doug and his parents Orazio and Billie—got a five-year lease on a handshake deal in 1974. They came down from Buffalo when Orazio got a job with defense contractor Tracor, the first Austin-based business to trade on the New York Stock Exchange.

"I just wanted to open a neighborhood bar like we had on every corner in downtown Buffalo," Doug Cugini said. While Doug was finishing college, his parents went into business together with Cugini's Truck City Cafes on Ben White and I-35 access road north. The Hole's first cook came from the truck stop.

"We had the marquee built before we even thought about having music," Doug said. "It was to advertise our food and to just basically tell everybody 'We're Here.'" At $2,500, the marquee was the biggest expense besides the liquor license of $5,000. But those two have paid for themselves—boy, have they ever!

That first year, Drag buskers John Garza, George Ensle, and Stephen Doster convinced Cugini to let them set up inside, and he moved a table from the south wall, so they played facing the bar. No stage, no PA, and no shoes, in the case of Garza.

One day an ambitious young singer-songwriter named Nanci Griffith came in and asked for a gig; Cugini gave her a Sunday, which became every Sunday for about a year. She brought her own PA and a bass player and demanded that the TV be turned off while she performed. "Nanci was the first act at the Hole who people came to see," said Cugini. "She was already playing real clubs like Castle Creek and she'd bring in about forty people, which packed the place."

The stage was built for the tenth anniversary in 1983 (the Hole celebrated the first anniversary on opening day) with Omar and the Howlers having first privilege. But another band from Hattiesburg, MS, would soon *own* the stage.

The Hole never had a door person—not with Nanci Griffith or Steve Earle or Sterling Morrison (as a member of the Bizarros)—until Suzy Elkins and the Commandos filled the joint, with a crowd outside the window looking in. One night a sign announced a three-dollar cover and only jerks bitched. Three dollars to have major label talent kick your ass from ten feet away?!

When JD Torian bought Austin's Pizza in 2005, the Hole was part of the package, but Torian didn't know any more about how to run a live music venue than his predecessors, so he looked for a buyer. And found a savior in Will Tanner, an El Paso club owner looking to relocate his young family to Austin.

Tanner has run the Hole with enthusiastic efficiency since February 2008, helping launch a new country music movement led by Clem N' Clyde's Whiskey Business, Mike and the Moonpies, Leo Rondeau, Ramsay Midwood, the Beaumonts, the Carper Family, Luke Bell, and more. Co-owned by former Hole booker Denis O'Donnell, the White Horse on the Eastside could be considered a spinoff club, but it's more about the dancing, packed with two-stepping hipsters.

It's been forty years since the LeRoi Brothers had a band brawl on stage that led to broken bones. Thirty years since Don Henley, hidden in a dark corner, jumped onstage to sing "Don Henley Must Die" with a stunned Mojo Nixon. And twenty plus since Courtney Love commandeered the men's room for a sniffing session the night before her rambling SXSW interview. It's been a long time since the entire crowd chased a guitar thief out the door, caught him, and returned the axe to Miles Zuniga of Fastball (then called Magneto USA). But the Will Tanner Hole was baptized in notoriety on Christmas night 2010 when a drunken Santa Claus smashed through the big front window while doing a karaoke turn.

Like most of his old-timers, founder Cugini has moved on, but a recent road trip to Florida with his twenty-four-year-old daughter pulled him back. "Have you heard this band called Spoon?" she asked, cueing up a favorite new track from *Lucifer on the Sofa*. Spoon played the Hole in the '90s more than any other band, besides maybe Buick MacKane and Pocket FishRmen.

"The old times are great, but we're looking to create some good ol' days of our own," Tanner told me in 2010. It's the cliché of the new owners of beloved clubs. But sometimes they prove true.

"I knew going in that when you run a live music club, you have to find some other payment besides money," said Tanner. "And I get that every night, when you see the interaction between the band and the people who come out to see them." That's always been the Hole truth, and nothing but.

The Hole in the Wall version of Spoon recorded debut LP *Telephono* in 1996. *L-R:* bassist Andy Maguire, Britt Daniel, drummer Jim Eno. Matador Records publicity photo.

Curly and Cody Hubach at the Austin Outhouse.
Courtesy of Chuck Lamb.

Austin Outhouse, 1981–95

Cody Hubach is one of the major unknown figures of the Austin music scene, going back to the '60s when he held court at the Red Lion on West Sixth with his friend Bill Wilson, a Bergstrom airman who would later record for Columbia with Dylan producer Bob Johnston.

Hubach's soulfully-sung folk/blues were a fixture at the 11th Door and Chequered Flag clubs, but the only time the *Statesman* profiled "the Manchaca Troubadour" was as a sculptor who sold a piece to Luci Johnson, for a Christmas gift to Tricia Nixon, in 1968.

After his favorite venues—the One Knite, Split Rail, and Spellman's—closed, Hubach found a new musical home in the late '70s at the Bentwood Tavern at 3510 Guadalupe. This was a classic neighborhood bar, with darts and shuffleboard and sweaty sports teams, but manager Chuck Lamb and harmonica-playing bartender Ed Bradfield started booking music around 1978. Besides Cody, regulars included Blaze Foley, Jubal Clark, Pat Mears, Rich Minus, Calvin Russell, Lost John Casner, and Townes Van Zandt. It was a stage of zero status, but where these hard-living friends could play the songs they just wrote in front of people.

That motley bunch of musical poets conveyed when Lamb bought the license plate-plastered joint in 1981 and changed the name to the Austin Outhouse. It was the club you went to if you'd been eighty-sixed from the Hole. The walk was a little too far for me, but when I did go to see Herman the German or the Horsies it was as crazy as any bar in town. True to its name, the Outhouse was a shithole supreme.

For a stamp of extra weirdness, 3510 was the new homebase of Curly Thompson, Austin's #1 musical savant, who was a fantastic drummer, played blues harp with just his hands and sang like Bon Scott when he wanted to. Curly lived with his mother, and after she shot herself in the head in the early '90s, a sister came down from Oklahoma to take him away. Curly's not been seen since, and because it's hard to imagine him living anywhere but Austin, he's most surely passed away, another character that made the Austin scene unique. Just like the Outhouse. "I loved those years, good and bad," Lamb recalled. "Music every night, good and bad. People you probably know, many you never heard of. It was real."

The club had been bailed out by benefits—most notably a Timbuk3 show, with their first Austin supporter Blaze Foley opening—in January '89 that paid two months back rent on the verge of eviction. A week after that jubilant celebration, Foley was shot to death by the son of a friend.

Folk singer Terri Hendrix plays the Austin Outhouse. Photograph by Randy Dees.

Perhaps coincidentally, perhaps not, the musical focus at the Outhouse gradually changed after Blaze's death to more indie rock. It became the new Beach, north of campus, with such bands as Happy Family, ST37, Texas Instruments (T.I.), Pocket FishRmen, Coz the Shroom, Go Dog Go, Brompton's Cocktail, Siddhartha Suns, and so on. Singer-songwriters were about 20 percent of the calendar.

In '93, Asylum Street Spankers packed the place every Wednesday with their old-time acoustic music and zany antics. It was a total scene. First Wednesday was Pajama Night—which some lovelies took as Lingerie Night. "At the end of the set we'd say, 'now let's go break into Barton Springs and go swimming' and half the crowd would come with us," recalled Forsyth, a Kansas City immigrant who, like so many from elsewhere, came to Austin because there were more places to play and more people to care.

"When you saw a great show at the Outhouse, you walked out feeling like you'd stolen something and gotten away with it," said Forsyth, who played the Outhouse until Flamingo Automotive bought the property for an expansion in 1995.

"I was sad the night we turned out the lights," said Lamb.

Party at the OAF House!
Photograph by David Sprague.

XXVII.

"Great Party! Who Lives Here?"

"You don't have to go home, but you can't stay here," is the standard clear-the-house line of bouncers and bartenders eager to close up for the night. No problem, boss. We just moved the party to an array of ramshackle houses, where last call was "we're out of beer."

On weekend afternoons, you'd use slacker sonar to detect bass notes, then follow the sound waves to the backyard keg. But to wander the streets of West Campus today is to visit a different town. As the rent at these quintessential party houses has quadrupled over the past fifteen to twenty years, there are no more couch carcasses on the front porch or Dino Lee props in the trees. Get ready to hear more about how cool Austin used to be as we go back to the years when it was all about finding something to do when there was nothing to do.

In the early '60s, you had "The Ghetto," an old WWII barracks across Nueces Street and down the alley from Dirty's, where the *Texas Ranger* (humor magazine) crew held court and the UT folkies like Powell St. John, Janis Joplin, Tary Owens, John Clay, and Lanny Wiggins coaxed sounds from guitars, banjos, harmonicas, and autoharps. Not a lot of homework got done at 2812 ½ Nueces, but Gilbert Shelton studied the cast of characters and eventually turned composites into *The Fabulous Furry Freak Brothers*.

The original slacker, Peter Chapa was an undergraduate student at UT for seventeen years, majoring in throwing massive house parties at 1508 San Antonio Street from the mid-'60s. "Party at Chapa's" meant champagne (BYOB) and music from Billie Holiday, Edith Piaf, and Louis Armstrong. This late-night hang was more for the professors than the students, with guests including author Tom Wolfe and directors John Waters and Jean Luc Godard.

In the '70s, there was always something going on in the 600 block of W. 33rd Street, "Hippie Row," where sometimes they'd block off a section with their cars and just party in the street. No permit needed. The hip crowd called Sixth Street west of Baylor "Oakland" because there was a big party scene around Oakland Street. Members of Beto y Los Fairlanes lived in one of those $250 a month four-bedroom houses. "We'd make enough money on one Thursday at Liberty Lunch to cover rent," drummer Mambo John Treanor told me.

Perhaps the most infamous West Campus party house of the '70s was the Twist-off at 2106 Pearl Street, where they held the wrap party for *Texas Chainsaw Massacre*. Residents included Big Boy Medlin and Bill Bentley, who left in '78 to help start *LA Weekly*, and ended up as bigwigs at E! Television and Warner Bros Records, respectively. Today it's home to six condos, but in '73, when the Twist-off hosted a big New Year's Eve bash, it was a six-bedroom house that shook to its foundation when hundreds of revelers danced to Creedence Clearwater Revival's cover of "I Heard it Through the Grapevine." The next day the hosts tried to clean up and ended up just hosing the living room.

When I got to town in the '80s, there was the "OAF House" at 28th and San Pedro and "House of Many Women" at 28th and San Gabriel, and of course there was the Colony at 2703 Rio Grande (same owner as OAF House, John Pieratt), where punk rockers would stay up all night every Saturday, so they could wake up the sorority girls with their racket in the parking lot Sunday morning. "Go ahead and complain. We're legal," read a banner facing the Contessa West next door. Colony "caretaker" David MacDonald would get a sound permit for the bands every week.

The OAF (One-Armed Farmers) House would have a big barbecue in the back yard every Sunday, even inviting the hobos who lived in the bamboo forest out back. Bands would play, including Pez, Technicolor Yawns, and Scratch Acid, whose singer David Yow was a resident. Then the cops would come to shut down the music. Back then, a party didn't count unless the fuzz showed up.

There was a lot of acrimony in the late '70s between the Raul's crowd and the Greeks, as exemplified by the meme, "I was punk rock when it was called 'Hey, f—t!'" The Big Boys answered with their first single "Frat Cars" ("Let's tow them away!") in 1980. Willie World didn't like punks either, with Austin Opera House stagehands brawling with the Big Boys and their fans onstage at the 1984 Austin Music Awards.

In the later '80s, a new "devil's triangle" of party houses was created to serve the Beach Cabaret scene of melodic guitar bands. There was the "House of a Thousand Beers" on West 30th across from Trudy's, "Big Yellow," which became the Spider House, and "the Lodge" at 2827 Salado, all housing a bunch of guys who know that the best way to make sure you get the last beer at a party is to hide one in the toilet tank.

Jennings Crawford, his Wannabes bandmate Hunter Darby, *Statesman* music writer Peter Blackstock, and a couple other guys rented the Lodge unseen. It had five bedrooms and rent figured out to eighty-nine dollars a man, so they took it. When Crawford unlocked the door for the first time, he found a dead rat on the floor. The kitchen was overrun by silverfish, and the back room, where the Wannabes practiced, creaked like it might fall off from the house (it eventually did). But for awhile, the Lodge was the most famous residence in town besides the Governor's Mansion. Junior's Beer & Wine store on 29th used to advertise that it was next door to the Lodge; second-term resident Ken Lieck would mention it as often in his *Austin Chronicle* column as his predecessor did his girlfriend Suzee.

Members of R.E.M., the Replacements, and Fishbone were some of the bands that stopped by after their shows, looking for the party. Once, when Crawford was home alone watching TV late at night, the mohawked members of the Exploited showed up, saying they heard there might be a party.

Nazi skinheads, led by Bay Area pus stain Mark Dagger, ruined the after-hours party scene for about a year. We'd be on the front porch arguing about the new Glass Eye lineup vs. the first one, and these amped-up bullies would show up for free beer and Doc Martin meat. Dagger's drug of choice was punching somebody in the face and laughing. That guy terrorized so many punk shows that a collection was taken up to hire a hitman. Today he's on Facebook and seems like a nice guy.

The era of the walking-distance party house and its open-door policy has gone the way of the Ark Co-op Coke machine, which stocked beer for seventy-five cents a can, so you could mellow your tweak twenty-four hours a day. Those days are left to the memory, because very few photos exist. Why take pictures when it's just going to happen again the next night?

ABOVE: Johnny Lee "Jukebox" Jackson of the Hickoids lived at the OAF and reportedly grew psilocybin mushrooms under the house. Photograph by David Sprague.

OPPOSITE: Old West Campus houses were the funnest, cheapest, all-ages venues. Photograph by David Sprague.

Tim O'Connor backstage at the Backyard.
Photograph by Scott Moore.

XXVIII.

"Why Don't You Run It by Tim?"

O'Connor Made the Music Scene Put On Its Big Boy Pants

No nonmusician has had more impact on the Austin scene than Tim O'Connor. Besides being Willie Nelson's promoter and business partner since the second Fourth of July Picnic in '74, O'Connor ran the Austin Opera House for thirteen years, then owned and operated the Backyard, Austin Music Hall, and La Zona Rosa. O'Connor's Direct Events brought more great roadshows to Austin than the Armadillo and Liberty Lunch combined.

Free of drugs and alcohol since 1988, Tim was addicted to the concert game, the work, the risk/reward rush, which eventually led to a slew of lawsuits and a 2013 bankruptcy. We'll get into all that in book two of this history, which picks up in the '90s, when O'Connor dominated the Austin concert scene. But by the end of the '80s, when he became an independent promoter, he "felt lost, without a home," he told Chris Riemenschneider of the *Statesman*.

He sold his share of the Austin Opera House and the fourteen acres around it in 1990, so he was rich enough to retire. But a framed note on his office wall from Willie kept poking him: "To Tim, What's Next?"

James Timothy O'Connor, his adopted name, came to Austin in 1972 to open Castle Creek with his Colorado buddy Doug Moyes. It was there in the former Chequered Flag folk club on Lavaca that O'Connor met new Austin resident Willie Nelson. "I'd sure like to play your joint," said Willie, who saw the acts being booked at the Creek—John Prine, Guy Clark, Steve Goodman, Steve Fromholz, Townes Van Zandt, Jerry Jeff Walker, etc.—and knew his songs were right for the room.

Tim was in charge of booking and crowd control, earning a reputation as a hard-ass with a soft heart. Willie had found his man! He didn't have to say "no" anymore, just "Why don't you run it by Tim?"

In 1975, O'Connor was outside the Alliance Wagon Yard at 505 Neches St. when things got heated with another group of men. One pulled out a knife, Tim pulled out a gun. His warning shot ended up going through a mobile recording trailer on the street and hitting the leg of a Columbia Records executive inside. It wasn't a bad wound and O'Connor wasn't charged, but he had to tell his boss what went down. "I think I'll let you negotiate all my deals with Columbia from now on," was Willie's response. Still, it was best for Tim to leave town for a year.

When he returned in the summer of '76, O'Connor opened Bull Creek Inn, ia former lodge with a marina, on 2222 past City Park Road (currently home to County Line BBQ). The Inn opened with Milton Carroll playing the 450-capacity indoor room the weekend after Labor Day, while the 2,000-capacity outdoor stage was christened by Rusty Wier in celebration of *Black Hat Saloon*, his stunning third album, and first for Columbia Records.

The venue abruptly closed in May 1977, after ten months of operation, and nobody knew why until it was announced that O'Connor and Nelson's new Southern Commotion partnership was opening the Austin Opry House as a classier Armadillo. When the Dillo closed on the first morning of 1981, the AOH was ready to own the '80s.

Tim O'Connor and Willie Nelson celebrate the ten-year anniversary of Austin Opera House. Photograph by Rick Henson.

Clubland Paradise: La Zona Rosa, 1989–Present

Called an "Ice House for the Arts," La Zona Rosa was a special place, curated and opened by Marcia Ball and husband Gordon Fowler in late '89. Located at the sketchy corner where Fourth Street ends and Rio Grande begins, "the Pink Zone" was inspired by crazy bordertown cafe/bars. With black velvet paintings, jarringly bright colors, and weird cutaways, someone dubbed it "PeeWee's Whorehouse." Each tabletop was painted by a local artist.

You'd go there for Sunday brunch and see Gov. Ann Richards, in shorts and flip flops, reading the *New York Times*. Molly Ivins would be three tables over, entertaining writers from *Texas Monthly*. Every poster artist in town was there. Sometimes there'd be a Mexican accordion player.

There was something about that room—maybe Sarah Elizabeth Campbell's "Bummer Night" on Tuesdays set the mood—but you'd get sadness at its most comfortable. Has Alejandro Escovedo ever sounded as warm as on the Sunday nights that closed SXSW? Some of the best Lucinda Williams shows in town were at La Zona.

By 1994, Fowler's "Two-Alarm Chili" money was almost gone, so he and his partners sold the club to World Series hero Kelly Gruber of the '92 Toronto Blue Jays, and his realtor wife Tosca. Westlake High alum Gruber, who had just retired from baseball due to injuries, was a rock 'n' roller, so that's where the bookings went. But LZR kept losing money until Tim O'Connor took over in 1997.

By then it was just a live music club with a dogleg, and a fifteen hundred capacity that was La Zona Rosa in name only. But saw some great shows there. The last act to play the club under O'Connor's ownership was Prince at SXSW 2013. Not a bad sendoff.

La Zona Rosa hosted a Woody Guthrie tribute in 1993. Lucinda and Butch at the middle mic. Photograph by Randy Dees.

Alejandro Escovedo plays La Zona Rosa with bassist Glenn Fukunaga and Chuck Prophet. Photograph by Lisa Davis. Courtesy of Austin History Center.

Jimmy Day on steel guitar at the Broken Spoke. Marcia Ball on keyboards, Alvin Crow fiddle, Gary P. Nunn guitar. Photograph by Rick Henson.

XXIX.

Country Clubs: Honky-Tonk Reality

Austin has had numerous country music nightclubs, but two stand out, in completely different ways—one for dancing and one for listening. What they had in common was Don Walser!

Broken Spoke, 1964–Present

Jerry Jeff Walker used to say that he didn't live in Texas, he lived in Austin. The opposite can be said of the Broken Spoke, where true honky-tonk Texas resides in the soulless heart of Condo Row.

The rustic red roadhouse used to be on the outskirts of town, but now it's smack dab near the middle, like the Alamo. South Lamar is almost unrecognizable from just ten years ago, but inside the Spoke it's still the '60s, the band is playing "Walking the Floor Over You," and the dancefloor is a counterclockwise swirl of bodies.

Along with Big G's in Round Rock and the Skyline on North Lamar, the Spoke was a stop on the honky-tonk circuit of the '60s and '70s.

The club was founded in 1964 by James White's stepfather Joe Baland, a gregarious carpenter in pinstriped overalls, who convinced Austin businessman Jay Johnson to not only lease him the old Al Ehrlich Lumber Co. property at 3201 S. Lamar but provide $5,000 worth of building materials.

Named after the cowboy movie *Broken Arrow*, the Spoke was just a beer joint that served great chicken-fried steak that first year. The dancehall, James White's baby, was built on in the back in 1965.

"One of the things Joe used to say was, `I've been drinking beer on this road for 30 years and always paid retail, but if I could build my own place and pay wholesale I'd save a lot of money,'" Johnson told John Kelso for Baland's obit in 1990. At age seventy-two, suffering from cancer and other ailments, Baland did what he told everyone he would, turning a shotgun on himself in the one-room shack he lived in behind the Spoke.

He'd officially turned the club over to James and Annetta White in 1980, but they'd always been running the place. James also booked the 661-capacity venue, a job he held until his passing in January 2021.

The first name act to grace the stage was Bob Wills and the Texas Playboys, White's all-time favorite group, in 1966. Their fee was $400 ($3,600 in current buying power—still a bargain). "Nobody believed they were gonna show, until Bob Wills himself walked through that door, smoking a big cigar," White said. "The fellas practically fell off their barstools."

The butt from that cigar is featured in the Spoke's "Tourist Trap" minimuseum, along with momentos from other acts who've played there, including Willie Nelson, Ernest Tubb, Roy Acuff, Tex Ritter, and Kitty Wells. There's also a cowboy hat from George Strait, who packed the Spoke with his Ace in the Hole Band once a month from 1975 to 1982.

Even with good home cooking and the souvenir shop, the Spoke is ruled by the dancefloor, and if it's not full you're playing the wrong songs. Club regulars Al Dean and His All Stars, from San Antonio, were hardwood heroes in the '60s for their resurrection of a forgotten fiddle tune called "The Cotton-Eyed Joe." The accompanying circle dance and "Bullshit!" response was developed at the Spoke and other Texas honky-tonks, fifteen years before *Urban Cowboy* (1980).

Acts like Jesse Dayton, who held a Thursday night residency for years, tailor their sets for the venue. "It's not about presenting yourself as a singer-songwriter—or even an entertainer—at the Broken Spoke," Dayton said. "The music is totally for the dancers, and we play the shuffles, waltzes, polkas, and 4/4 beats they love."

Dale Watson wrote a Texas two-step song—"Quick Quick Slow Slow"—as a template for new dancers, who share the floor with expert twirlers. As for nondancers, they quickly learn to respect the sign that says, "No standing on the dance floor." That elbow was on purpose.

The most successful Spoke bands have been the ones like People's Choice—who packed it every Wednesday from the late '70s through the '80s—that present perfect copies of the hits old and new. The Spoke is the most famous cover band bar in Texas.

One longtime Spoke act who did sing original compositions was Don Walser, which worked because his songs sounded like classic country.

Dubbed "the Pavarotti of the Plains" by Charles M. Young in *Playboy*, the magnificent yodeler received a standing ovation at the Erwin Center when he opened for Johnny Cash in 1996. Walser was then signed to Sire Records, the home of Madonna and the Ramones, and sang with the Kronos Quartet when they played Austin in '97. But he picked up his career so late, at age fifty-six, that he had only a decade of relevance. In the early 2000s, weighing well over three hundred pounds, his health deteriorated to the point that fans were openly concerned. The last club to book him was the Broken Spoke. "Don just loves to sing, but it broke my heart to watch him perform when he was ailin' so badly," White said. The decision in 2003 to scratch his good friend from the schedule was the toughest he's ever made. But the people made it for him by not dancing like they used to.

"When you come to the Broken Spoke, you're coming to the same place that folks have been coming to for 50 years," James White said in 2014. The Spoke experience is still one of the coolest, most authentic things about Austin, a visitor's favorite stop at night after a day at Barton Springs Pool.

"Texas has a dance culture unlike any state in America," said Dayton. "Asking someone to dance without any intention of picking them up is just a part of who we are. And it started at places like the Broken Spoke."

Henry's Bar and Grill, 1981–92

It can't be easy to impress a member of Led Zeppelin, especially on Burnet Road, but when Jeff Pinkus of the Butthole Surfers took John Paul Jones to a country music club the size of his closet in early 1992, the exalted bassist rebooked his flight out of Austin so he could have another couple weeks of Henry's.

In town to do preproduction for *Independent Worm Saloon*, the Buttholes 1993 major label debut, Jones couldn't believe that was Jimmy Day playing with Don Walser one Monday night. The former Hank/Elvis/Willie sideman was tucked in the corner with his head down like he was on the lam. But there was no disguising Day's magnificence on pedal steel, an instrument Jones was learning to play.

Walser was a one-man authenticity machine, even making Emo's country, when the punk club booked him at the insistence of Ministry's Al Jourgenson. This round mound of pure country sounded like the last forty years didn't happen.

"There was a feeling that Henry's was the last of a dying breed of Texas clubs and everyone was there to savor the mood," said John Conquest, a Brit whose *Music City Texas* (later *3rd Coast Music*) championed Henry's early and often. "Whenever you had visitors from out of town you'd take them to Henry's and the pure Texas honky-tonk experience would just blow them away." Junior Brown filled the club every Tuesday night.

Other nights it was a scene out of *Bakersfield 90210*, with such fresh-faced traditionalists as Kelly Willis, High Noon, Chapparal, Wayne "the Train" Hancock, Teri Joyce, and Monte Warden working on their credibility badges.

There wasn't much to the windowless, cinder block building, not even a stage, but graffiti in the men's room said it all. "I dreamed I went to heaven. It wasn't as good as Henry's." There was no cooler twang scene anywhere—definitely not in Nashville or LA—than at 6317 Burnet Road, where the masters and disciples played for vintage two-steppers and punks in mohawks.

But it wasn't as profitable as an Auto Zone would be, so this box of Austin soul was flattened after a Halloween 1992 blowout with the Cornell Hurd Band. The line to get in for that final night stretched almost to the Poodle Dog Lounge! Thirty years later, folks are still talking about Henry's, but it was open just eleven years—and had been a destination only for the last two. There were a lot of groovy things happening elsewhere in Austin at that time, but for where it was—in the sofa and Sealy

James White passed away in 2021 after fifty-seven years of greeting fans at the Spoke.
Photograph by Rick Henson.

showroom corridor—Henry's was something special.

As is so often the case in Austin clubland, the owners and staff deserve much of the credit. "James fostered an environment that was just so much fun for the musicians and the crowd," said Ted Roddy. "The audience was appreciative, and the tips were great," added fiddler Howard Kalish, who originally played with Walser at Henry's in August 1990 as a duo. "It's amazing that it was all gone by '92."

James and Gayle Henry, who married when he was nineteen and she fifteen, were hardcore country music fans from Leander whose yellowed memorabilia covered the walls, with the spirit—and cigarette smoke—filling the air. Henry's regulars learned to disrobe at the front door when they got home to let their clothes air out.

Arkansas-born James Henry opened his namesake beer joint in 1981 after retiring from Lone Star Paper at age fifty-five. Gayle grew up working in the country music club business, with her parents Buck and Marie Wickson running the Hilltop Inn, a Western swing dancehall on far north Burnet Road in the '50s and '60s. James was there most nights, helping out and digging the sounds.

"I used to sleep in a basket under the bar," said the Henrys' oldest daughter Linda Troutman. Younger siblings Laura, Jimmy, and Tommy graduated from the same "honky-tonk daycare."

When James and Gayle fulfilled their longtime goal of opening their own country music venue, they continued the family tradition, with the kids serving ice-cold beer and above-average cheeseburgers, while James and Gayle held court at the big, round "King's Table." If they called you over to sit with them and their hillbilly friends, it was better than an Austin Music Award.

In the '80s, North Austin was full of quirky beer joints, including the Poodle Dog, Lala's Little Nugget and Hector Alvarado's Taco Flats, but what set Henry's apart was the high quality of live music. The amount of talent per square foot was just crazy!

"Because of the stuff they played on the radio, I didn't know much about real country music until I started going to Henry's," said former High Noon bassist Kevin Smith, who replaced Bee Spears in Willie Nelson's Family in 2011, when Spears died after a fall outside his Nashville home in freezing weather. "Being 10 feet away from Don Walser when he'd sing was just incredible exposure to the bare, primitive soul of that music and the people who love it."

The Henrys were devastated when they got the notice to vacate, as were the bands and fans, but a "Henry's Appreciation Night" at La Zona Rosa in October 1992 buoyed the spirits. James vowed that it wasn't the end of Henry's! Location #2 was announced for Research Blvd., but a lack of parking killed the rezoning request. Ginny's Little Longhorn, in the former Rustic Lounge location ('63–'72) on Burnet Road, started booking Henry's bands like High Noon to fill the void. Henry's Bar & Grill eventually resurfaced in a much bigger building near the Henry home in Liberty Hill, but Williamson County is apparently where scenesters draw the line. Even Conquest had to talk himself into making that trek.

James and Gayle Henry, married since they were teenagers, made a home for real country on Burnet Road. Courtesy of Henry family.

Don Walser and Junior Brown and Kelly Willis and the Robison brothers, Charlie and Bruce, went on to score major label deals and tour the world. The hip country bands moved on to Jovita's, Babe's, Ego's, the Continental, and elsewhere, but the Henry's dream was shattered by the wrecking ball of late '92. So many things have to come together at the right time to create a magical environment for music. It's almost impossible to duplicate. Especially with all the red tape.

James Henry passed away from Hodgkin's lymphoma in 2008, at age seventy-two, and Gayle from COPD in 2017 at age seventy-seven. Because they loved the music so much, they were willing to put in the work to make it happen for everybody, making a lasting impact on the Austin music scene. Their club was not an excuse to dance, though some did. You went to Henry's to watch country music being made in its natural habitat. Who needs a stage?

Don Walser and the Pure Texas band at Henry's.
Bert Rivera on steel. Courtesy of Linda Henry Troutman.

Jay Clark, who came to the Carousel as a member of the Velvetones in 1967, could play a bit of everything. Courtesy of Nicki Mebane Carousel Lounge.

XXX.

Virtue of Blindness on the Music Scene

For decades the only public schools for the blind in Texas—one for whites and one for Blacks—were in the state capital, and since playing music is one of the vocations where sight is not required, musical training was a focus. Some notable blind musicians have passed through Austin, including gospel pioneer Arizona Dranes, country music great Leon Payne, "King of the Whistlers" Fred Lowery, and Pat McGarrett's daughter Elizabeth, who wrote the state song of New Mexico.

Other sightless players stayed here and made an impact. Singer-pianist Bobby Doyle was signed to Columbia and eventually overshadowed, but never forgotten, by his high-harmonizing bass player Kenny Rogers. Blind George McLain stomped out country piano blues in the '70s like he was part Ray Charles and part George Jones. Sid Fisher, whose Hammond organ virtuosity earned him a daily 11 a.m. slot on KVET in the '40s, played all over town, from swanky lounges to the Tally-Ho Waffle Shop on 19th St. Legally blind clarinetist Hub Sutter led the popular Hubcats, and Johnny Morrison and His Texas Ramblers, a Western swing band of the early '50s, were billed as consisting entirely of former students from the Texas School for the Blind.

Clubland Paradise: The Carousel Lounge, 1963–Present

Then there was Jay Clark, the one-man swing band who'd been flying people to the moon at the Carousel Lounge for almost thirty years before being discovered by whimsical hipsters and mad trippers in the '90s. Wonder if one-time 8 ½ Souvenirs singer Chrysta Bell took her friend and collaborator, *Blue Velvet* director David Lynch, to the club. How could she not?

Remember the first time you walked into the hallucinogenic Carousel—it doesn't matter the year—and wondered why it took so long? The CL was cool without having to let everyone know about it. But eventually everyone did.

What most don't know is that, as of 2023 when it turned sixty, the Carousel has hosted live music, continuously, for longer than any club in Austin, beating the Broken Spoke by a year. The Continental Club is older, opening in 1955, but it didn't have live music for almost all of the '70s, when it was a day drinker haven.

The Carousel's founders were Cecil and Myrtle Meier, a couple who grew up dancing at the SPJST ("some people just sit there") Hall in Taylor. On a visit to New Orleans circa '61, they had drinks at the Carousel Lounge in the Hotel Monteleone and fantasized about opening their own one-ring circus in Austin. Their dream came true at 1110 E. 52nd near the freeway. But they kept their day jobs—Cecil delivering bread for Butter Krust and Myrtle working in an insurance office.

It was 1963 and another Carousel club in Dallas would soon be made infamous by its owner Jack Ruby. But that was a seedy burlesque joint. Austin's Carousel was for older couples dancing to combos playing the music of Frank Sinatra, Glenn Miller, Patti Page, and the like.

Even more than the club's pink elephants and circus décor, Clark's effervescent arrangements of timeless classics defined the Carousel's surreal personality. The eccentric living jukebox retired in 1998 after a stroke limited his ability. He passed away in 2006 at age eighty-six.

"I've never known a finer man than Jay Clark," said Stella Boes, the patriotic dancing bartender at the Carousel, who passed away the year after he did, at age eighty. Boes met the Meiers when she was a volunteer aid to cancer patients, and Cecil Meier was on her route.

Clark was born with sight, but he lost both eyes in separate mishaps, the first at age three and the other at eleven. A native of McKinney, John W. "Jay" Clark moved to Austin in 1931 to attend the Texas School for the Blind and Visually Impaired. It was there that his passion for music was born.

After graduating, Clark played saxophone, clarinet, and keyboards in area big bands in the '40s and early '50s, especially Cecil Hogan and the Swingsters (and other names), which featured local WWII hero Hogan on guitar, backed by blind musicians Clark, Sid Fisher, and clarinetist Hub Sutter. Jay had three kids to support so he ran the concession stand in the basement of the *Austin American-Statesman* for several years before pursuing music full time.

The Carousel's chief competition early on was the Playboy Club on 53½ Street near Airport, which featured the Velvetones, who did justice to big band standards with only five members. When the Playboy burned down in '67, the Velvetones hired on at the Carousel to play seven nights a week, but the grind of that schedule (for not great pay) made it hard to keep musicians, especially as popularity waned for this "music for squares" during that time of the cosmic cowboy. The Velvetones started shrinking until there was only one member, Jay Clark, who bought a four-track recorder and dubbed in the sax and clarinet parts, then played along on his organ with programmed beats.

The Carousel hit a rough patch in the '80s when the original clientele dwindled and was not replaced. The turnaround came when the Meiers's daughter Nicki Mebane hired a pair of popular UT coeds as bartenders after she inherited the club in '88. The word got out on campus about "this crazy circus bar," and it became a secret hangout for kids in the know.

Then the quirky musician crowd came out just to hear Jay. "I loved that guy," remembered King Coffey of the Surfers. "He could play anything: rock, country, soul, blues, show tunes; his knowledge was deep. To this day, whenever I hear 'From a Jack to a King' or 'Kansas City,' I think of Jay Clark, not Ned Miller or Fats Domino."

Frank Zappa and his opening act Blind George McLain hit it off at the Armadillo in March 1973. Blind George came to Austin to attend the blind school and ended up staying for club work. Photograph by Burton Wilson.

The folkie. The rocker. The roots king. Jerry Jeff Walker, Roky Erickson, and Doug Sahm were a living Austin music Mount Rushmore on May 16, 1977, Margaret Moser's twenty-third birthday party. The only ones missing were Willie Nelson and Stevie Ray Vaughan. This superjam was captured at Gemini's, the club on the Drag that would become Raul's by the end of the year. Photograph by Ken Hoge. Courtesy of AusPop archives.

SXSW cofounders Roland Swenson, Louis Meyers, Louis Black,

XXXI.

SXSW: Birth of the Mid-March Monster

When my son Jack was eight, I gave his mother a break one day by taking him with me on my SXSW party rounds. We walked down the alley behind Yard Dog to see two winos urinating against a wall, and soon were hit with an airspace grapple of cigarette smoke, sizzling hot dogs, marijuana, and BO The backyard of the outsider art gallery was jampacked, loud, and rowdy. Nowhere to go and only one way out. A mortified Jack alternated between pinching his nostrils and plugging his ears; we didn't last ten minutes. When we walked back to the car, Jack asked, "When you decided to become a music critic, did you know about South by Southwest?"

Hell, kid, I was there from the very beginning, when SXSW moved into the spare downstairs office of the *Austin Chronicle* at 28th and Rio Grande. It was the room where we used to go and sit on old *Chron* bundles and smoke joints.

I actually go back even further when SXSW was called the New Music Seminar (NMS) and held in New York City each July. NMS was the model for the music conference former Standing Waves manager Roland Swenson and booking agent Louis Meyers wanted to bring to their hometown. With connected advisor Ed Ward and the support of the Austin Chamber of Commerce, Swenson talked NMS owners into producing an Austin spinoff. The debut of New Music Seminar Southwest was set for spring 1987.

The Austin music scene was "what's hot," with big spreads in *Rolling Stone* and *Spin*, and a devoted hour on MTV. The Fabulous Thunderbirds, Timbuk3, and Charlie Sexton all had Top 20 hits in '86. Stevie Ray Vaughan was the new guitar hero, Zeitgeist and True Believers signed major label deals, and outsider songwriting savant Daniel Johnston was the feel-good story of the year. This new conference/festival would solidify Austin as the *Third Coast* its monthly magazine claimed it to be.

Showing NMS owners around town, though, Swenson was disappointed that "it became obvious that we were not going to play any part" in the new venture. It would still be a good thing for the Austin club scene, but the conference would be New York-owned and operated.

But just a couple months before the maiden event, NMS pulled out. Not enough time. That was great news for Swenson, who worked at the *Chronicle* in a distribution and marketing capacity (he got the paper into H-E-B, despite protests from the relig-o-right over the personal ads). He went to publisher Nick Barbaro and editor Louis Black and convinced them that the *Chronicle* could do this event without New York. The clubs and hotels welcomed this "South by Southwest" (reflecting Black's Hitchcock affinity) because it was scheduled for one of the slowest weeks of the year—when all the students were on spring break.

One day in early '87, I heard something I thought I'd never hear in the *Chronicle* offices: "We need the room." What movie is that from? "C'mon, guys, clear out," Roland said in my direction. Shit, that meant me too.

Especially me. I had a big mouth and a column, and they didn't want any word of this Austin conference to get out until it was all set. I called those first meetings "reindeer games" because I was Rudolph, the red-nosed Irishman they wouldn't let play. What did I care? Nobody

SXSW embraced the hate, selling a bunch of the t-shirts Mojo Nixon is wearing, circa 1989. Also pictured Miles Zuniga, Bill Davis, and Rickie Gelb. Photograph by Linda Earley. Courtesy of Austin History Center.

ABOVE: Daniel Johnston on the job before music became his career. Photograph by David C. Fox.

Singer Junior Medlow and guitarist Chris Duarte perform at SXSW in 1989. Photograph by Martha Grenon. Courtesy of Austin History Center.

thought SXSW would draw much more than the best up-and-coming bands from Oklahoma, Arkansas, and Louisiana—plus Giant Sand.

Almost forty years later SXSW is still a regional conference, but the region is Planet Earth. Austin in the '80s was about as international as a house of pancakes, but in recent years flights from all over the world land at ABIA every March. With attendees from every continent except Antartica (home of a very pissed off trip-hop duo), SXSW has come to represent a full range of cultures, in a city not known for diversity.

Austin isn't really Austin during SXSW. It's a dead buffalo, and all the people who come are the Native Americans who use every piece of the animal. Every building, every parking lot, every side street, every park. They dance to tribal beats and go a little crazy in the spirit of celebration. And when they go home there are always a few braves and maidens left behind.

It's different for the townsfolk, who cue the *Jaws* music when the calendar flips from February to March, and start freaking out in a mix of horror and excitement. Fear of missing out (FOMO) was launched at SXSW—year two. "We're gonna do it right this year!"

Except for the pandemic torpedo strikes of 2020 and 2021, when we understood how Chicago Bulls fans felt when Michael Jordan quit to play baseball, our town becomes an almost unrecognizable Super Austin every March. But one thing hasn't changed since the 1987 debut: SXSW brings out the best *and* the worst in us. The humble become entitled, but they do work their asses off.

Organizers didn't know what to expect that first year and were delighted when seven hundred people registered, at thirty-five dollars a badge. There were fifteen panels during the day, and fifteen showcase venues at night. Wristbands to see the 170-act lineup were ten dollars.

ABOVE: Waiting for the speedboats on festival beach, circa 1967. Courtesy of Austin History Center.

ABOVE: Rod Kennedy was president of Aquafest in 1966 when he announced that Melody Patterson of F Troop would be guest of honor that year. Courtesy of *Austin American-Statesman* Photographic Morgue at the Austin History Center.

The first breakout star was Austin—where the music was good stuff from road-tested professionals, the clubs were right next to each other, and the weather was better, the beer cheaper, and the people friendlier than back home. We didn't even need breakfast tacos.

SXSW legitimized Austin as a music industry town; Nashville with soul, an affordable LA, Manhattan with free parking.

SXSW Music added about six hundred registrants per year in its first twenty but flattened out when internet streaming started killing much of the music business. Added in 1994 as a way to figure out CD-ROMs, SXSW Interactive (originally "Multimedia") topped music registration for the first time in 2010 with over fourteen thousand badges. It's been the dominant component ever since.

SXSW is now known as much for being the launchpad for Twitter, Foursquare, and HomeAway as it is for unknown future headliners like Kendrick Lamar, the Strokes, Mumford and Sons, Amy Winehouse, Florence and the Machine, Billie Eilish, and White Stripes.

Austin has become a favorite bar overrun by trendies. You can't even remember that night the girl who's now your wife surprised you by rubbing her bare foot on your crotch from across the table. That booth is still there, but it's not available to you after about 7 p.m. Or when there's a festival in town (aka "the weekend").

A couple of ironies to point out: SXSW was started by the *Austin Chronicle*, a liberal weekly with an anti-growth agenda, and it was held the third week of March because all the college students would be out of town.

In recent years, as the buzz got out about celebrity sightings and free concerts and free booze at music industry parties, Austin became a Spring Break *destination*. Padre Island still gets the bronzed and the blasted, but the more parsimonious and musically adventurous collegians head to ATX to get their free(k) on. It's the party of the year if you know how to work it, and if you don't and you have forty dollars you can get one of the RSVP services to enter your name in as many free party lotteries as they can.

Aqua Fest: Death of the August Godzilla

During the first couple years of South by Southwest, if you were in a bar and said that "one day this is going to be bigger than Aqua Fest," you'd be cut off. That was as overserved a prognostication as saying rooms at the San Jose Motel would be over a hundred dollars a night in a few years. Can I call you a cab, sir?

During its '80s heyday, Aqua Fest was the biggest annual music event in town by far. Every August it would squat on the shores of Town Lake like Godzilla in a white sailor suit, swatting at local club business, sending big growls of sound up the hills of South Austin, overloading the streets with cars parked like tossed magnets. In its biggest year, 1985, Aqua Fest attracted 252,000 during a nine-day run. Most club owners would schedule their vacations to coincide with "Aqua Pest."

But by 1998 it was a floater, done in by greed, cluelessness, and ridiculous sound limits. The emergence of SXSW made Aqua Fest look like the glorified county fair it was.

When the Austin Aqua Festival began in 1962, water was the star, as the event celebrated the completion of Longhorn Dam, which created Town Lake. It was held at Fiesta Gardens, where thousands would stake their square of the shore to watch speedboats roar. Bikini-clad water-skiers waved as they sliced the water, and there were kiddie fishing derbies, Boy Scout canoe races, and the unveiling of the Aqua Fest Queen and her court.

In the evenings, couples two-stepped on a concrete dancefloor to local country bands, or they danced the polka on "Czech Night," one of several ethnic heritage nights. The neighborhood came out on "Noche Mexicana," and Eastsiders crossed the freeway for "Soul Night."

Aqua Fest got the whole city involved, with Bergstrom AFB opening up to civilians for its AeroFest sky ballet and Rod Kennedy presenting the Festival Teen Hop at Municipal Auditorium, a battle of the bands.

The national-caliber boat drag races were the biggest draw, with thirty thousand rubber-neckers crowding Festival Beach (not a beach). But since speedboats sound like lawn mowers on the porch, the predominantly Latino neighborhood protested hard about the noise. The Brown Berets stepped in, and the controversy was covered in the *Statesman* for a year before Mayor Carole McClelland cast the deciding vote to ban speedboats on Town Lake in 1978. That year Aqua Fest moved to the more spacious Auditorium Shores, and live music became the main attraction.

The Fest's best years, musically, were '86–'90 when attorney Cindi Lazzari and Eric Johnson's manager Joe Priestnitz booked it. The music industry veterans, dating at the time and later married, put Jimmie and Stevie Ray Vaughan back together in 1987. They booked a magnificent performance by Roy Orbison in 1988, just four months before he passed away. But 1989 was unbeatable, with a lineup that included George Jones, Dwight

Jimmie Dale Gilmore plays the Sixth and Brazos stage at SXSW97. Photograph by Jana Birchum.

Yoakam, NRBQ, Ray Price, the Reivers, Clint Black, Guadalcanal Diary, Patty Loveless, and Chuck Berry. For eight dollars a night.

In 1988, the nine-member staff, led by Fest president Newt Youngblood, decided to give themselves nice salaries (Youngblood's was $130,000 a year), since things were going so swimmingly. Before that, Aqua Fest was run by volunteer "Commodores," who resented the new paid leadership.

Perhaps because the staff's bonus incentives were tied to net profits, they decided to up the ante, getting bigger names and charging more money for admission. But when the cost went up to twelve dollars per night, attendance dropped. Expensive acts like Kenny Loggins, Three Dog Night, and Damn Yankees lost money. As they should have.

Aqua Fest used to hit paydirt by booking bands months before they broke out, like George Strait in 1981, and Billy Ray Cyrus in '92. They paid "Mr. Achy Breaky" $7,500 and drew seventeen thousand. The same year Dolly Parton got $80,000 and drew only seven thousand. That's show biz.

When 1992 booker French Smith didn't have his contract renewed, he ran a competing festival on Sixth Street the next year. Only forty-four thousand came through the turnstiles at Auditorium Shores in '93 and Aqua Fest lost $600,000. During the next three years, the fest would lose the rest of the $2 million reserve they'd spent thirty years accumulating.

Aqua Fest was never cool, just something to do if you lived in Austin. SXSW, on the other hand, grew from the national music scene's best-kept secret into the world's largest—and wildest—music conference and festival. Added in 1995 was SXSW Film (originally chided as "Friends of Louis Black Festival").

NMS went badge-up in 1996, leaving SXSW alone at the top. The only thing louder that year than the music on the free stage at Sixth and Brazos was the sound of the NMS guys kicking themselves. They were Wally Pipp, who took himself out of a game with a headache, and Southby was Lou Gehrig.

The '96 confabfest was the first I covered for the *Statesman*, which had a history of ragging on my old pals at SXSW. Since the *Austin Chronicle* owned the conference, they weren't going to write anything really negative, so that became the *Statesman*'s role as the paper of record. Like a coach who's especially tough on his son, I continued the critical onslaught lest there be a scent of favoritism. No *friendola* here.

I'd taken some shots at Reindeer Games before I hired on at the *Statesman*. When I was advancing SXSW for the *Dallas Morning News* in '94, I advised a money-saving approach to readers. "You don't need a badge," I wrote, "just buy a wristband and hang out in the lobby bar of the Four Seasons." When I went to pick up my credentials that year, I was handed an envelope that included a wristband and directions to Austin's swankiest hotel. The look on my face had to be Nick Barbaro's favorite SXSW moment that didn't involve softball, though he did hand me a badge after the laughter died down.

On deadline for a 1A scene report/wrap-up in '96, I found Roland standing at Seventh and Brazos, overlooking the biggest crowd yet at SXSW, about twelve thousand packed next to the Driskill to see a free Iggy Pop show. "Not now," he snapped, when I pulled out my notebook. I just needed one innocuous quote, so I could file the story and start partying with everyone else.

Luckily, a clueless driver on Seventh gave me my lead. He pulled up to Roland, amidst the raucous music cranking out of every open doorway, as well as outdoor stages, and rolled down his window. "Excuse me," he yelled. "Could you tell me how to get to South by Southwest?"

That was like pulling into Vietnam during the Tet Offensive and asking which way was the war.

SXSW is Austin's signature event, but the foliage has overgrown base camp. Southby lost Sixth Street years ago, and the afterparty now goes on before, during, and after the main event. "Influencers" are as important as people who've worked hard to actually create something, and RSVP service? In the old days, you just slipped the guy at the door a couple joints.

This town in the early years of SXSW was a moveable beast rivaling Paris in the '20s. But in recent years it's become the Burning Brand Festival.

It was like young love. Did you think it was going to be that way forever?

Oh, how things have changed.

Overheard at SXSW, 1989

1. "Do you know where Saturday's day party is?"
2. "Austin learned its lesson from the Armadillo. No way they're tearing down Liberty Lunch for an office building."
3. "I'm in such a hurry I'm gonna have to grab lunch from a food truck. Where's the nearest construction site?"
4. "Let's just take a cab to Salt Lick. How much could it be?"
5. "So, besides the Austin Music Awards, what else are you excited about this week?"
6. "Holy shit, that's Peter Zaremba!"
7. "SXSW is a good idea, but they're gonna need to rely on the revenue from the *Austin Chronicle* to survive."
8. "They need to get someone hip, with an opinion, to keynote. Someone like Michelle Shocked."

Epilogue

Thus concludes this history of the Austin music scene. Even though I wrote "Welcome to Mediocre, Texas" in 2012, I don't read any of those longform pieces about how Austin isn't cool anymore. If you want to ponder change, look in the mirror and ask yourself: How would you feel if Austin wrote a big article about how you're not as fun, affordable, or skinny as you used to be?

Though the quantity of live music goes down when musicians are forced to live in the real world, there will always be something worth hearing in Austin seven nights a week. Even if it's looking harder for you than you are for it. This book would not be the one you hold in your hands without the photographers who, in most cases, donated their work to this project. The goal was to put out a history book that would outlast us all. Time will tell.

Read more about Austin musicians in these previous Michael Corcoran books:

All Over the Map: True Heroes of Texas Music
(UNT Press 2017)

Chapters on Stevie Ray Vaughan, Blaze Foley, Johnny Gimble, Alejandro Escovedo, Nick Curran, Don Walser, Doug Sahm, and Butthole Surfers

Ghost Notes: Pioneering Spirits of Texas Music
(TCU Press 2020)

Chapters on Roky Erickson, Arizona Dranes, Camilo Cantu, the Gant Family, Bobby Doyle, Johnny Degollado, Henry and Virginia Leberman, and B. L. Joyce.

About the Author

A native of Honolulu, and reborn in Austin as a young man in 1984, Michael Corcoran went from The Alternative Press to the Dallas Morning News when he was hired as the paper's first country music critic in 1992. Twenty years later he retired from the Austin American-Statesman to spend his working hours researching and writing Texas music history. Corcoran's book and CDs on gospel pioneers Arizona Dranes (2012) and Washington Phillips (2017) were both nominated for Grammys in the historical album categories. He is also the author of All Over the Map (2017) and Ghost Notes (2020), which profile Texas music heroes and pioneers.

Index

B

C

D

E

H

I

J

K

L

P

Q

R

W